AVOIDING THE DARK

To Karin, Marcelo and Caetano

DAMES

Dansk Center for Migration
og Etniske Studier

**EUROPEAN RESEARCH CENTRE
ON MIGRATION & ETHNIC RELATIONS**

Avoiding the Dark

Race and the forging of national culture in
modern Brazil

DARIÉN J. DAVIS
Middlebury College, Vermont, USA

Ashgate

Aldershot • Brookfield USA • Singapore • Sydney

Published by
Ashgate Publishing Ltd
Gower House
Croft Road
Aldershot
Hants GU11 3HR
England

Ashgate Publishing Company
Old Post Road
Brookfield
Vermont 05036
USA

Ashgate website: http://www.ashgate.com

British Library Cataloguing in Publication Data
Davis, Darién J.
 Avoiding the dark: race and the forging of
 national culture in modern Brazil. - (Research in migration and
 ethnic relations series)
 1. Blacks - Brazil 2. Nationalism - Brazil 3. Brazil - Race
 relations
 I. Title
 305.8'00981

Library of Congress Catalog Card Number: 99-73478

ISBN 1 84014 874 8

Printed and bound by Athenaeum Press, Ltd.,
Gateshead, Tyne & Wear.

Contents

List of Figures and Tables

List of Abbreviations

(APP):   Arquivos das Poliçias Politicais do Estado de Rio de Janeiro, Rio de Janeiro.

(AN):   Arquivo Nacional, Rio de Janeiro.

(BN):   Biblioteca Nacional: Seção da Musica, Ministerio da Cultura, Rio de Janeiro. (BN)

(CPDOC): Centro de Pesquisa e Documentação: Fundação Getúlio Vargas, Rio de Janeiro.

(SPHAN): Serviço do Patrimonio Histórico e Artístico Nacional, Ministério da Cultura, Rio de Janeiro.

Preface

Avoiding the Dark: Race and the Forging of National Culture examines the impact of the African legacy on modern Brazil's national discourse. It seeks to indicate ways in which Brazilians have marginalized the contribution and the presence of Africans in the post-abolition era, while attempting to understand regional trends in race relations from independence movement till the end of World War II.

On the one hand, this work is interested in race relations as they impact blacks and whites in Brazil, with a close scrutiny of the role of the mulatto as a group that is neither black or white to paraphrase Carl Degler. At the same time, this work is interested in the forging of a national identity by the political and cultural elite who are to a large extent responsible for promoting a given sense of blackness, *mulatismo*, or mulatto-ness, and whiteness.

This book traces the construction of a national identity in search of modernity and progress that avoided associations with Africa or blacks. Other scholars have begun to show that the construction of a dominant national identity was not limited to a black-white discourse, but that the contribution of natives and other 'immigrants' were also 'avoided' or 'integrated' into a dominant mestiço-white complex.

Racial identity, like all identities is a malleable construction depending on region, politics, economics and history. Who constitutes 'a white' may change over time within some limits. Views of racial identities also change depending on the historical era. The changing nature of racial identity in Brazil together with the numerous ways in which Brazilians have of describing one another (such as *branco, moreno, mulato, preto, caboclo*, to name a few) gives credence to the widespread social scientific belief that race is a social construct. At the same time, it is important to understand that the construction is closely related to relations of power. Difference can be and has been accentuated or camouflaged by individuals for a number of reasons. Still, it is important to understand that only some social constructions are malleable. Brazilian colonization, like colonization elsewhere in the Americas, was predicated on the idea of white supremacy. Non-whites, however defined, suffered under the system but also learned and internalized social practices over four centuries.

For years, pseudo-scientific theories relegated people of mixed ancestry to obscurity, seeing them as degenerate and incapable of reproduction as the root of *mulato* indicates. All this despite (or perhaps because of) the growing *mulato* and *mestiço* populations in the nineteenth century. Latin American intellectuals and nationalists in quest of positive national identities could not shake off the colonial mentality which subjugated the slave, that is to say the African, and secondarily those who were tainted by Africa, the *mulatos*, and so forth. It was not uncommon for nations such as Brazil to promote white images of itself, and for many *mulatos* from 'good families' to see themselves as white. Mass European immigration, the growth of the middle sectors, coupled with advances in social sciences and the pursuit of national symbols after World War I would all contribute to the cultural changes in the first two decades of the twentieth century.

Thanks to anthropologists such as Franz Boas, Latin American scholars such as Gilberto Freyre, for example, were able to refute theories of the degeneracy of the mulatto. Thus began in the 1920s a promotion of a mulatto identity, now in positive terms. But very often *the mulato* was promoted at the expense of blacks. More often than not, however, even *the mulato* was not accepted as a part of white society.

Intellectuals and politicians play important roles in the construction of nationhood, but they are not the only partners nor are political rhetoric and published materials the only fora through which individuals comment on race and national identity. For the general population numerous forums exist for their participation, although not all of them reach national attention. Music is one exception. The rise of mass media in the 1930s, allowed for the emergence of popular voices on the national level. The radio was particularly important in this endeavor. While black and mulatto musicians commented on race and nationhood, they were rarely the spokesmen or women of their musical productions. White entrepreneurs brought the music of the popular classes to national attention. Nonetheless, we can glean a sense of the popular view from important and widely popular compositions from this time period. What is apparent is that even in musical texts we see an avoidance of blackness in favor of a celebration of multiculturalism, sometimes the mulatto, but there seems to be an implicit sense of celebration of Brazilian whiteness.

From the 1930s to the 1950s, various black activist groups emerged to galvanize the black voice. Those groups that attained national attention came mostly from Rio or São Paulo where blacks constituted a minority and where the sense of blackness was more readily definable in monolithic terms. Still, the effectiveness of these groups as mass movements were doubtful. Moreover, these organizations had little impact on the perceptions of Brazilians. The Frente Negra, or the Black

Front, for example, gave unwavering support to President Getúlio Vargas, and forged a sense of blackness within a broader construction of *brasilidade* rather than in opposition to it. The Teatro Experimental do Negro was faced with immediate goals of survival and recognition. In the beginning it relied on a number of individuals interested in Afro-Brazilian culture, including many such as Gilberto Freyre or Jorge Amado who were not necessarily interested in promoting black consciousness.

'Afro-Brazilian culture' was a term that went beyond personal identity, for example. Indeed Freyre and Amado, both biologically mulatto or *mestiço*, were part of white Brazilian culture, yet saw 'Afro-Brazilian culture' just as much 'theirs' (i.e. part of their national identity) as any black Brazilian. This discourse cannot be overlooked since, on the one hand, it is indicative of a sense of consciousness among some white Brazilians. Recognition of importance does not necessarily translate into political support of rights, however. Indeed, for many years individuals such as Freyre and Amado saw no need for specific laws outlawing discrimination. This attitude has been described by Florestan Fernandes as the prejudice of having no prejudice.

Throughout the text, I employ Brazilian racial and cultural terminology in Portuguese and in English translation. The Portuguese terms are italicized. Thus I may use the English 'mulatta' and the Portuguese '*mulata*'. All translations of Portuguese names, terms, lyrics and texts are mine.

This work is hardly the definitive work on race relations and national identity in Brazil, but rather it seeks to look at the inter-section of both from a new perspective. National identity emerges from a dialogue among texts. Here, I examine many of them while showing how some texts are privileged over others. Popular culture and civil rights rhetoric emerged under a powerful framework of patriotism, and Brazilian race relations in the modern era cannot be understood without understanding the overwhelming power of patriotism and nationalism in Brazilian history.

Acknowledgments

Many people and institutions have helped bring this work to fruition. Thanks go to Robert Levine for his comments on an earlier version of this work. I would also like to express my gratitude to Dan Mack and Andrew Davenport, two of my students at Middlebury College, who helped me with various tasks during the preparation of the manuscript. I am indebted to many Brazilians who helped me gather and interpret information for this project. I am also grateful to the staff at the National Archives in Rio and at the Museum of Image and Sound in Rio, as well as to those at the Center for Latin American and Caribbean Studies at New York University. Special thanks go to Middlebury College for its generous research support. Comments from the many anonymous readers and to the staff at Ashgate helped me shape this text. Finally, I wish to thank my family for their patience during the research and writing of this work.

1. Race and National Identity in Brazil: A Latin American perspective

> Ideology is an unconscious tendency under-lying religious and scientific as well as political thought: the tendency at a given time to make facts amenable to ideas, and ideas to facts, in order to create a world image convincing enough to support the collective and the individual sense of identity...the total perspective created by ideological simplification reveals its strength by the dominance it exerts on the seemingly logic of historic events, and by its influence on the identity formation of individuals.
>
> Eric H. Erikson, *Young Man Luther: A Study in Psychoanalysis and History*

Since the transition of the Brazilian political system from military to civilian rule in 1985, Brazilian and American scholars, civil rights activists, and politicians have intensified their studies and debates on race and race relations in Brazil. One result has been a healthy growth in the number of scholarly manuscripts and journal articles on a wide variety of subjects. Unfortunately, much of the debate still centers around questions about Brazilian *racial democracy*. Critics in this country and in Brazil have continually charged that the image of Brazil as a *racial democracy* with few racial antagonisms was essentially a myth constructed by the Brazilian elite. Defenders of Brazilian culture who point to many examples of racial cooperation, particularly in the realm of popular culture, have responded that even so, blacks and whites in Brazil have encountered less tensions throughout history than many of their Latin American counterparts and certainly less than their counterparts in the United States. Few scholars have sought to address the historical roots of the Brazilian racial ethos, although many agree that the 1930s was a crucial decade in the formulation of the modern discourse on race and national identity in Brazil.

Less than fifty years after abolition in 1888, Brazil saw the emergence of a new political regime with a nationalist world view. This nationalist period coincided with an age of technological developments in communications and media, which saw a proliferation of newspapers and

1

radio stations around the country. This was also the decade that witnessed the emergence of Brazil's first national civil rights organization, the *Frente Negra Brasileira* (Brazilian Black Front or the FNB). The relationship between patriotic nationalism and ethnic nationalism in the 1930s would impact the discourse on Brazilian national identity for the remainder of the century.

This work examines the position of blacks and the idea of 'blackness' within Brazilian patriotism and national identity from the turn of the century to the end of World War II, placing particular emphasis on the period from 1930-1945 when national icons and symbols became institutionalized thanks to the effort of President Getúlio Vargas who consolidated the federal system of Brazil for the first time. It assesses the dialogue between the struggle for black political and cultural representation and the larger developments of Brazilian patriotic nationalism paying close attention to popular mediums of communication.

Brazilian nationalists under Vargas forged and propagated an all-inclusive national identity which promoted the idea of a racially harmonious Brazilian national family. Vargas' generation succeeded in encouraging Brazilians to identify with 'the nation' above other possible communities such as racial, ethnic or regional ones. In the process, nationalists created enduring national myths and symbols which successfully marginalized racial consciousness for the rest of the twentieth century. This introductory chapter aims to place the Brazilian process within the larger Latin American discourse on race and national identity. The marginalizing of ethnic movements coexisted with a denigration of the African influence and a general de-legitimization of blackness as a viable component of national identity. While contemplating the value of minorities to the nation, intellectuals in the 1920s and 1930s, Vargas' generation, promoted Latin American's hybridity and racial mixing above an authentic appreciation of separate cultural identities within one nation. Moreover the views of miscegenation and the mulatto in particular, was often stereotypical or one-dimensional.

Given the legacy of slavery, and the association of blacks with that institution, official Brazilian nationalism had for decades successfully avoided associating blacks and blackness with Brazilian nationhood. By focusing on economic, cultural, political, and racial unity, Brazilians established a national rhetoric of *brasilidade*, or Brazilian-ness, based on the uniqueness of a so-called Brazilian cosmic race comprised of Africans, Europeans, and native peoples. Aided by a host of optimistic intellectuals, and a popular faith in the country's potential, as late as the 1960s, Brazilian authoritarianism had successfully avoided introspection and any meaningful discussion of its history and the role of blacks within the nation.

The military, which had suspended all civil rights in 1968, had in 1964 rebelled against the government of João Goulart, a protégé of Getúlio Vargas. Vargas was Brazil's most controversial and longest serving chief statesman who served as president from 1930-1945, and again from 1951-1954. The nationalist tactics perfected under the military regime in the 1960s first emerged in Brazil with the rise of Getúlio Vargas to national prominence in 1930. Technological developments in print journalism, together with new developments in the radio industry allowed the regime to create Brazil's first national propaganda machine with widespread, yet ambiguous duties. Benedict Anderson's *Imagined Communities* (1983) has already shown that a nation's means of communication plays a significant role in establishing links among individuals with shared experiences within a nation. Earlier, Karl Deutsch iterated those claims in *Nationalism and Social Communication*. This is particularly true of the forging and propagation of a dominant national identity--how a nation defines itself. And Ernst Gellner likewise reported that nationalism invented nations where they did not exist.[1]

While the invention of the printing press aided in the propagation of national identities, newspapers were not the only, or even the most important, forms of communication. Indeed non-written texts such as musical compositions, oral traditions and the like, have been crucial to the propagation of national entities. In countries where there are low literacy rates, oral modes of communication have played important parts in maintaining a cohesive sense of national self. This is particularly true of Latin American nations in general and Brazil in particular. In the twentieth century, music has not only helped to disseminate myths of 'the national', but musical styles and rhythms have become inextricable intertwined with individuals' identity.

National identity, like any label, however, is a starting point which, upon closer examination, is quickly fragmented by individual human experience. Race, not surprisingly, represents one of the most important social parameters that have affected our visions of 'the national'. Despite widespread miscegenation which facilitated a Brazilian culture based on the combining of distinct cultural elements, 'race' remained an important indicator of privilege in society. Moreover, Brazilian society continues to maintain an unofficial caste system based on color in which *brancos* (whites) remain at the top, people of mixed racial ancestry *(mulatos, mestiços, morenos, coboclos, etc.)* occupy the middle sector, and blacks *(pretos)* occupy the lowest rung. Racial prejudice aside,

Brazilian writers have often employed the term *raça* to refer to the Brazilian nation, made up of members of all races.

While exploring the state, intellectual, and popular conceptualizations of Brazil's identity through important national institutions, it will be important to document the Brazilian nationalist desire to distance modern Brazil from slavery (which implied avoiding associating Brazilian-ness with blacks or blackness). The inability of black Brazilians to affect or contribute to the discourse of national identity relates largely to the social position of blacks in Latin American society and the relatively few mechanisms which allowed for social mobility. In seeking to place this study of Brazil in a larger Latin American, if not, American framework, two tasks must first be accomplished. First, it will be important to examine the contribution of scholars whose work has informed this study. Second, this introduction surveys Brazil's historical discourse on race and national identity in relation to the wider Latin American discourse of the nineteenth century.

The Scholarly Contribution

The work of many scholars have informed this book. Indeed this work seeks to dialogue with other works in the fields of nationalism and race relations. The scholarship on Brazilian nationalism is varied and uneven. The now classic work by Nelson Werneck Sodré, *Raízes histócas do nacionalismo brasileiro* attempts to explain the roots of Brazilian nationalism, while Olympio Guilherme's work, *O nacionalismo e a política internacional do Brasil* looks at foreign relations, particularly from 1930s, and emphasizes Brazil's economic nationalism. José Perreira Lira's book *Temas de nossos dias: Nacionalismo, corrupção, presença das massas*, published during the same period, is more critical and contains diverse essays on nationalism from the 1930s to the 1950s.[2]

Recent book-length publications have revisited the Vargas years from diverse perspectives. Two were most helpful. Lúcia Lippi Oliveira, *A questão nacional na Primeira República* provides an analysis of nationalism in the period prior to the Vargas' Estado Novo. Arturo Ariel Betancur examines Brazilian nationalism from the outside in *Getúlio Vargas: nacionalismo e industrialización en el Brasil, 1930-1945.*[3] The author traces Vargas' economic policies an its impact on neighboring countries.

Several articles by Brazilians have helped shaped my ideas, and are properly cited in the text. Many others will be of immense importance to students of Brazilian cultural nationalism. They include works by Regina Maria do Rego Monteiro Abreu, 'Emblemas da nacionalidade: o culto a Euclides da Cunha'; Aracy A. Amaral, 'Oswald de Andrade e as artes plásticas no modernismo dos anos veinte'; Maria Luiza Tucci Carneiro, 'Sob a máscara do nacionalismo: autoritarismo e anti-semitismo na era Vargas, 1930-1945'; and Mônica Pimenta Velloso, 'A brasilidade verde-amarela: nacionalismo e regionalismo paulista'. Leonardo Senkman's 1997 essay which compares the nationalist and populist tactics of Juan Perón in Argentina to those of Getulio Vargas provided a framework for future intra-American comparisons.[4]

Works in English have, of course, been equally as important. Victor Alba's 1968 book on the tensions between the oligarchy and the masses, *Nationalists Without Nations* helped lay the foundations for future studies of nationalism in Latin America. While few works have been dedicated specifically to nationalism under Getúlio Vargas, Robert Levine's work on Vargas has been indispensable, particularly his 1998 *Father of the Poor? Vargas and His Era.* In an earlier work, *The Vargas Regime: The Critical Years 1934-1938*, Levine includes a chapter on patriotism and nationalism in the 1930s that place these ideologies within the Brazilian twentieth century context.[5]

Studies on race in Brazil have tended to focus on abolition and the pre-abolition era, although that may change in the near future. Many compare race relations in Brazil with other American national formations, particularly the United States. Donald Pierson for example, emphasized that conflicts were not racial but cultural in his article 'Os africanos da Bahia'.[6] He tended to support the theory of the forerunner of comparative race relations, Frank Tannenbaum, who portrayed the African slave of Latin America in a rather positive light in comparison to the slave in the southern United States.[7] Stanley Elkins followed with a similar study that developed Tannenbaum's thesis, arguing that slavery in the U.S. was a result of rampant capitalism while in Latin America the presence of the Church and laws of manumission did not allow the slave to be reduced to the status of commodity.[8] This line of thinking served to enhance Brazilian nationalist writers who claimed that the uniqueness of the Brazilian racial experience engendered a Brazilian 'cosmic race', based on the construction of the 'Casa Grande'.[9]

Many others, such as Seymour Drecher, have argued the contrary. In his article, 'Brazilian Abolition in Corporate Perspective', Drecher points to various local factors that made Brazilian slavery not milder, but more distinct from American slavery.[10] Meanwhile, Robert Brent Toplin in his *The Abolition of Slavery in Brazil* and in *Freedom and*

Prejudice documented the abolitionist movement, implying that abolition in Brazil was rushed through by often violent means in order to avoid social revolution, or anything similar to what occurred in Haiti.[11] Arthur F. Crownin follows Toplin's lead, explaining that emancipation liberated blacks in name only. As evidence, he states that today blacks still occupy the bottom of the socioeconomic scale. The debate will undoubtedly continue and invlove many scholars who are not listed above. Luckily, Stuart B. Schwartz provides a comprehensive assessment of the literature in the first chapter of *Slaves, Peasants, and Rebels: Reconsidering Brazilian Slavery* (1992).[12]

The period from 1888-1945 has not received the same amount of attention as the nineteenth century. The seminal work to date on race relations and national identity in this era is undoubtedly Florestan Fernandes' *The Negro in Brazilian Society*.[13]   Florestan Fernandes has written a plethora of articles and books on race and national culture.[14] Fernandes, however, dealt specifically with the status of blacks in São Paulo. Numerous scholars follow in Fernandes footsteps looking at racial relations from a socio-historical perspective.[15]   Carl Degler's *Neither Black nor White* briefly looked into color consciousness in his work on race relations. Degler concludes that whites dilute their prejudice, but as blacks educate themselves and become more stable economically, prejudices will manifest themselves as in the United States.[16] Abdias do Nascimento goes one step further in his *O Genocídio do Negro Brasileiro* that chronicles the cultural and physical genocide of blacks in Brazil.[17]   Finally, Clóvis Moura's *Brasil: As Raizes do Protesta Negro* has contributed to the historiography by looking at the black movement in São Paulo from 1930-1970.[18]

Other studies have reinterpreted the ideas of Gilberto Freyre and Tannenbaum using modern social science techniques.[19]   In *Democracia racial: ideología e realidade*, Thales de Azevedo has gathered a series of views on racial democracy in Portuguese that has yet to be translated.[20] Alberto Guerreiro Ramos makes a poignant attack on the myths of nationhood by looking at the differences between facts and myths about race relations in Brazil.[21]   Other studies have shown the complex relationship between race, class, and regional perceptions. Robert Toplin, for example, has looked at racial relations in the context of Brazil's boom in development,[22] while Charles Wagley has looked at race relations in the backlands.[23]

A handful of studies have looked at the role of intellectuals and the connection of their ideas to the politics and events of their respective eras. Intellectuals and their forging of national identity is the focus of a superb collection of essays edited by Richard Graham. Thomas Skidmore investigates racial attitudes and social policy in Brazil from 1870-1940,[24] and Bolivar Lamounier has looked at the political implications of whitening and the co-optation of lower classes by national ideals that stymied the successful mobilization of black consciousness movements as well as any form of non-white solidarity.[25] A decade earlier, Edison de Sousa Carneiro studied the inclusion of blacks as part of national culture in his acclaimed essay 'La nacionalización del negro en el Brasil'.[26]

In the 1950s, Era Bell Thompson's popular piece posited one of the more important questions and problems of co-optation and absorption of cultural minorities in 'Does Amalgamation Work in Brazil?'[27] This question was one of the main focuses of several good essays and literary texts. Many have attempted to articulate the contribution of history and literature to national image and identity. Among the more salient are Antônio Cândido's 'Literature and the Rise of Brazilian National Identity',[28] and Wilson Martins' *The Modernist Idea*.[29] Martins' work is the best historical study of modernist influence in Brazilian history during the period 1910-1950, although John Nist has also produced an excellent appraisal of the modernists in their quest for a nationalist aesthetic.[30] David T. Haberly has also published a work that looks at racial identity, mixture, and ethnic diversity as depicted in Brazilian literature.[31]

João Cruz Costa and Emilia Viotti da Costa have produced the most decisive works that analyze intellectual thought and political myths in modern Brazil. Cruz Costa's work represents one of the few studies which has provided an evolution of ideas in Brazil to date. He provides a thorough analysis of the influences of European philosophy on Brazilian thinking and the adaptation of some of those ideas to Brazilian reality. In the Hegelian tradition, Cruz Costa discusses the constant dialectic between the idea or desire and the material reality.[32]

Emilia Viotti da Costa's *The Brazilian Empire: Myth and Histories* provides another historical analysis of Brazilian social history. It deals extensively with ideas in Brazil from liberalism on to the 1930s nationalist ideology. In chapter nine, she looks closely at the myth of racial democracy as an idea, and attempts to explain how ideas are both products of their time as well as reflections of the people that espouse them. She provides a refreshing reappraisal of race relations in the twentieth century from a philosophical perspective, taking into consideration evolving social relations.[33]

More recently, scholars such as George Reid Andrews, *Blacks and Whites in São Paulo, Brazil, 1888-1988* (1991), and Michael George Hanchard, *Orpheus and Power: The Movimento Negro of Rio de Janeiro and São Paulo, Brazil, 1945-1988* (1994) have explored black political organizations in the post-abolition era.   Kim Butler's recent *Freedoms Given Freedoms Won: Afro-Brazilians in Post Abolition São Paulo and Salvador* (1998) is an important contribution to the study of black political and social life.   Butler provides an array of insightful information on black social, cultural and political activities, while carefully placing them into the broader national contexts.   Still, information on the role of race in the construction of Brazilian national identity remains an understudied field of inquiry.   No work to date has examined how Brazilian nationalism in the 1920s and 1930s succeeded in forging and institutionalizing a dominant national identity based on cultural inter-mixing, but with a clear aversion to 'blackness'.   Nor have scholars paid enough attention to the nascent media, particularly the developments in print journalism, radio and the record industry that allowed these forums to be exploited in the forging of Brazilian national identity.

In many ways, Brazil is both typically a Latin American country with its transference of Iberian culture and its reliance on indigenous and African labor, and unique in its struggle for independence while depending almost exclusively on Africans and peoples of African descent for its economy.   It is often said that after Nigeria, Brazil has more people of African descent than any other country in the world.   After Tokyo, Brazil's industrial city of São Paulo is home to more Japanese than any other place in the world.   There is also a sizable German, Italian and Jewish population in Southern Brazil.   Yet as a rule, even today, Brazilians remain more nationally conscious than racially so.   As in other areas of Latin America, ethnic nationalism, although growing in some areas such as Uruguay has never matched the fervor of patriotic nationalism.[34]   No discussion of race and national identity in modern Brazil is possible, however, without first examining the historical construction of Latin American nations in general and the Brazilian nation in particular.

The importation of African slaves to Brazil began as a measure to supply a much needed labor force.   In 1559, a triangular trade route began between Brazil, Portugal, and Africa.   The impetus for the slave trade was the commencement of a way of life that privileged the Portuguese colonizers.   As Colin MacLachlan has indicated, the plantation system based on African slavery began the ideal model for the Portuguese's American colony.[35]   The slave population in Brazil in 1798 was estimated at over a million and a half, and before 1850 another million and a half would reach Brazilian shores.

In multiracial or multiethnic societies such as the American nations, national identity is necessarily a product of the racial or ethnic tensions that have developed over time. In the United States, for example, dual categorization of racial identity ensured that race and class were closely related. The colonial class structure engendered a caste system in so far as the white colonizers, by virtue of their race, were inherently of a higher status.   People of African descent, regardless of economic considerations, occupied an inferior social status. The dominant national identity in such a system was synonymous with one's social class. Although whiteness did not always indicate privilege, blackness signified the lack of it. In most Latin American societies a similar social structure emerged, although official recognition of miscegenation blurred the dual relationship of power.   The first stage of colonization excluded the participation of European women, therefore European men took native women and later African women as sexual partners. Henceforth began a widespread process of miscegenation, creating a new people of mixed racial heritage. As history would have it, a large population of mulattos and mestizos emerged as a distinct social category, but still inferior to the white.

Naturally, these distinctions varies from region to region and in some cases from town to town. Given the historical autonomy of Brazilian *captaincies*, which later developed into states, for example, strong state identities emerged over time.   Nonetheless, the general distinctions between the conquerors and the oppressed in Latin American colonial societies paralleled other European frameworks of empire. This European framework where difference was treated as inferior assured European settlers of superior positions in societies. Thus, Europeans born on the peninsular, (*renois* in the case of the Portuguese, *peninsulares* for the Spanish) were socially superior to Europeans born in the Americas, (*Creoles* in Spanish America, *mazombos* in Brazil). Indians and Africans occupied the lowest level of the social hierarchy, and the mixed population facilitated ethnic fluidity.

The emerging class system in Latin America was incompatible with the Iberian categorization of race. Theoretically, Africans and Indians or those who were tainted with their bloods were not considered *gente boa* (good people). However, many Spaniards and Portuguese raised their *mestizo* or *mulato* children as white.   In turn, the society at large considered them such, affording them privileges based on their class status. Other *mestizos* and *mulattos* not recognized by their fathers lived and were raised by their African and indigenous mothers and attained the consciousness of the lower classes. Thus patriarchy established a male-determined pattern of power and privilege in society which served as a model for the construction of the national family, that is the nation.

By the end of the eighteenth century, European Enlightenment had produced a new philosophy of liberalism which called for the equality, liberty and fraternity of men. These were the supposed tenets of the French Revolution of 1789 which would have a direct impact on Latin America. But liberty was shaped in terms of an anti-colonial discourse. Equality referred to equal standing of Creoles with *peninsulares*. Only in Haiti, a colony that was overwhelmingly black did abolition of slavery and independence go hand in hand. In other regions, independence preceded abolition in some cases by twenty to thirty years, and in the case of Brazil almost seventy! Nonetheless, the promise of abolition helped Latin American independence leaders attain the support of their slaves.

With the exception of Haiti, the wars of independence were detrimental to most blacks in Latin America. Blacks and mulattos, slave and free, participated disproportionately in these fights, and hundreds died for a Creole cause. Mulattos such as José Antonio Paez were instrumental in Simón Bolivar's struggles in northern South America. The expression 'damned if you do, damned if you don't' surely applied to blacks and mulattos in the wars of independence, since despite the fact that they gave their lives for the nationalist cause, they were often looked upon suspiciously. The 'Temor del Negro/Temor do Negro' or 'The Fear of the Black' lingered as Creoles and *Mazombos* dreaded the possibility that blacks would somehow take over the country as they did in Haiti. It takes no stretch of the imagination to see that this fear could only result in the marginalization of blacks from future national economic and political possibilities.

Prior to the nineteenth century, national consciousness, where it existed, was an upper class luxury. Latin Americans from the upper classes derived their identity from their class positions, in part reflecting racial overtones. Although Spaniards strongly identified with regions in Spain, in Latin America they also identified with a central metropolis symbolized by the monarchy. The major obstacle to economic and political dominance of the Latin American upper classes, were the European *peninsulares* who controlled trade and commerce and reinforced the distinction between *peninsular* and Creole. National consciousness was predicated on racist beliefs that European dominance was justified by natural law, and thus excluded other non-white racial groups from their discussions of regional identity. Even after the wars of independence, in which many non-whites participated, when Latin American writers wrote of the Mexican or Brazilian nation, they essentially meant Creole Mexico or Luso-Brazil. Their writings dominated due to access to the means of communication of the time (especially newspapers). Indians and Blacks as well as the lower class mestizos were absent from this formulation. This should come as no surprise considering the fact that only in the latter part of the twentieth century are we beginning to hear diverse ethnic voices, even in the United States where access to capital far outstrips Latin American possibilities.

Aversion to 'blackness' has been fundamental to all American nations which have attempted to promote a 'modern' image, as if 'modern' meant eliminating history. In the absence of a concerted social and political program that would guarantee black citizens' rights, Latin American leaders have traditionally carved out a place for blacks in its static formulations of national culture and history. At the same time, many states pursued immigration policies, discrimination and other mechanisms which have succeeded in marginalizing blacks from any opportunities of power. In this regard, black pride movements such as *negritude*, which began with French Caribbean and African writers in Paris in the 1930s, were important anti-nationalist revolutions of the twentieth century which brought the question of race to center stage. Black intellectuals exposed Western societies' aversion to blackness, and their dismissal of black culture to the West, a world that was their own. While no strong *negritude* movement has ever emerged in Spanish or Portuguese-speaking Latin America, the black contribution to the modern nation formation is undeniable. Unfortunately, official avoidance of discussion of that contribution is equally so.

Independence, Race and Nationhood

Simón Bolívar (1783-1830), the South American independence revolutionary hero, was like most Creoles of his day, intensely skeptical of the ability of the masses to partake fully in the new United States of South America that he envisioned. Disdain for the masses became a general of his stature regardless of his political persuasion, as did a racist ethos which pervaded Latin America since the time of Columbus, and which held Africans and Indians in considerably low esteem. Still, at the turn of the nineteenth century, Africans, Indians, and their offspring constituted a majority of the population of the Americas. Add to that the growing numbers of mulattos, mestizos and other *castas*, Creole men such as Bolívar were an absolute minority. Still, with history, morality, and liberalism on his side, Bolívar, armed with both pen and sword, galvanized the masses to create a unified front against Spanish oppression, tyranny, and the rape of American soil. Independence!

Bolívar was initially reluctant to include blacks in his campaign against the Spanish, but prejudice gave way to political expediency.[36] Among the former African slaves who participated in the independence wars were Lieutenant Leonardo Infante, the mulatto general José Laurencio Silva, and the black Colombian admiral and popular personality, José Prudencio Padilla, hero of the Colombian Navy, who saw battle in Venezuela. Padilla served as a vivid reminder of the price of independent thought. He was eventually executed in 1828, supposedly for attempting to murder Bolívar. Padilla is only one story among many. Blacks, of course, participated in the campaigns of San Martín in the Rio de la Plata region, and in the struggles of Mexico and Central America. In Uruguay the famous 'Black Battalion' gave their support to the Uruguayan independence. During the Cisplatine War, 1825-1829, Afro-Uruguayans such as Dionisio Oribe and Joaquin Artigas showed valor, as had many others in the creation of the Banda Oriental del Uruguay, the youngest South American republic. After independence, the race question centered mostly on slavery and its role in the modern nation, not on the welfare of blacks. As the nation-states defined their geopolitical territories, national consolidation and order became of primordial importance. Within this context, the post-colonial elites wanted to ensure that their nations possessed the appropriate labor to guarantee the proper functioning of their economies.

Bolívar's Creole identity served him well, for despite his privileged position he was able to claim solidarity with his 'American' brothers, both slave and free. The common enemy-Spain-had provided a cause around which he galvanized the support of the popular masses for whom he had a genuine sympathy although his social background would not allow him to regard any of them as his equal. The masses had proven loyal in the attack on French colonialism in Saint Dominigue, and Bolívar counted on them to fill the ranks of his armies. Bolívar employed the language of unity like a politician who is about to run for office despite the anti-black feelings that he and his class harbored.[37]

To fight colonialism, Creoles planted the seeds of nationalism which espoused the creation of American nations.[38] While nationalism urged identification with (if not adoration of) the community of people we call nation, seeing that identification as fundamental to its political, economic, or cultural survival, strictly speaking, the wars of independence were not nationalist wars. Men like Bolívar were interested in the creation of states, political units, that would have responsibility for the laws of the land. The rhetoric of an incipient nationalism was at best romantic praise of some abstract notion of *patria*. Creoles did not dream of a multiethnic nation of citizens; rather their larger goals of freedom from Spain had no vision aimed at resolving racial disparities. The nineteenth century seemed like a Pirandello play: 'Creole Nationalists in Search of Latin American Nations'. Indeed as Edward Said has argued, nationalism which accompanies decolonization passes though two stages: resistance against an outsider and secondly, ideological resistance when efforts are made to reconstitute a shattered community, to save or restore the sense and fact of community against all pressures.

Resistance against the Portuguese metropolis in Brazil was not as torrid as in the Spanish-American cases. Brazil's road to independence represents one of the many Latin American anomalies in the formation of the modern Brazilian nation-state. The famed Joaquim Jose da Silva Xavier, popularly known as Tiradentes, launched the *Inconfidência Mineira*, an attack against the Portuguese colonial government in late 1788. The Portuguese thwarted this effort, however, executing Tiradentes in 1792.

The War of the Tailors, an eighteenth-century revolt by soldiers, sharecroppers, and mulatto artisans who espoused the abolition of all existing governmental structures including slavery compounded their fears. Nonetheless, it created a conservative backlash resulting in the capture and death of the leaders of the revolt, and the precarious slaves saw no amelioration in their condition. Slave protests, riots, rebellions and growing philosophical opposition to slavery accelerated the process of abolition, and the eventual signing of the *Lei Aurea*, or the Golden Law in 1888. Despite anti-Portuguese attitudes and the emerging abolitionist movement, the socioeconomic system remained unchanged. Moreover, the absence of a national university and the limited Catholic authority in Brazil (since the Jesuits had been expelled in 1759) meant that no other authority could challenge the elite's world view.[39]

With the French Revolution, one year after the independence cries of Tiradentes, news of the abolition of slavery by the French reached slaves' ears.[40] The 1791 success of the Haitian Revolution led by blacks and mulattos against the white aristocracy also shook Brazil. Although the threat was closer to Cuban shores, Brazilian elites suffered from the 'Fear of the Negro'.[41] Events in Brazil compounded their fears. The liberal ideas which in western Europe meant the struggle against absolutism and the power of the Church, as well as against any obstacles to free trade and material progress, were also adopted by Latin American elites of the nineteenth century. The supporters of liberalism in Brazil were traditionally those agricultural lords connected with the import-export economy, who supported slavery as well as progress, which they saw as closely linked. Though many pushed for more autonomy, compared to other Latin American nations, the Brazilian independence movement was weak.[42]

Events on the Iberian peninsula ultimately set the independence movement in motion. In 1808, with the Napoleonic invasion imminent, the Portuguese royal family fled to Brazil where they would remain for fourteen years. Once in Brazil, the Crown opened Brazilian ports to foreign shipping, enhanced the beauty of the new capital, and eventually elevated Brazil's status from colony to kingdom. When the Portuguese crown reluctantly returned to Portugal in 1822, King João left behind his Brazilian-born son, Pedro, who would later declare independence from Portugal on September 7, 1822. The monarchy, as symbol of Brazilian unity, endured until a little more than a decade before the end of the century.

Throughout the nineteenth century, slavery brutalized Africans and natives in Brazil, but also relied on them to populate Brazil. On the arrival of the crown to Rio de Janeiro for example, for every white there were ten blacks, three mulattos, and three *caboclos*. African slavery steadily increased until the abolition of the slave trade in 1850, although the institution was not abolished until 1888. All this despite João's signing of a treaty to limit the practices. The success of the Haitian Revolution led by blacks and mulattos against the white aristocrats also shook Brazil, and the Brazilian elites likewise suffered from what has been called the 'Fear of the Negro'.[43]

The 'Fear of the Negro' in particular, and of the masses in general, was so great that abolition was virtually impossible until the end of the nineteenth century. Despite the slaves' importance to the Brazilian economy, white Brazilians emphasized the European aspects of the land. Their image in the international arena was of utmost importance, and Brazilians had begun an impressive trade with the United States by the middle of the nineteenth century.[44] Class alliance, in this context, became even more important than political affiliation. Indeed very little differentiated the Liberal Party from the Conservative except that they alternated in power in the Parliament. Both despised and feared the masses and had worked out an accord in 1852 known as the *conciliação*.

Still, it is instructive to mention that prior to the 1880s, the image of Brazil as a *senzala*, a slave quarter, was partially balanced by its image as a monarchy. The monarchy provided unity, a connection with Europe, and a royal figure which provided moral authority. While slavery, had become a major set back to European immigration, many Brazilians, even abolitionists, claimed that Brazilian slaves were better off than many of the

European free workers, and certainly better off than the freed slaves in the United States. Joaquim Nabuco (1849-1910), a major spokesman for the abolitionist-republican movement, indicated that the relationship between abolition and immigration was not incidental. Essential to his anti-slavery stand was his hope for *embranqueamento*, or whitening, of seeing Brazil as becoming more European.[45] For this reason, Nabuco also opposed the immigration of East Asians as it would 'complicate the situation'.[46] Despite his motives, he argued that blacks had a right to freedom as 'creators of Brazil', setting the precedent for a rhetoric that would inspire writers in the 1930s. Similar to other Brazilian writers, Nabuco compared the plight of blacks in Brazil to blacks in the United States, stating that there was some mobility of Brazilian blacks who were better off than their counterparts in the United States. Nabuco believed that Brazilian culture had afforded Africans opportunities that the United States had denied them.[47] His indictment of blacks in Brazil is undeniable. He attributed the problems in Brazil to the African presence, asserting that the vice of African blood came into widespread circulation, not owing to the African, but to the system of slavery. 'Without slavery', he explained, '... Brazil could have been like Canada or Australia'.[48]

Nabuco's discussion of race reflected two important perceptions of his class and his generation. First, the slave was not inferior because he was African, but because he was a slave. This was an attempt to justify abolition, while downplaying the 'Fear of the Negro'. Brazilians still considered blacks culturally inferior, and their inferiority was associated with their ethnicity. Brazilian national identity would not, indeed could not, include blacks as equal participants in the nation. This construction was not uniquely Brazilian. Latin American intellectuals from Mexico to Peru had somehow managed to avoid discussing blacks by dismissing race as a non-issue, or by focusing on a romantic view of the native.

The Cuban martyr and national hero, José Martí, is a case in point. Martí, the Cuban independence fighter *par excellence* positively defined his identity within a national framework. He attacked the myth of the inferiority of the mixed blood at a time when Cuba's population was more than half *mulato*, or mixed.[49] Martí continuously stressed the lack of racial conflict among Cubans in an address to a New York audience in 1895: 'In Cuba there is no fear whatever of racial conflict. A man is more than white, black, or mulatto. A Cuban is more than white, black or mulatto'. Martí's Cuba was undoubtedly plagued by racial prejudice, yet this rhetoric of unity attempted to rise above it.[50]

As in Cuba, Brazilian blacks and particularly mulattos such as José de Patrocinio, Machado de Assis, Luiz Gama, and João da Cruz e

Souza, supported abolition. But few voices problematized or challenged the Brazilian silence on issues of race relations, particularly after abolition. Moreover, after 1889, the liberal ideas of nationhood based on liberty, fraternity, and equality seemed to apply only to whites and *near whites*. The popular masses would remain invisible until their co-optation in the 1920s. For now, the Brazilian elite called for European immigration to solve what they perceived as Brazil's cultural backwardness, just as Sarmiento had done in Argentina almost a century earlier. As Katia M. Queiros' insightful comment recalls: 'Very few slaves saw their dreams of freedom come true... Rejoicing was short. Freedom was the freedom to remain poor and indigent'.[51]

That the Brazilian elite ruled with little or no political opposition until the 1880s indicated the lack of social or political change throughout the century and the class-based imperative of any semblance of national consciousness. The liberal ideas which in Europe meant the struggle against absolutism and the power of the Church, as well as against any obstacles to free trade and material progress, in Brazil, continued to be the rights of a selected elite class.[52] Hayden White has aptly indicated that 'historical situations are not inherently tragic, comic, or romantic. All the historian needs to do to transform a tragic event into a comic situation is to shift his point of view or change the scope of his perceptions'.[53] Prior to the 1950s, Brazilian writers such as Gilberto Freyre had for a very long time looked back on its uncharacteristic Latin American history with pride in its benign conflicts and apparent solidarity.

In neighboring Argentina, the dictatorship of Juan Manuel de Rosas, 1829-1852, and a vociferous and respected intelligentsia in exile, provided a wealth of written materials on Argentine society which was not paralleled in the case of Brazil. The Argentine intellectual discourse against dictatorship also provided a curious window into views on blacks and blackness in the 19th Century. Rosas had been rightly criticized for his autocratic rule, particularly in the 1830s, but Argentine intellectuals such as Juan Domingo Sarmiento and Esteban Echeverría utilized a discourse of race that vilified Rosas, associating him with blacks, mulattos, and the popular masses, or what Sarmiento calls 'barbarism'. Thus blacks were used as an effective way to criticize Rosas and to call for change. After Rosas' defeat in 1852, Sarmiento and others would call for the importation of 'civilization' which meant European immigration.[54]

From 1830-1888, race remained a subversive force in Latin American politics and society, masked by lofty republican ideals of citizenship and modernity. Creole disdain for the masses had much to do with an aversion for 'anything' associated with the slave classes, and protection of their elite position.   As Roderick J. Barman informs us, 'Blacks were dispised, but indispensible'.   Indeed, most of Brazil was either black or mulatto, yet the elite believed slavery to be crucial to their social and economic well-being.[55]   Unlike our modern concept of prejudice which has promoted segregation and avoidance of racial interaction, the post-independence Latin American society was one of tolerance--in the Erasmian sense of the word-- 'the acceptance of a necessary evil'.   Indeed as scholars such as Rebecca Scott and Stuart Schwartz have already emphasized, slavery was not *one* aspect of Latin American society, but *the* model around which all activities were based: conomic, social, political and cultural.   After abolition, many Latin Americans continued to discrimate against blacks, while the states pursued policies that whitened their nations.

Within this context race took on an all-important meaning that determined one's every activity.   Race, however, meant different things to different people, and more than one meaning to many.   Brazilian racial categorization differed substantially from region to region, and like other Latin American cases relied both on biological traits, social and economic parameters.   But this too must be classified.   Indeed it was (and still is) only for the middle sector mestizos and mulattos that class and other social consideration predominates over biological determinants.   For *pretos*, dark blacks, the so-called mulatto escape hatch was virtually insignificant, although blacks, those sons and daughters of slaves, and some *mulattos*, children of slaves and their masters had long acquired a new world sense of identity *(crioulos)* distinct from their African forebears.

Yet the *mulato*, that brave hero that would be celebrated in the 1930s, was destined to be an escape hatch for whites, an invention that would soon be seen as evidence of the Portuguese benign conquest. Aluísio de Azevedo's classic text, *O mulato*, published in 1881 is at once a daring criticism of Brazilian racism at a time when Brazil was not yet prepared to officially recognize its mixed origins, and a reflection of elite views of the mulatto.   The themes of order and chaos, civilization and barbarism, are likewise present here.   Raimundo, a light-skinned mulatto with blue eyes falls in love with a white woman, but is eventually killed because he dared to dream that such a union was possible.   While Azevedo's work exposed the brutality of racial prejudice, it is the prejudiced reader who received the benefit of the final catharsis, as it imposes order and punishes the upstart to 'save the race'.   Kim Butler has insightfully described that phenomenon as a general imposition of order which 'has prevented the equitable participation of blacks in national society'.[56]

Azevedo had, nontheless, scandalized decent society just as his contemporary José Ferraz de Almeida Júnior had with his famous painting, *The Wooodcutter*, in 1879. These men must been seen as precursors of the modernist intellectuals of the 1920s, fostering a romantic vision of miscegenation and racial mixing in general and of the mulatto in particular. Azevedo's mulatto was talented, handsome, strong and not belligerent. He becomes as much as a national fetish, a stereotype as the white girl, representative of the beauty, with whom he falls in love. While some mulattos had gradually assimilated into dominant Brazilian society, many blacks and mulattos had been resisting Portuguese and Brazilian authorities since colonial rule.

In 1850, Brazil outlawed the slave trade, and although many slaves entered Brazil illegally after this time, this move helped consolidate a sense of Brazilian-ness among blacks with the number of foreign born slaves gradually diminishing. Still, given the Haitian Revolution, the upper classes feared becoming a black nation. Abolition, which meant freedom for the slave, and added security for the free men and women of color, meant the possibility of becoming modern for the whites and distancing themselves from slavery, that is, blackness.

History has a serendipitous nature for some. Even before abolition, Brazilian blacks would have an opportunity to serve their nation and to gain limited social mobility during the Paraguayan War or the War of the Triple Alliance (1865-1870) in which Uruguay, Argentina, and Brazil stripped their powerful Paraguayan neighbor of all military power, and decimated almost one third of its population. The war was detrimental to the black Brazilian population. According to Julio José Chiavenatto, the war was the first time in Brazilian history that the black population declined in absolute numbers. Between 60-100 thousand blacks perished.[57] Wars allowed Brazilians, however inadvertently, to diminish significantly their 'race problem'.

Abolition, too, was necessary to 'save the race', a term Brazilians often used to evoke the Brazilian desire to become more European, less African. But there was no clear sense among Latin Americans in general or among Brazilians in particular of what this actually meant. For blacks abolition signaled the potential for becoming full citizens to pursue economic and social opportunity previously denied them. Abolition also meant integration into 'the national', and unfortunately integration meant an acceptance of a white world view which carried with it the concept of *melhorar a raça*, or whitening. For whites abolition signaled the eradication of slavery associated with backwardness and a projection of a new nationhood free of the African past.

Nationhood, in the tradition of the French Revolution--which implied equality, liberty, and brotherhood among the members of the national community--in reality meant equality, liberty and brotherhood among the Creole classes or whites. After the independence movements of the nineteenth century, liberal ideas along with the developments of positivism reinforced the possibility of nationhood and American consciousness. At the same time, new ideas began to transform upper-class thinking. The Brazilian abolitionist movement, which developed out of liberal thinking saw slavery as inconsistent with national independence and national development. Since the international community perceived forced labor and illiteracy as signs of backwardness, free labor and education became a panacea for the ills of the colonized regions.

The emerging class system saw a new market in the growing wage earners, and late nineteenth-century industrialization inadvertently acknowledged the lower classes as an important consumer population. With the decline of the institution of slavery, a slow disjointed process of industrialization engendered an expanding wage-earning class with few political rights, but enjoying a slightly better standard of living. Urban industrialization, however, could not keep pace with Brazil's rapidly expanding city populations due to new European immigrants, and rural to urban migration. The Brazilian state joined other Latin American governments in encouraging European immigration to cleanse themselves of the 'backward populations'. The immigrants climbed up the social hierarchy at a more rapid pace than the ex-slave populations.

Even liberals who supported abolition did so not because they wanted slaves to be citizens, but because it was detrimental to their international image and their elite concept of nationhood. Joaquim Nabuco, one of Brazil's leading abolitionists, best reflects this view when he wrote in 1886, two years before abolition that:

> We do not want to eliminate slavery simply because it is morally illegitimate, but because slavery ruins the country economically, debases its politics and prevents immigration. Indeed it is a system which prevents our incorporation into modernity.[58]

This pessimism toward the darker elements of Latin American society is reflected in the public discourse throughout the nineteenth and early twentieth century, emerging, however, in distinct national or regional clothing. The Argentine Domingo Sarmiento, living in exile in Chile, had became the most eloquent and well-respected *letrado* of this pessimism creating a paradigm of national identity that Latin Americans would later adopt.   In his 19th century essay, *Civilization and Barbarism*, he characterized Argentina, then a typical Latin American society, populated by Creoles on the one hand and blacks and Indians on the other.   Latin America's ability to survive would depend on its ability 'to become like the United States, a nation that has successfully transferred European values in the Americas'.   Barbarism was all that was South American; its indigenous roots, its African slavery, its miscegenation, and its cultural mixing.   All this, Sarmiento associated with economic and political backwardness that had to be either eradicated or absorbed.   For Sarmiento, the conflict in Argentina raged between two parties; one European, liberal and of the City; and the other barbarous and South American.

Within Latin America, Argentines have continued to be villainized for being racist Europhiles who harbor anti-Latin American sentiments.   Sarmiento merely represented the views of a host of Latin American liberal thinkers.   Sarmiento's disdain is echoed in the work of Echeverría, who had like himself called forth his talents to criticize their greatest enemy, Juan Manuel de Rosas, who not coincidentally was easily ridiculed and villainized not only for his political butchery, but for his immense popularity among the popular class, largely black, mulatto and mestizo.   Brazil had no Rosas, nor did a perfidious system of oppression pit liberal intellectuals against an emerging nation; yet Brazilian liberals shared the desire to transform their society along more European lines as well.   What distinguished Argentina from the other South American republics at the turn of the nineteenth century was that Argentina's astute immigration policy succeeded in shifting its demographics drastically in three decades.   Argentina had become a 'civilized nation', and this necessarily meant the eradication of all that was barbarous, particularly the remnants of slavery.   It had adopted a constitution similar to the U.S., and attracted foreign investment like no other Latin American nation.

While Argentina celebrated, in many countries such as Brazil, Uruguay, Paraguay, Cuba, and the Dominican Republic, Creole intellectuals and politicians lamented the failure of liberalism to increase their well-being and transform their societies.   While all Latin American societies embraced abolition by the end of the nineteenth century, the newly created republics had not yet resolved issues of integration, or had not adequately developed mechanisms for the integration of its free and productive citizens, nor could many of them justify being called modern.   Rather, abolition assumed a freedom, not yet conquered, but nonetheless created a climate which would allow for the absorption of freed blacks into national life.   The distinction between integration and absorption is not incidental.   It was as if abolition signaled the disappearance of the black, and an intense regionalist rhetoric of union and consolidation would emerge within the writings of the Latin American modernists who celebrated cosmopolitanism and republicanism.   Racial and ethnic marginalization remained a 'non-topic' for generations to come.

At the turn of the century, notices about the deplorable conditions for workers in Brazil circulated throughout Europe discouraging any mass exodus from desired countries such as England and the German-speaking areas.   Still between 1904-1929 Brazil received a host of European immigrants not only from Portugal, Spain, Italy, and Japan respectively, but also from Turkey, Russia, Germany and Austria, most of whom settled in southern Brazil.   Indeed, before World War II, Latin America received more immigrants into the region than it sent out.   Implicit in the call for European immigrants was the notion of whitening, and thus Japanese immigration policy was often surrounded by a xenophobic discourse.   New capitalist investors and industrialists in South America preferred European labor to blacks because blacks represented backwardness and the past which Latin Americans wanted so badly to escape.   This was not necessarily the only course to be taken.   In Central America, economic projects such as the railroads and the Panama Canal depended upon skilled and unskilled cheap laborers from the Caribbean islands, black in their majority.   The demographic changes in Central America represents the only American example of a region becoming more black rather than less. Still, black political and economic associations were discouraged by a host of autocratic leaders, or in the case of Cuba, by national law.

By the Spanish-American War (1898), Latin American patriotism had shifted from the days of independence and so had the role of race within the country-loving ideology.   The growth of U.S. hegemony would also provide a new force, towards which Latin American nationalists could direct their efforts.   By the turn of the twentieth century, the United States had become the dominant economic and political hegemony in the region. President Theodore Roosevelt reinforced the 1823 Monroe Doctrine in his annual address to the U.S. Congress in 1904 in another edict that would come to be known as the Roosevelt Corollary.   The Corollary essentially attempted to ensure U. S. economic and political hegemony in the region and to warn European powers that their interference in the Western hemisphere would not be tolerated.   However, the Corollary also served as a justification for U. S. military presence in the region.

For many Latin Americans, Anglo-America became synonymous not only with progress and economic development, but with colonizer and oppressor.   The infusion of North American culture likewise became a major threat and an important aspect of the construction of Latin American identity.   In asserting its hegemony, North America's English-derived culture became the springboard off of which Latin Americans carved their own distinctiveness.   Anti-Americanism served Latin American nationalism by providing an economic and cultural imperialist enemy against whom the promotion of 'the national' could be fashioned. Brazilians (and later American scholars) would claim with pride that slavery in Brazil had been better for blacks than slavery in the United States, as if degrees of oppression could somehow overlook the debasing experience of this most insidious way of life.   Latin American heroes from Tijuana to Patagonia evoked the negative aspects of the United States with zeal.

José Martí, Cuba's greatest patriot, claimed in 1895 that Latin America's greatest danger was the scorn of the United States.   Marti contrasted what he called 'Anglo-America' to Latin America ('Our America') which he described as a distinct Creole reality that incorporated diverse cultural elements such as the African and the Indian into its spheres.   While Martí held to a positive vision of brotherly Latin American union, his discourse on race relations united him to the Latin American tradition of avoidance of racial tensions.   Martí, the Cuban independence fighter *par excellence*, positively defined his identity within a national and regional framework.   He attacked the myth of the inferiority of the mixed blood at a time when Cuba's population was predominantly *mulato*/mestizo and continuously stressed the lack of racial conflict among Latin Americans in general and Cubans in particular.[59]

In this regard, Martí shared much in common with an unlikely contemporary, the Uruguayan, José Enrique Rodó when he wrote in his 1900 classic *Ariel*:

> We Latin Americans have an inheritance of Race, a great ethnic tradition to maintain, a sacred bond which unites us to immortal pages of history and puts us on our honor to preserve this for the future. In the United States...(t)he typical hero is he who wants... North American life, indeed, describes Pascal's viscous circle in a ceaseless seeking for well-being with no object outside of itself...Its prosperity is as immense as its incapacity of satisfying even a mediocre view of human destiny.[60]

Rodó and Martí provided an ideological resistance which sought to forge nationhood against a common outsider.   Inverting Sarmiento's dichotomy, by the turn of the century, Latin America had somehow become 'civilized', not through economic, political, or social change, but in the realm of culture.   Latin America possessed an ability to unite individuals of different racial backgrounds underneath the Creole umbrella, while the U.S. and its unchecked expansion were barbaric.

This vision of unity was just that--a vision.   In 1900, intellectuals throughout the region were neither entirely optimistic nor necessarily proud of their unique heritage, as the case of Aclides Arguedas indicated with the title of his 1902 essay *Pueblo Enfermo.*   The opening of a new century did provide a forum for speculation for the republics---and new republics such as Brazil (1889) and Cuba (1902) led the way in the search. While Cuba focused its energy on defining its nature in the shadow of the Colossus of the North, Brazil was about to re-embrace its Portuguese heritage in a newly found national pride that would be unleashed by the military's brand of republicanism and come to fruition in the 1930s.

That Brazil became a republic in 1889, one year after the abolition of slavery, indicated a clear relationship between the theoretical freedom of all citizens and the rights of citizens under a republic.   Despite all the changes that accompanied the dismantling of slavery, the plight of the former slave remained precarious.   Although many historians have contended that abolition in Brazil was slow and calculated and thus no social movement emerged to disrupt the social system, what is clear is that the political and social climate after abolition virtually ignored the slave.

At the end of the nineteenth century, Latin American militaries also began to become professional and to exert their presence in the Latin American political arena.   Positivism, in part, accounted for Latin American militaries' roles in the development of national economies.   The rank and file provided men from the lower and middle classes with opportunity, albeit limited, for social mobility and a sense of belonging to a national territory, while many civilians were still regionalist and localized.

The Twentieth Century

Republicanism assumed a high degree of mobility, educational possibility, and a church with limited power.   Despite the anti-American rhetoric, Latin American states officially pursued economic bilateral agreements and sought to emulate many of the political practices.   Modeled after the United States of America, the Republican Constitution of February 21, 1891 governed Brazil until 1934.[61]   The Constitution reiterated the individual's rights as citizens which included liberty, security, and property.   All were equal under the law, but despite the new citizenship of ex-slaves, their access to mobility was limited by the liberal oligarchy. Lack of general education in the population at large, a Constitution which ill-defined individual rights, and an authoritarian capitalist model of development which valued property above individual rights, weakened civil rights. Brazil entered industrialization without destroying its pre-abolition attitudes and practices. The state regarded social questions as a matter for the police.[62] Still, the period of transition saw the proliferation of black associations and newspapers and Afro-Brazilian presence in the military.[63]

Indeed the military had become one of the most prestigious national institutions since the Paraguayan War Paraguay in 1864. Positivism as a conservative ideology which emerged out of liberalism, pervaded state thinking. In 1882 Miguel Lemos founded the Positivist Church of Brazil. The military, now under the command of Benjamin Constant, promoted what Robert Nachman has called 'practicing positivism', which called for the reformation of mentality, habits, and customs, but within a paternalistic, hierarchical and corporatist framework which relied on education and access to capital.[64] It is no surprise that it is within these quarters that one of the first social revolts registered, and led by a black Brazilian, João Cândido.

How would Brazil come to speak of its African population in this framework? While race and color affected society on all levels and writers did not cease from discussing race in private, race relations did not become a public issue to be resolved or discussed. Economic development, national formation, the threat of regionalism, education, and the growing urban centers, all received priority. Moreover, the Latin American tradition has continued to claim that racial problems are a subset of larger class problems. Underneath that rhetoric an aversion remains. World War I helped to shatter the myth that progress was exclusively a European cultural ideal. Brutal war ravaged Northern Europe resulting in the death of millions. In the interim between World War I and World War II, the pessimism about Western culture directly influenced the construction of nationalism in former Western colonies. European intellectuals such as Osvald Spengler, joined by Neitzsche, Sartre, and a myriad of others predicted the decline of the West.[65] These ideas paved the way for patriotic nationalism in Brazil to emerge in the face of the imminent Western decline. The interim period between the two world wars was a time of economic and social crisis, calling for an urgency of change, which was met in the short term in Brazil by the successful middle-class revolution signaled by the election of Getúlio Vargas in 1933. It was also a time of development and expansion of national industries.[66]

Centralization and urbanization in Brazil had a direct effect on the system of education. These processes clearly favored the urban areas, and were directed by a more centralized system guided and directed under the auspices of the respective branches of the state. The rapid rate of urbanization and the increase in the middle sectors occurred at a pace that outstripped the ability of government to provide a proper education to respond to its needs. Historically, the highly selective nature of entrance into centers of education, from the primary school to the university, gave an advantage to the middle and upper classes, and thus the educational system responded, by and large, to the needs of those classes.[67]

Nationalism, the ideological commitment to the pursuit of unity, independence and interests of people who conceive of themselves as forming a community relied on patriotism, the idea that the belief in and propagation of one's own culture is necessary to the preservation of the sovereignty of the *patria*. Ethnic nationalism, has been and continues to be at odds with the Latin American form of patriotic nationalism. Furthermore, economic marginalization has restricted the capacity of black Latin Americans to organize. When blacks in the United States organized pan-African conferences, which were predicated on the belief that peoples of the African diaspora share a similar heritage rooted in the African continent, and have endured a similar set of social experiences, Latin American participation was negligent.[68]

By the 1920s, immigrants, blacks, mulatto, and mestizo masses had begun to swell the major urban centers. The city became the center of national development and cultural production. During this time, writers began to recognize the historical contribution of previously ignored racial sectors to the formation of national identity. Latin Americans began to project positive racial images, celebrating the mixture of native, European, and African traits. Students of history will note that this era in Latin American history coincided with the post World War I period when European intellectuals and artists became interested in the so-called 'primitive cultures' of the non-Western world. The Harlem Renaissance was a cultural manifestation of this age. Marcus Garvey gained attention with his call to 'return to Africa', and the Negritude Movement began as a cultural revolution somewhat later in Paris. In Latin America, the Mexican José Vasconcelos noted that *miscegenation* had created what he called a *cosmic race*.[69] Similar theories arose in the 1920s and 1930s throughout Latin America. Writers such as the Brazilian Gilberto Freyre and the Cuban Elías Entralgo wrote about *miscegenation* between the European and the African in a positive manner. These views, in part, reflected the twentieth-century nationalists' attempt to view their Latin American identity and development in positive national terms, and not in racial terms.[70] But underneath the celebration of the mestizo and the mulatto lay a repudiation of blacks and Indians.

The political ideology of populism which attempted to create alliances among classes within a national framework informed the emergence of new Latin American moderate political parties, and centrist thinkers such as the Peruvian Haya de la Torre. De la Torres' Popular Alliance Party, founded in Mexico, failed to have any real affect on the political process however. Moreover, his views towards the black populations remained surprisingly ambiguous while he promoted an *indigenista* view of Latin American identity. In *¿A dónde va Indoamerica?*, for example, de la Torre makes a case for calling 'Latin America' 'Indo-America' because the economic development of the region occured as a result of the exploitation of indigenous labor. De la Torre merely mentions Africans in his references to Haiti.[71] Populism, in general, proved to be another ideology which sought to co-opt blacks who were still viewed as an undefined constituency of the popular sector.

The period after World War I proved an important time period for the emergence of home-grown national movements. The idea of the nation-state accepted now by the League of Nations, became important for Latin American nations as new mythologies emerged. In the 1930s, for example, Uruguay under José Batlle y Ordoñez constructed the ideal nation-model, projecting four national myths: the myth of the 'median', a concept that expressed that there were no poor or rich in Uruguay, but only a 'middle class'; the myth of non-Latin American country or *uruguayidad;* the myth of the consensus: equality of all before the law; and the myth of Uruguay as a country of cultured citizens. Economic hardship in the 1950s caused Uruguay to pursue economic and structural changes and integrate itself into the Latin American community. The economic crisis destroyed the socioeconomic structure on which the national myths were based and in so doing rendered them invalid.[72]

Like their Spanish-speaking neighbor, Brazil pursued a path that would attempt to accentuate its uniqueness in an era of economic, political, and social reorganization. The development of cultural nationalism in the 1930s, however, must be seen as the third stage of three important stages in which the state ceased to be an elite phenomenon divorced from the popular sectors and transformed itself into a legitimate representative of the nation. The stages can be loosely defined as: (1) forging citizenry, (2) questioning, and (3) institutionalization.

The first stage of forging citizenry began with the abolition of slavery and the dismantling of the monarchy. In 1888, the last theoretical barrier for all Brazilians to participate in nation formation as citizens fell, and the political framework changed with the establishment of the republic. In this period 1902, Euclides da Cunha published *Os Sertões*.

The questioning phase, 1902-1929, was a battle between the optimism signaled by 'progress' of the belle époque and the pessimism and the lingering feeling of backwardness. This was also the era of the undisputed rise of U.S. imperialism. Political and cultural movements such as the young lieutenants of the military (the famed *tenentes*) staged their assault on the political order, as the modernists called for cultural rejuvenation in the 1920s. These rebellions questioned the moral, economic, and political order of the First Republic and the legitimacy of the political elite in the face of their declining economic power which culminated with the stock crash of 1929.

In 1930, the institutionalization process began with the emergence of a new state that claimed to be the legitimate representative of the nation. In the 1930s, the Brazilian nation-state became the legitimate unit for the promotion of national development and the legitimate representation of all sectors in the international arena. The state capitalized on the new developments in technology and reorganized the relationship between the people and the government. It also established a federal bureaucracy, the first Ministry of Education and Public Health responsible for the promotion of a national culture and the education of citizens. Meanwhile, like other major Latin American economies, Brazil began to connect its budding urban centers of growth to the world capitalist system. Middlemen connected to the export-oriented economies and upwardly mobile professionals connected to international trends usurped many of the old regional patriarchies. Traditional landowners saw their position gradually erode as their national economies became internationalized. The sons of the traditional agricultural elite inherited their father's tales of the 'good old days' when society functioned in a nation characterized as coherent, and where peace and order reigned. In this final stage, evident are the three aspects of decolonization that Edward Said has described as an essential part of constructive nationalism: the insistence of seeing a community's history as whole, coherent and integral, the development of the concept of a national language--in many respects a new form of communication; and organization of cultural memory as intellectuals reconstruct their past.

Brazil constructed a populist cultural nationalism based on the notion of *brasilidade*, a sense of Brazilian-ness. Although an ambiguous national essence at best, *brasilidade* meant a commitment to Brazilian national culture. But what national culture? Invariably, the national culture reflected the centralized power of the state in Rio de Janeiro and of the urban cultural elite mostly in southern urban cities such as Rio de Janeiro, São Paulo, and to a lesser extent Belo Horizonte. *Brasilidade* also celebrated Brazil's ethnic diversity and the forging a cosmic race free of racial discrimination. Cultural populism of the 1930s allowed a new generation of politicians and writers to present themselves in their various nations as the voice of the popular classes. In this context 'nation' became synonymous with race.

Brazilian populism arose as a sociopolitical agenda to bridge the gap between the upper and popular classes, calling for the rights of workers and underscoring their importance in the building of the nation. It continued to promote the elite version of patriarchy in the realm of culture as their fathers had exerted that influence in the realm of politics and economics. National populists utilized the rhetoric of 'the popular'. They criticized those citizens who sold out to foreign influences, thus encouraging an identification with that which was Brazilian. Concomitantly, they usurped grassroots, class, and race-determined movements, as well as internationalism and pan-ethnic collaborations by co-opting them into their concept of nation as a diverse family.

But what role did blacks play in the creation of this process?

Nineteenth-century national identity, we have already determined, was primarily an elite construct. The twentieth-century quest for national identity led by nationalist intellectuals and politicians promoted cultural unity by casting the nation as a cohesive unit. Nationalist rhetoric exploited the popular sector's desire to belong. In so doing, grassroots race consciousness movements in particular became difficult to sustain or have an impact on the constructing of national identity. Seen in this light, national identity remained a class construct well into the twentieth century. In the nationalist fervor of 1930s and 1940s Brazil, blacks explored possibilities of racial edification within this nationalist framework, avoiding the rhetoric of ethnic nationalism or segregation.

The national myths that attempted to unite were strongly utopian in nature. By excluding blackness as any official representation, Brazilians saw certain indications of that utopia in their countries. Nationalist writers defined the national cultural identity vis-à-vis Western culture often symbolized by the United States, the dominant political force in the region. National ideals, heroes, and essences were important embodiments of the cultural identity that was distinct and often presented as superior to that of the United States. Speaking of Brazil, for example, Nabuco remarked that:

> Slavery among us remained open-ended indiscriminately
> extending its   privileges to all... a flexibility immeasurably
> greater than it would have possessed had it been the
> monopoly of one race as it was in North America. The
> system of absolute equality certainly opened a better future
> for the black race in Brazil than in the United States.[73]

The nation-state was the only legitimate unit for the promotion
of national development; and the state was the legitimate representation of
all social sectors in the international arena. In order to represent the ideas
of the nation-state, the new political and intellectual elite believed that they
legitimately represented the people in the quest for freedom, equality, and
fraternity. Culture, we must insist, is a multi-faceted dynamic entity.
Nonetheless, in an attempt to answer the question 'who are we?', national
writers responded from a macro-perspective, glossing over many
contradictions such as regionalism, race, and class in the attempt to
describe symbolically a diverse, complex nation. Furthermore, the
perceptions of the elite continue to dominate our perceptions of 'national
culture', and these views are often reflected in mass culture.[74]

The power relations implicit to this framework manifests itself
upon examination of the national means of communication utilized to
reinforce the individual's place within the nation. All members of society
exploit the means of communication available to them to promote their
ideas both within and outside the community. In modern capitalist Brazil,
dominant intellectuals served the state by interpreting the political agenda
on a cultural level. They organized national culture through the mass
media, particularly through radio and the press. The press was the major
medium for nationalistic rhetoric in the form of art, poetry, essays,
histories and literary criticism in Brazil.[75] Radio programs and recorded
music aired on the radio provided a rapid forum for the promotion of
brasilidade.

The importance of a national canon cannot be underestimated in
our modern societies in which education is of primary importance to social
mobility. The emergence of the classics of national interpretation in the
Latin American setting was intimately linked to issues of national identity
and independence. Those texts created in the revolutionary spirit of the
1930s, once institutionalized, were assured a place in the national canon.
The agreement between the intelligentsia and the political elite was an
essential step in the monopolization of the means of communication and
the inculcation of the nationalist agenda. Institutionalization of national
classics was dependent on the owners and major users of the means of
communication, and hence the existing social structure.

To evoke the cause of the nation in Brazil, the intelligentsia encountered a native vernacular to express its respective notion of *patria*. Language remains one of the essential parts of a national classic since it is the nation, or parts of the nation who must recognize, communicate, and see to some degree their reflection within the classic. A relatively small group of associations usually of *letrados* or advisers to the Ministry of Education have had enormous power in framing public discourse on national identity at any particular point in time. The role of those classic texts, that attempt to organize and order Latin American reality is best described by Julio Ramos:

> what is thought of as Latin American is a created field,
> ordered, in the same politically predetermined disposition,
> from the discourse that names and on naming engenders the
> field of that identity.[76]

Two major details are important here. First the essay of national interpretation, even if it loses validity as an historical event, maintains an incredible referential power as it becomes established in the national *mentalité*. This will be vividly seen in the case of popular Brazilian music which provided a rich source of oral texts.[77]

Texts which promote national myths that reflect the status quo depend on a patriarchal system inherited from the metropolis. In such environments the classic as reference point is a text to be revised, negated, or embellished, but never discarded. In 'La escritura de lo Nacional y los Intelectuales Puertorriqueños', María Elena Rodríquez-Castro makes the connection between a society's classics and patriarchy. In the spirit of paternalism and corporatism, many privileged Latin American writers have tended to assume the position of caretaker of national culture or of the popular sectors.[78]

The cultural elite of the 1930s were ideally situated to forge the myths of the nation. Aided by a nationalistic state, they were also able to direct the national thinking of citizens. In creating their national history, they reconstructed the national cultural memory. But 'cultural memory', by definition is relative and dependent on when, why, and who is doing the remembering. As a tool of the intelligentsia, nationalism arose with the destruction of the traditional patronage and its stability was based on traditional modes of societal relationships of the plantation economy. To avoid being usurped by a growing working class and incipient industrialization, the sons and daughters of a traditional elite became authorities of culture, interpreters, examiners and guides of the new social order.[79]

This work is interested in how the ideas of nationhood also came to be established in the popular mind. How were blacks encouraged to contribute to a non-racial nationalism, while images of blackness remained relatively static and often negative? The written and musical texts examined here were manifestations, or interpretations, of the idea of nation prevalent in the cultural matrix of the time.

A national classic defines, in one way or another, an essence or myth that is perceived to be true by a sufficient number of citizens. At the same time, the national classic becomes entrenched in the spirit of the times and therefore is central to the 'cultural matrix', aiding in the consolidation and institutionalization of the ideas of the national culture. This process is clearly related to the centralization of economic, political and psychological power.[80]

Applying the ideas of the institutionalization of a classic to texts of national interpretation, Rodríguez-Castro, offers us several factors that aid in its effective canonization: the rise of middle sectors, the increase in literacy and minimal education, the rise of professional classes, the relations with the popular masses, and the reorganization of the state. As we will see in the case of Brazil, all of these characteristics were present.[81] In search of a national identity, letrados accounted for the 'others' within the nation who, according to elitist thought, could not represent themselves. These subcultures were assimilated into mainstream culture through folklore, a devise that would be critically looked at by intellectuals of the sub-cultures in subsequent generations. The nation defined as a basic unit that symbolizes a heterogeneous group of people, will, in its definition, contain traits favorable to the group or groups which have defined it. Its acceptance by the masses at large is dependent on the mechanisms available to those intellectuals responsible for the propagation of nationalistic ideas. The dominant intellectuals vehemently opposed illegitimate power, but included their voices in their histories and literature.[82]

Divided into four main chapters, this work follows a chronological development from 1888-1945. Chapter two (Race and Patriotism Beyond Abolition, 1888-1930), focuses on the construction of patriotism and the forging of a dominant national identity. It pays particular attention to the interrelationship of race and national identity from the turn of the century to the beginning of the Vargas Revolution of 1930. Desperate to join the select company of modern nations, Brazil fashioned a modern view of itself which grappled between the pessimism of the *fin de siècle* and the optimism of the *belle époque*, between past and the future, between black and white. Crucial to the historical search for a positive national identity were the modernists of the 1920s. Chapter two illustrates how modernist thought created a cultural paradigm through which nationalists searched for the nation's essence, *brasilidade*, while avoiding or downplaying black contributions.

Chapter three (The Getúlio Vargas Regime and the Institutionalization of National Culture) examines the institutionalization of patriotism and a Brazilian national identity (*brasilidade*) under President Getúlio Vargas (1930-1945). Elected to the presidency by the Brazilian legislature in 1933, Vargas created a federal bureaucracy which allowed nationalist-minded intellectuals to promote a 'new' national identity based on the promotion of civil sentiments above all others. Crucial to this process were the Department of Education and Public Health and the Department of Print and Propaganda which promoted an idealized image of the 'new Brazil', and the idea of a 'Brazilian race'.

Chapter four (The Nationalization of Popular Culture), examines the nationalization of Brazilian popular culture by focusing on the emergence of two of Brazil's most vibrant popular manifestations: soccer and *música popular brasileira*, or popular Brazilian music. By the 1930s, soccer had developed from an elite Brazilian sport to a national pastime, and a symbol of racial integration, despite practices which barred many black players from national attention. At the same time, through new developments in the Brazilian radio and record industries, Brazilian popular music became an important vehicle for the promotion of nationhood. Performers such as Carmen Miranda and Almirante, Ary Barroso, and others were instrumental in this process. Brazilian popular music celebrated nationhood, cultural and racial mixing while perpetuating static and often marginalized images of 'blackness'.

Chapter five (Blacks and Civil Rights: Ethnic Consciousness versus Cultural Nationalism), presents a detailed appraisal of dominant black voices and their views on Brazilian nationhood and the role of race within it. Placing black social, cultural, and political mobilization within the nationalist contexts, it becomes imperative to examine the definition of civil rights and how it emerges within the Brazilian national discourse. While the chapter provides an overview of important black figures in Brazil from the marine rebel, João Cândido, at the beginning of the century, to Abdias Nascimento, founder of the Teatro Experimental do Negro in 1944, the major focus is the Frente Negra Brasileira which emerged as the first national black civil rights movement during the Vargas years.

Chapter six concludes this work by reiterating the major arguments of the preceding chapters before treating the legacy of Brazilian nationalism and national representation and its effects on black movements in the post-Vargas era.   When Marxist parties gained momentum after World War II, many blacks joined the movement in the hope of changing the fundamental economic system which discriminated against them. In so doing, once again race became secondary to wider problems of class transformation. The 1960 Castro Revolution, for example, spurred the nationalism of racial unity.   For Castro, 'nation' implied the popular sectors, and he vowed to eliminate both racism and elitism.[83] While Castro initially had some success, racism continues to be an eroding force in the Cuban society, as it still is in other Latin American countries today.

While revolutionary rhetoric stymied autonomous black movements on the left, right-wing military dictatorships that emerged in the 1960s and 1970s prohibited any form of grassroots movements or developments. The political opening of the 1980s, known in many countries as *abertura*, provided a political space that continues to be filled by black movements and community development throughout the region. Blacks have traveled a long and tiring road from conquest in the sixteenth century to new movements of racial pride and consciousness in the 1980s. Still so much more needs to be done particularly as we enter a new post-revolutionary period in which international cooperation, and as NAFTA, MERCOSUR, and other global economies emerge.   Racial identity, admittedly, will never be as salient a social factor as it has been in the United States. African-Americans have inherited a different political and cultural tradition which have allowed them to define themselves in different ways from their counterparts in Latin America. In addition, as an underdeveloped region, issues of national development will continue to take precedence over internal problems for some time to come.

Notes

[1]
See Benedict Anderson, *Imagined Communities* (London and New York: Verso, 1983). Karl Deutsch, *Nationalism and Social Communication* (New York, 1966). Ernst Gellner, *Thought and Change* London: Weidenfeld and Nicolson, 1964.

[2]
Nelson Werneck Sodré, *Raízes histócas do nacialismo brasileiro* 2nd edition (Rio de Janeiro: Ministério da Educação e Cultura, 1960).   Olympio Guilherme's work, *O nacionalismo e a política internacional do Brazil* (São Paulo: Editôra Fulgos, 1957). José Perreira Lira's book *Temas de nossos dias:*

Nacionalismo, corrupção, presença das massas (Rio de Janeiro: J. Olympio, 1955).

[3] Lúcia Lippi Oliveira, *A questão nacional na Primera República* (São Paulo: Editora Brasiliense, 1990). Arturo Ariel Betancur, *Getúlio Vargas: nacionalismo e industrialización en el Brasil, 1930-1945* (Montivideo: Fundación de Cultura Universitaria, 1991).

[4] Regina Maria do Rego Monteiro Abreu, 'Emblemas da nacionalidade: o culto a Euclides da Cunha', *Revista Brasileira de Ciências Sociais* 9: 24 (Feb 1994), 66-84; Aracy A. Amaral, 'Oswald de Andrade e as artes plásticas no modernismo dos anos '20', *Revista do Instituto de Estudos Brasileiros* 33 (1992), 68-75; Maria Luiza Tucci Carneiro, 'Sob a máscara do nacionalismo: autoritarismo e anti-semitismo na era Vargas, 1930-1945', *Estudios Interdisciplinarios de América Latina y el Caribe* 1:1 (Jan-June 1990), 23-40; Mônica Pimenta Velloso, 'A brasilidade verde-amarela: nacionalismo e regionalismo paulista', *Estudos Históricos*, 6:11 (Jan-June 1993), 89-112. Finally see the comparative work on Vargas and Peron by Leonardo Senken, 'La lógica populista de la identidad y alteridad en Vargas y Perón: algunas implicaciones para los inmigrantes', *Cuadernos Americanos*, 66, (Nov-Dec 1997), 130-152.

[5] Robert Levine, *Father of the Poor? Vargas and His Era* (Cambridge: Cambridge University Press, 1998). See also *The Vargas Regime: The Critical Years 1934-1938* (New York and London: Columbia University Press, 1970).

[6] Donald Pierson, 'Os Africanos da Bahia', *Revista do Arquivo Municipal* (São Paulo) 7, no. 78 (August-September 1941): 39-64. See 'Diluicão da linha de côr na Bahia', *Revista do Arquivo Municipal* (São Paulo) 8, 89 (March-April 1943): 105-127.

[7] Frank Tannenbaum, *Slave and Citizen: the Negro in the Americas*. (New York: Vintage Books, 1946), 112. Tannenbaum is an American who writes in the mid nineteen forties at a time that he was witnessing the aftermath of the social problems due to racism in this country.

[8] Carl Degler, *Neither Black nor White: Slavery and Race Relations in Brazil and the U.S* (New York: Macmillan, 1971). See also Stanley Elkins, *Slavery, a Problem in American Institutional and Intellectual Life*. (Chicago, 1959).

[9] The 'Casa Grande' was the self-contained plantation which Freyre presented in a romanticized light. See Gilberto Freyre, *Casa Grande e Senzala* 5th ed. (Rio de Janeiro: Livraria José Olympico Editora), 1941.

[10] Seymour Drescher's article appears in a book edited by Scott called *The Abolition of Slavery and the Aftermath of Emancipation in Brazil*. (Durham: Duke University, 1988), 429-460.

[11] Robert B. Toplin, *Freedom and Prejudice*. (Westpoint, Conn: Greenwood Press, 1940), 57.

[12]   See Arthur F. Crowlin's article 'Afro-Brazilians: Myths and Realities', *Slavery and Race Relations in Latin America* (Westpoint, Conn., 1974), 385-437. See Staurt B. Schwartz *Slaves, Peasants, and Rebels: Reconsidering Brazilian Slavery* (Urbana and Chigago: University of Illinois Press, 1992). 1-38.

[13]   Florestan Fernandes, *The Negro in Brazilian Society*. Jacqueline D. Skiles trans. (New York: Columbia University Press, 1969).

[14]   Florestan Fernandes, 'El drama del negro e del mulato en una sociedad que cambia', *Mundo Nuevo*, 33 (March 1969): 11-21. He treats the subject of immigration as it relates to race relations in 'Imigracão e relacões racias', *Revista Civilizacão Brasileira*, (Rio de Janeiro) 1, 8 (1966): 75-95. See also 'Immigration and Race Relations in São Paulo', *Présence Africaine* (Paris) 61 (First Quarter, 1967): 103-120.

[15]   See for example, Jean-Claude García-Zamor, 'Social mobility of Negroes in Brazil', *Journal of Inter-American Studies and World Affairs*, vol. 12, no. 2 (April 1970): 242-254. Octavio Ianni highlights the role of race in economic exploitation in his *Escravidão e Racismo* (São Paulo: Editora Hucitec, 1978). One study conducted by Annani Dzidziendo and Lourdes Casual examines briefly the position of blacks in Cuban and Brazilian society. See *The Position of Blacks in Brazilian and Cuban Society* (London: Minority Rights Group, 1979).

[16]   Carl Degler, *Neither Black nor White: Slavery and Race Relations in Brazil and the United States* (New York: MacMillan Company, 1971).

[17]   Abdias do Nascimento, *O Genocídio do Negro Brasileiro* (Rio de Janeiro: Paz e Terra, 1978).

[18]   Clóvis Moura, *Brasil: As Raizes do Protesta Negro* (São Paulo: Editora Global, 1983).

[19]   Charles Wagley has edited a sociological survey of race relation in the rural North East. Wagley and other authors discuss the element of color prejudice within a variety of settings, but that many people of different colors are present at many levels of Brazilian society. See Charles Wagley (ed.) *Race and Class in Rural Brazil* (New York: Columbia University Press, 1963).

[20]   Thales de Azevedo, *Democracia racial: ideologia e realidade* (Petrópolis, Brazil: Editôra Vozes, 1975).

[21]   Alberto Guerriero Ramos, *Patología social do 'branco' brasileiro* (Rio de Janeiro: *Journal do Commercio*, 1955).

[22]   Robert Brent Toplin, 'Brazil: racial Polarization in the Developing Giant', *Black World* 22 (November 1972): 15-22.

[23]   Charles Wagley, 'Attitudes in the Backlands', *Courier* (Paris) 5 (August-September, 1952): 12-14.

[24]   See Richard Graham ed. *The Idea of Race in Latin America, 1870-1940* (Austin, University of Texas Press, 1990). Thomas E. Skidmore, 'Racial Ideas

and Social Policy, 1870-1940' 7-36. Aline Helg, 'Race in Argentina and Cuba, 1880-1930: Theory, Policies and Popular Reaction', 37-70. Alan Knight, 'Racism, Revolution, and Indigenismo: México, 1910-1940', 71-115.

[25]   Bolivar Lamounier, 'Raça e Classe na Politica Brasileira', *Cuardernos Brasileiros* 47 (May-June 1968): 39-50.

[26]   Edison de Sousa Carneiro, 'La nacionalización del negro en el Brazil', *Cuba Professional* (Havana) 3, no. 10 (April-June 1954), 16-18.

[27]   Era Thompson Bell, 'Does Amalgamation Work in Brazil?' *Ebony* 20 (July 1956): 27-34.

[28]   *Luso-Brazilian Review* Vol. IV, no. 1 (1968): 27-43.

[29]   Wilson Martins, *The Modernist Idea* (Westport, Connecticut: Greenwood Press, 1971).

[30]   John Nist, *The Modernist Movement in Brazil: A Literary Study* (Austin, Texas: University of Texas Press, 1967).

[31]   David T. Haberly, *Three Sad Races: Racial Identity and National Consciousness in Brazilian Literature* (Cambridge, England: Cambridge University Press, 1983).

[32]   João Cruz Costa, *A History of Ideas in Brazil: The Development of Philosophy in Brazil and the Evolution of National History* (Berkeley, California: University of California Press, 1964).

[33]   Emilia Viotti da Costa, *The Brazilian Empire: Myths and Histories* (Belmont, California: Wadsworth Publishing Company Inc, 1985).

[34]   See, for example, the discussion of the growing racial consciousness among Afro-Uruguayans in *No Longer Invisible:Afro-Uruguayans Today* London: Minority Rights, 1995).

[35]   Colin M. MacLachlan, 'African Slave Trade and Economic Development in Amazonia, 1700-1800', *Slavery and Race Relations in Latin America* Robert Brent Toplin ed. (Westport, Conneticut: Greenwood Press, 1974): 112-145. The relationship between ideology and institutional change is treated in 'Slavery, Ideology and Institutional Change: The Impact of the Enlightenment on the Slavery in Late Eighteen Century Maranhão', *Journal of Latin American Studies* (May 1979): 1-17.

[36]   See Leslie Rout, *The African Experience in Spanish America, 1502- Present* (Cambridge: Cambridge University Press, 1976), 126. Maurice Belrose, *Africa en el Corazón de Venezuela* (1988). Laureano Vallenilla Lanz, *Cesárismo democrático: estudios sobre las bases sociológicas de la constituición efective de Venezuela* 4th Edition (Caracas, 1961), 9.

[37]   It is difficult to forget that it was the Spanish Crown who welcomed Jews, Arabs and sub-Saharan Africans into their fold, provided they converted to Hispanic Christianity, and later created the Inquisition. In the Americas, the

Crown instituted a hierarchical class system based on race which assumed miscegenation, while outlawing marriage among different races.

[38] Karl W. Deutsch, 'Nation Building and National Development: Some Issues for Political Research', *Nation Building* Karl W. Deutsch and William J. Foltz, eds. (New York: Atherton Press, 1963), 1-16.

[39] For a good summary of the colonial period in Brazil, see James Lang, *Portuguese Brazil: The King's plantation* (New York: Academic Press, 1979).

[40] Joaquim José Da Silva Xavier (Tiradentes) 1746-1792 was the leader of the revolt against the monarchy in favor of independence in Minas Gerais. He was captured, hanged and quartered as a lesson to other would be rebels. He later became a hero and precursor to Brazilian independence.

[41] This fear was accentuated due to the lack of women. In addition to fearing revolt, the Portuguese feared that their women would be taken away by runaway Africans. See Appendix.

[42] Viotti da Costa, *The Brazilian Empire Myths and Histories*, Belmont, (California: Wadsworth Publishing Co., 1988), 53-77.

[43] This fear was accentuated due to the lack of women. In addition to fearing revolt, the Portuguese feared that their women would be taken away by runaway Africans. For information on slavery in the nineteenth century see Mary C. Karasch, *Slave Life in Rio de Janeiro, 1808-1850* (Princeton: Princeton University Press, 1987). Katia M. de Queirós Mattoso, *To Be A Slave in Brazil, 1550-1880* Arthur Goldhammer trans. (New Brunswick: Rutgers University Press, 1986). Stuart Schwartz, Slaves, *Peasants and Rebels: Reconsidering Brazilian Slavery* (Urbana and Chicago: University of Illinois Press, 1992).

[44] A good presentation and analysis of demographic information in Cuba can be found in Martínez-Alier, *Class and Colour in 19th Century Cuba*, 3.

[45] Joaquim Nabuco, *Abolitionism, The Brazilian Anti-slavery Struggle* (Urbana, Chicago and London: University of Chicago Press, 1977), 223.

[46] Thomas E. Skidmore, 'Racial Ideas and Social Policy in Brazil 1870-1940', *The Idea of Race in Latin America* (University of Texas Press, Austin, 1990), 9.

[47] Nabuco, *Abolitionism*, 21.

[48] Ibid, 98-100.

[49] As in Brazil, in Cuba the belief that Cuba did not have any racial conflict can be summed up in the well known statement, 'Aquí no pasa nada' (Nothing's wrong here). This will be explained at various intervals within the text. The diffusion of myth in a given society takes place on two levels; the conscious and the unconscious. The psychoanalyst Carl Jung explains it best. (See the section under ideology in Chapter I).

[50] Martí, José, *Our America* Philip Foner ed. (New York and London: Monthly Review Press, 1977): 278-279.

[51]   Katia M. Queirós Mattoso, *To Be A Slave in Brazil, 1550-1880*, p. 211.

[52]   Viotti da Costa, *The Brazilian Empire Myths and Histories* (Belmont, (California: Wadsworth Publishing Co., 1988), 53-77.

[53]   See Hayden White, 'The Historical Text as Literary Artifact', *Tropics of Discourse* (1978).

[54]   See Sarimiento *Civilization and Barbarism* (1845) or Echeverría, *El Matadero* (published 1871).

[55]   Roderick J. Barman, *Brazil: The Forging of a Nation, 1798-1852* (Stanford: Stanford University Press, 1988), p. 15-16 and 193.

[56]   Kim Butler, *Freedoms Given, Freedoms Won: Afro-Brazilians in Post-Abolition São Paulo and Salvador* (New Brunswick: Rutgers University Press, 1998), p. 17.

[57]   Julio José Chiavenatto, *O Negro no Brasil: da Senzala á Guerra do Paraguai* 4th edition (São Paulo: Editora Brasiliense, 1987), 194-205.

[58]   Joaquim Nabuco, *Abolitionism, The Brazilian Anti-slavery Struggle* (Urbana, Chicago and London: University of Chicago Press, 1977), 223.

[59]   José Martí, *Our America* Philip Foner ed. (New York and London: Monthly Review Press, 1977): 278-279

[60]   José Enrique Rodó, *Ariel* Margaret Sayers Peden trans. (Austin, Texas: University of Texas Press).

[61]   *Constituições Brasileiras*, 517.   Deodoro created a commission of five members to elaborate the Constitution.

[62]   Many of the ideas come from Hasenbalg who in addition to the above mentioned reasons for the lack of Civil Rights states that the rapid increase in population, especially through immigration, diminished the likelihood that natives construct an authentic Civil Rights movement.   In fact, many parliamentarians began to propose anti-immigrant attitudes and legislation. Social movements such as communism and anarchism, and anarcho-synicalism were blamed on immigrants.   See Hasenbalg, *Discriminacão e Desigualdade Racias no Brasil* (Rio de Janeiro: Graal, 1979), 256-259.

[63]   Note that Afro-Brazilians were always present in many national institutions. However, slavery even divided the Afro-Brazilian population.   There were many Free People of Color throughout the existence of the institution of slavery.   Several documents have left rich sources of information for regional studies.   Magazines and newspapers with such names as *O Bandeirante*, *Senzala*, and *Libertade* attempted to address the national issues as they related to blacks.

[64]   Robert G. Nachman, 'Positivism, Modernization and the Middle Class in Brazil', *Hispanic American Historical Review* 57 (Feb. 1977) No. 7: 1-23.

[65]   Oswald Spengler, *The Decline of the West* Vol. I (New York: Alfred A. Knopf, 1926), 96-97.

[66] The importance of the centralization of power after the depression and the role of the government, even in the United States, using Keynsian economics for the first time, expanded. In this case, both public and private education were indispensable in the inculcation of national ideals.

[67] Robert J. Havighurts and J. Roberto Moreira, *Society and Education in Brazil* (University of Pittsburgh Press, 1965), 18.

[68] Ronald W. Walters, *Pan-Africanisms in the African Diaspora* (Detroit: Wayne State University Press, 1993), 326.

[69] *La raza cósmica: misión de la raza ibero-americana* (Mexico: Aguilar S.A. de Ediciones, 1961).

[70] See Gilberto Freyre's Brazilian classic, *The Masters and the Slaves* (1933), in which he developed his theory of lusotropicalism, crediting Portuguese racial tolerance as critical to their colonization efforts. Elías Entralgo proposed his ideas about mestizaje and miscegenation *La liberación étnica cubana* (1953).

[71] Victor Raul Haya de la Torre, *A dónde va Indoamerica?* (Santiago, Chile: Bibleoteca America, 1936), 22-31.

[72] Juan Rial, 'El imaginario social urugauyo y la dictatadura. Los mitos políticos de (re)-construcción', *De mitos y memorias politicas*. Carina Perelli and Juan Rial. Montevideo: Ediciones de la Banda Oriental, 1986), 15-36. As a result of this period of crisis, the Partido Colorido, which had maintained political control over Uruguay for 96 years, lost control. In the late 1960s this process is further exasperated with the emergence of armed violence movements from the left.

[73] Nabuco, p. 121.

[74] E. Bradford Burns, 'Ideology in Nineteenth-Century Latin American Historiography' in *Hispanic American Historic Review*' 58, (3): 409-431.

[75] *Novo Diccionario de Historia do Brasil* (São Paulo: Indústrias de Papel, 1970), 349. In Brazil, however, the journalistic tradition began in Great Britain with the establishment of the *Correio Brasiliense ou Armazén Literário* in 1808 by Costa Pereiera Furtado de Mondónça. This newspaper was an instrumental forum for the events of 1822. Between 1808 and 1822, inspired by the accomplishments of Mendonça, a great deal of newspapers and journals appeared. Local writers and thinkers were supported by the *Impressão Régia* founded in Rio de Janeiro by the Portuguese Royal family who had fled the peninsula due to the Napoleonic wars. Although the Impressão Régia allowed for the expansion of the press, the ideas which came from its quarters were monitored by the Crown. In 1815, censorship was 'softened' and the press was allowed to print invitations, announcements and the like. In 1821, official censorship was abolished, resulting in the emergence of several newspapers, including the *Réverbero Constitucional Fluminense*. Newspapers were the major forum for the dissemination of ideas throughout the nineteenth century,

followed by magazines and journals which did not develop until the latter part of the nineteenth century. Illiteracy and the lack of a bourgeoisie were two factors which did not allow for the development of more matured genres until the early part of the twentieth century. The 1920s marked the commencement of what could be called the Brazilian 'Golden Age'.

[76] T.S. Elliot, *What is a Classic?* (London: Faber and Faber Ltd, 1946), 15. See also Frank Kermode, *The Classic: Literary Images of Permanence and Change* (New York: Viking Press, 1975) which is a further elaboration of the Elliot text. The definition of a classic comes from Julio Ramos, *Desencuentros de la modernidad en America Latina* (Mexico: Fondo de Cultura Económica, 1989), 229. Ramos also best describes the relationship between myth and classic in another work: 'un clásico es un evento discutivo que, institucionalizado en diferentes coyunturas históricas, asumen un enorme poder referencial. Un texto que en la historia de sus lecturas pierde su cáracter de acontecimeinto discusivo y se lee en función de la presencia del mundo representante y inmediata del mundo representatitivo'.

[77] A very apparent case is that of Argentina. Sarmiento's *Civilization and Barbarism* is justifiably a required text for students of Argentina, and arguably Latin American, history. Despite the contemporary assaults on Sarmiento's work (even his contemporaries like Bartolomé Mitre who was opposed to some of his ideas), Sarmiento helped establish the myth of Argentina and, by extension, Latin America-(Barbarism) as opposed to Europe (Civilization). Domingo Faustino Sarmiento, *Facundo*.   (Mexico: Nuestros Clásicos, Universidad Nacional Autónoma de México, 1972), 1. Mitre founded the Junta Historia y Numismática American in 1893.   Born in Buenos Aires in 1821, Mitre served in various cabinet positions after the fall of Rosas, but he is best known as one of Argentina's foremost writers of the nineteenth century.

[78] Maria Elena Rodriquez-Castro, 'La escritura de lo nacional y los intelectuales puertorriqueños'. Ph.D. Diss. Princeton University, 1988.

[79] Antonio Gramsci, *Los intelectuales y la organization de la cultura* (México: Juan Pablos Ed, 1975), 11-28.

[80] Rodriquez Castro, 27-28.   Refer to Michel Foucault, *Vigiliar y castigas* (México: Siglo XXI, 1976).

[81] Rodriquez Castro, 27-28.

[82] Angel Rama, *La ciudad letrada* (New Hampshire: Ediciones del Norte, 1984), 30.   See especially Chapter I, 'La ciudad ordenada'.   Rama discusses the historical development of the medieval city as a center of authority which was later transferred to the Spanish colonies in the Americas.

[83] Fidel Castro, *La historia me absolverá* (La Habana: Imp. Nacional de Cuba, 1961), 47-48.

2. Race and Patriotism Beyond Abolition: Forging national citizenry, 1888-1930

O regime político das massas é da ditadura. Não há, a estas horas, país que não esteja à procura de um homen carismático ou marcado pelo destino, para dar às aspiracões da massa uma expressão simbólica... Não ha hoje um povo que não clame por um César.

Francisco Campos, Minister of Justice, Estado Novo

Literature and to a lesser degree history has always been a part of nation building in Latin America.

Antônio Cândido, 'Literature and the Rise of Brazilian National Self-Identity'.

A nation may function with slaves, but if it is to function well, it must cultivate citizens. By the 1870s, Brazilian slavery was becoming less and less important, and the country already possed a large population of freed blacks and mulattoes. Between 1888 and 1889, however, Brazilians dismantled the last theoretical barriers for the theoretical participation of Brazilian citizens in the cultural, political, and economic activities necessary for nation formation. Brazilians abolished slavery in 1888, and one year later Brazil ceased to be a monarchy when it established the First Republic under the tutelage of a patriotic national military. On the brink of a new century, Brazil was entering modernity with a new state and new citizens. Within this post-colonial, post-abolition context, patriotism, the phenomenon that Leonard Doob calls a conscious conviction/belief that one's welfare is dependent upon the power and culture of his/her society, emerged. At the turn of the century, this meant an importation of European ideas, and an imitation of French cultural ideas and behavior. That emulation would also mean that elites would largely ignore the social reality of the downtrodden in general, and blacks, in particular.[1]

Patriotism, nonetheless, implies a tension, a dialectic, in which opposing forces, euphoria and pessimism, must battle and in which

41

euphoria must ultimately prevail.   Post-colonial patriotism, a natural precursor to nationalism, an ideology which implies action in the economic, political, or cultural realm seeks out cultural and political formulae of unity.   From 1888-1930, Brazil's new citizens, many of them freed slaves, remained on the fringes of national culture, as Brazilians grappled with questions of national identity and progress.   Before World War I, the answers to this question were largely one-dimensional and often superficial.   After all, this was the *belle époque*, and Brazilians participated with a vengeance, and with all the euphoria of a bohemian in Paris.   The voices of pessimism, stemming largely from a national inferiority complex or concern, lurked in the corners of post-monarchy Brazil.   They would not be adequately addressed until World War I transformed the Brazilian views of European superiority.

Two institutions would play critical roles in the process of national consolidation, during this time: the military and the cultural elite. The former had become a force of integration since the Paraguayan War (1865-1870), while the latter would, for the first time begin to diffuse through means of mass communication, particularly journalistic forums, ideas about nationhood, its identity and its aspirations under republicanism.   Brazilian Aryanism, in all its flexibility would allow for little advancement of blacks.   Indeed black images and voices before the 1930s were largely absent from national political and cultural life. Mulattos faired somewhat better both in national politics and in literature, but (as we will see) many mulattoes, avoided a discussion of racial background in public forums.

This chapter will trace the construction of patriotism in relationship to race and its black citizens from the turn of the century to the beginning of the Vargas revolution of 1930.   How did the non-white voices and images emerge?   And in which contexts?   The aspirations and limitations of national development at the expense of ethnic consciousness, in the broadest sense of the word, surely would set the parameters for these responses.   Brazil would have to construct itself between the prevalent moods of the *fin de siècle* and the *belle époque* (1880s-1920s), between optimism and degradation, future and fear, salvation and slavery, white and black.   This is the context within which the *mulato* would emerge as a nation icon, a product of racial cultural intermingling, but it was a *mulato* constructed by whites.

By the late 1920s, patriotic nationalists, from what Angel Rama would call the 'lettered cities', who constituted a cultural elite, emerged to construct the cultural identity of the nation.   In their image, they created the mulatto and within their conceptualization of the nation they discussed the meaning of miscegnation and cultural mixing to Brazilian identity. The image of the mulatto was at the crux of the idea of racial democracy, or the Brazilian lack of racial prejudice. The discussion of miscegenation remained in the realm of the European-African type, with a strong emphasis on the absorption of the latter into the former. No major works, for example, looked at Africans and Indigenous relations.

Optimism would permeate Brazil throughout the *belle époque*, paving the way for the more incipient institutionalized nationalism of the 1930s. But the two and a half decades after abolition were not easy ones, particularly for blacks. Indeed, while many of Brazil's elite celebrated Brazilian cultural icons based on a bohemian life whose blueprint came from Paris, others began to plant the seeds of national consolidation, posing difficult questions about the nature of Brazil and Brazilians. How did Brazil cultivate citizens in the wake of abolition and how would their participation in this new nation-state be guaranteed? What importance was placed on race relations in general and the black populations in particular? And how did that influence the Brazilian emerging patriotism that would feed the nationalism of the 1930s? The answers necessarily begin with the legacies of slavery. Abolition forged a social system flexible enough to allow for the social ascent of exceptional blacks and mulattos, particularly those who could successfully blend into elite circles.

Blacks, Ethnicity and Nationhood, 1880s-1920s

During the abolitionist campaign, Joaquim Nabuco, the best known of the Brazilian abolitionists, divided the abolitionist movement into two main camps: the activist and the moderates. According to Thomas Skidmore, the activists, men like José do Patrocinio, Fereira de Menezes, Vicente de Souza, Nicoláu Moreira, and João Clapp (not included is Luis Gama, who served under Furtado de Mendonça, delegate and law teacher at the University of São Paulo) appealed to public opinion while moderates such as Nabuco, André Rebouças, Gusmão Lobo, and Joaquim Serra, spoke of saving Brazilian culture in order to appeal to the nationalist sentiments of members of Parliament.[2] This dichotomy suggests the two primary ways that black advocates would attempt to engage in a dialogue with the nation: appealing to the public sense of morality, and framing their agenda within a wider desire for the betterment of Brazilian culture. At the same time, blacks would have the additional challenge of raising consciousness within the diverse Afro-Brazilian community, and promoting a strategy of self-betterment.

Abolition as a white solution to slavery and as a national solution to the problem of the Brazilian image meant that the few blacks who joined the abolitionist movement expressed themselves within the political and cultural framework of whites. (From a practical standpoint, this meant that in order for their words to be effective, blacks and mulattos were obliged to express themselves in a language understood and accepted as authentically Brazilian by whites.\ As Roger Bastide has so poignantly shown, many mulattos and mestizos separated themselves from Africa in an effort to avoid the social stigma associated with blackness.[3] Afrânio Peixoto, for example, has shown that mulatto writers such as Machado de Assis avoided referring to his African heritage. Indeed, Assis' work hardly focused on slavery or the life of mulattos or blacks.[4] A closer analysis reveals that many mulattos, and even some blacks avoided the discussion of race allowing them to join national circles.

Many freed Afro-Brazilians, nonetheless, participated in the abolitionist campaign, among them the journalist José Carlos do Patrocínio (1854-1905), André Rebouças (1838-1898) and Luis Gonzaga de Pinto Gama (1830-1882). These men were freed men, citizens who spoke vociferously against the institution of slavery, not for racial rights or equality. Mulattos such as Luis Gama (1830-1882) and João da Cruz e Sousa (1862-1893), one of Brazil's few romantic black poets, defied racial exceptionalism which selectively allowed given mulattos to attain a higher status in a racialized pre-abolition society.[5]

Republicanism assumed a high degree of mobility within national boundaries, and the liberal ethos proposed education, and limited the role of the Church. Modeled after the United States of America, the Republican Constitution of February 21, 1891 governed Brazil until 1934.[6] The Constitution reiterated the individual rights of Brazilian citizens which included liberty, security, and property. [Despite a law which guaranteed equality of all its citizens, black access to mobility was limited. Lack of general education in the population at large, a constitution which ill-defined individual rights and the authoritarian capitalist model of development which valued property above individual rights, weakened civil rights. Brazil entered industrialization without breaking down its pre-abolition society's framework and attitudes, and the state often resolved social conflict with force.[7]

The period from the turn of the century to the beginning of the Vargas Revolution in 1930 was marked by a tension between optimism and a search for Brazilian roots. At the same time, (white intellectuals carved out the basis for what would become an official denial of ethnic conflict under Getúlio Vargas' cultural policy. Traditional scholarship has explained this phenomenon in terms of the extensive miscegenation and cultural intermingling that blurred the lines between blackness, and whiteness, but this phenomena hardly explains why *pretos* as an entity among themselves did not organize in droves or why some mulattos did. [Cultural nationalism which asserted civic duty over so-called primordial groupings largely shaped the tone of the black movement of the 1930s.] ←

The 1910s and 1920s saw the emergence of black protest and participation in local and specific conditions.   It is no coincidence that only in the 1930s did the first national black movement arise with its own ideas of nationhood.   But the first rebellion which occurred within the navy, led by João Cândido, was not solely a racial affair, although it was perceived as such by many. [Still lacking a middle class, in the first two decades of the twentieth century, black protest in Brazil encompassed issues of ethnic identity as one ingredient of a mass mobilization that called for changes that would benefit the working class.] A dominant Brazilian ethos as antithetical to blackness as to popular class defiance would quickly control it before it spread to the civilian sector.

In the aftermath of the rebellion, the racial significance was not lost on the general population.   Important national dailies published photographs of the sailors.   The important, *Jornal do Brazil*, published a series of photographs in the September 27 and 28 additions, indicating the extent of black participation. João Candido features prominently among the sailors, along with another young sailor who the paper describes as 'a major aid to João Candido...' was a 'caboclo-looking man with blond hair of *franzinha* complexion...'. The group photograph aboard the São Paulo on November 28, 1910, depicts a group of black and mulatto men during the *distribuição do rancho*.   One of the men is holding a sign that reads: 'Long Live Liberty!'[8]

The case of the cargo ship, known as the 'Satellite' provides further evidence on the republican state's inability to treat its black population as citizens, underscoring the unwritten laws that blacks had a place in society but that they were not to challenge the system, much less to call civil rights into question. On December 25, 1910, ex-sailors, more than 40 women from the Detention Center (female prison), thieves and vagabonds, as well as sympathizers of the revolt bordered the cargo ship, *Loide Brasileiro Satellite*, headed for the Amazon.   The majority of the passengers never arrived. According to Mario Filho, the cargo ship looked like an old slave vessel carrying African slaves to the interior of Brazil. Its passengers were maltreated, many of them were executed and dumped in the water, others died of diseases. Those who survived the trip were sent to forced labor camps in the interior---forgotten by official history.[9]

Writers covering the revolt at the time were neither unanimously in support or against the revolt, although many journalistic pieces contributed to the anti-black and anti-popular attitude, while reinforcing the status quo. The *Estado de São Paulo* displayed its displeasure with the amnesty, and criticized the 'brutal force of the enlisted men' who needed to be taught through corporal punishment.[10] The popular weekly magazine, *Careta*, also criticized the government for offering amnesty.   The magazine caricatured Candido as a large bowlegged animal with large ears dressed in an officers' uniform above the legend 'The Discipline of the Future'. Behind him stood two white marine officers barefoot, their lips covered with lipstick, to make them appear effeminate---an indication that they were wimps or homosexuals.[11] *O Malho*, another *carioca* weekly whose mascot the *salimbanco* arms himself with a pen in one hand and a hammer in the other, caricatured João Cândido as a strong black sailor pointing a revolver at a young girl who purportedly represented the city of Rio de Janeiro. The legend below read 'Order and Progress', clearly a satirical representative of the much revered positivist-minded philosophy.[12]

The short-lived revolt among the enlisted men took place during an era of growing euphoria and patriotism, but less than two decades after the abolition of slavery. The official rhetoric against the sailors was never explicitly racist, nor were the demands of those revolting framed in racial language.   Race, nonetheless, played a critical role in establishing the rhetoric of confrontation, demonization, and ultimate condescension which allowed the established regime to dishonor its amnesty. The popular classes could not be trusted, much less blacks from the popular classes. For many, particularly among the press, capital punishment remained a legitimate tool of the status quo to maintain order.

Eight years before the Russian Revolution, Brazilian blacks had challenged the class and race-based prejudices that robbed hundreds of Brazilians of the dignity of citizenship. Despite an ill-conceived sense of civil rights ironed out by a manipulative state, blacks along with other members of the rank and file were able to assert their human rights within a new republican framework. As one anonymous cadet remarked to the *O Estado de São Paulo*, 'Sir, you know that we are not dogs. We are people like them (the officers)'.[13] Unfortunately, despite the bravery of these few men, neither the Brazilian state under Hermes de Fonseca, nor the Brazilian elite viewed this assertion as positive for Brazilian republicanism underlined by a positivist penchant for 'order and progress', with emphasis on the order.

In Cuba after the 1912 insurrection led by black Cubans under the banner of the Independents of Color, the Cuban government banned any associations based on one race to avoid blacks joining forces again. In Brazil, no such legislation was necessary. The Brazilian state thoroughly isolated the black rebels, sending a strong message to the population that challenges to the national order would not be tolerated. Most of the rebels were executed, imprisoned, or banished to the interior of Brazil. João Cândido, who was eventually dismissed from the Navy, died in poverty, and to this day has never been given his rightful place in Brazilian social history.

Patriotism, Cultural Production, and the *Belle Époque*

The abolition of slavery and the creation of the republic fueled the consolidation of the republican nation-state. Brazil would enter into its first phase of modern nationalism in which it would change the relationship of the government with the people. Underlying this nationalism were two important assumptions: first, the nation-state was the legitimate unit for the promotion of national development. Second, the cultural elite became the legitimate representation of the nation by virtue of their class and education. The myth of a national family was in the process of uniting Brazilians from Manaus to Matto Grosso, from Rio Grande do Sul to Maranhão. The military would play a crucial role in consolidating the territory, but the cultural elite would provide the conceptual framework for decades to come.[14]

In an attempt to answer questions such as 'who are we ?', by the 1920s, national writers responded from a macro-perspective, glossing over many contradictions such as regionalism, race, and class in the attempt to describe symbolically a diverse, complex nation.[15] In modern capitalist Brazil dominant intellectuals organized national culture through the press, particularly prior to World War I, after which other means of mass media, including radio and cinema would come into use. Newspapers and other forms of print journalism, however, remained the most important source for nationalistic rhetoric, particularly through essays, literature, and poetry.[16]

The *patria* in Latin America depended on both land and language. To evoke the cause of the nation, its writers, members of the intelligentsia, developed a native vernacular by the 1920s to express their respective notion of *brasilidade*.[17] Language remained one of the essential parts of the national, as Mario Andrade attempted to convey in his article 'Fala Brasileira' in 1929.[18] A Brazilian language, proud and defiant, distinct from the mother tongue of Portugal emerged in this period in texts which have since become classics.

The role of texts of national interpretation assisted in ordering Brazilian reality, as Julio Ramos Best has explained.[19] Two major details are important here. First the classic, even when outside of its historical context, maintains referential power as it becomes established in the national canon. Juan Domingo Sarmiento's *Civilization and Barbarism*, for example, retains its authority eventhough his later work in which he criticizes some of the European immigrants could not overcome the power of his own classic.[20]

Indeed, classics which promote national myths that reflect the status quo depend on a patriarchal system inherited from the center of power. In such environments the classic as reference point, is a text to be revised, negated, or embellished, but never discarded. In 'La Escritura de lo nacional y los intellectuals puertoriqueños'. María Elena Rodríquez-Castro makes the connection between a society's classics and patriarchy. In the case of Latin American privileged writing in the search of multi-cultural identity in the spirit of paternalism and corporatism, writers tend to assume the position of caretaker, and they include in their writing those sectors of society they deem important. As we will see in the case of the decade of the 1930s, the popular masses would become of particular importance to nationalism.[21]

Intellectuals, influenced by these ideas, participated in cultural populism and corporatism. The cultural elite of the 1930s ideally situated themselves to forge the new national myths aided by a nationalistic state already intent on directing (if not controlling) how citizens imagined the nation. [In creating their national history, Brazilian intellectuals reconstructed the national cultural memory. But cultural memory is relative and dependent on when, why, and who is doing the remembering. In the case of both Brazil, and to a certain extent all of Latin America, the writers with access to the national media were overwhelmingly white and from elite backgrounds.]

As a tool of the intelligentsia, nationalism arose with the destruction of the traditional patronage and its stability based on traditional modes of societal relationships of the plantation economy. To avoid being usurped by a growing working class and incipient industrialization, the sons and daughters of a traditional elite became authorities of culture, interpreters of the new social order which began at the turn of the century.[22]

Fin de Siècle **Brazil**

There was much to celebrate as Brazil entered the twentieth century, free of the hideous trappings of slavery. Even before abolition, liberals had favorably compared their societies with the economic power of the North. Speaking of Brazil, for example, Joaquim Nabuco remarked that:

> Slavery among us remained open-ended indiscriminately extending its privileges to all... a flexibility immeasurably greater than it would have possessed had it been the monopoly of one race as it was in North America. The system of absolute equality certainly opened a better future for the black race in Brazil than in the United States.[23]

With slavery gone along with the monarchy, Brazil was well on its way to becoming the envy of the world, or so many nationalist thought.

1900 signaled, after all, the beginning of a new century, and marked the 400 anniversary of Cabral's discovery of Brazil for the Portuguese. One year later, on October 19, 1901, the Brazilian Alberto Santos-Dumont (1873-1932) would circle the Eiffel Tower with the modern airplane, and become the 'First Man to Conquer the Air'. Santos-Dumont's short trip was the perfect metaphor for Brazilian intellectuals pursuing French customs and idioms in a modern era.

It was not difficult to feel especially proud of Brazil in this period given the influx of immigrants from Europe, and the zeal with which the Brazilian military followed the positivist assumptions, order and progress! Brazil was on its way to becoming a power to be reckoned with, and under a carefully orchestrated military-oligarchy alliance the young nation would develop, although late, what Benedict Anderson terms 'the possibility of a new form of imagined community, which in its basic morphology set the stage for the modern nation'.[24] Technological advances during the *belle époque* would nonetheless lay the infrastructure that would facilitate national communication without which nations cannot exist. Three of Brazil's most important cultural developments revolutionized the means of communication which greatly enhanced the creation of the images of 'the national' including journalism, and the radio and record industry.

Newspapers, of course, were not new to Brazil. The first Brazilian newspaper, the *Correio Brasiliense*, was published in London by Hippolyto José da Costa in 1808, and the oldest Latin American newspaper was *O Diario de Pernambuco*, founded in 1825, but circulation was limited mostly to the northeastern coastal city of Recife. A host of important newspapers would join their rank before the onset of World War I, including the *Jornal do Brasil* (1900), *Correio da Manhã* (1901), and left-wing papers such as *O Amigo do Povo* (1902) and *O Protesto* (1899). As Thomas Skidmore has already indicated, most intellectuals first began publishing their materials in newspapers and magazines because of the limited distribution of manuscripts. This necessarily required a given marketable format within which writers had to express their ideas.[25]

Newspaper circulation grew exponentially from 1900 to 1930, and so did their political importance. Print capitalism did not only create what Benedict Anderson has called 'the language of power', but also models of discourse which would, for the first time, direct itself to a supposed national audience. This was particularly true of the essays of national interpretation.[26] The power of print media was evident by the modern buildings which they moved into in all the major capitals. The close connection of the intellectual class to the established political structure was not incidental. When opinions differed from given political interests, it was not difficult for politicians and capitalists to buy them.

With the expansion of print capitalism, it was not long before national associations appeared. The socialist Gustavo de Alacerda's Associacão Brasileira de Imprensa or Association of Brazilian Journalists, (A.B.I.) established in 1908, aimed to safeguard the freedom of expression, and to protect journalists from the type of corruption outlined by Campos Salles. One year later Lima Barreto's *Recordações do Escravão Isaías Caminha* (1909) staged a concerted attack on the careerism and elitist perspective of journalists who had formed a pact with the economic elite. Both Barreto and Alacerda directed their criticism to a national audience rather than a local one. Criticism notwithstanding, essays of national interpretation with patriotic underpinnings were common. Such were the cases of *Patria* published in 1900 by Alfredo Varella and *Porque Eu Ufano do Meu Pais* (*Right Or Wrong, My Country*) by Affonso Celso, both of which reflected the sense of optimism and blind faith in Brazil.

Graça Aranha's *Canaan* (1902) provided a forum for a more intense battle under patriotism. Skidmore justifiable notes that the sentimental nature of the text is secondary to 'the Brazilian dilemma'.[27] In *Canaan*, Aranha displays an uncanny patriotism with his choice of title--- the biblical promise land of Canaan and describing the *mestiços*/mulattos as the true Brazilians. *Canaan* emphasized Brazil's bright future as long as it resolved its conflicts which included both the question of blacks and miscegenation, and immigrants. Insofar as *Canaan* is pessimistic it arises from a number of areas, including Aranha's perceived disorder that resulted from the legacy of slavery, the lack of homogeneity of the population, and the question of integration of the masses of European immigrants. Moreover, *Canaan* forges a discourse over national identity seen from the eyes of two immigrants, Lentz, 'the farmer by instinct' and Milkau, 'the hunter'.[28]

The story opens with Milkau riding into the majestic city of Cachoeira in Espirito Santo. And it is through the eyes of the immigrants that the reader sees Brazil. Prior to World War I, Brazilians constructed their national image gazing towards Europe. Europe remained the standard to which Aranha and others measured Brazil. Eurocentrism aside, Aranha novelized a national region, its landscape and its people, creating a national text to discuss issues of 'the national'.   While Aranha raised questions about the future of Brazil, Brazil was in the midst of territorial consolidation. This was also the time of one of Brazil's greatest statesmen, José Maria da Silva Paranhos, the Baron of Rio Branco.

Well-revered among Brazilian intellectuals, Rio Branco almost single-handedly expanded and defined Brazil's national borders with its South American neighbors.   In 1895, he successfully argued the case against Argentina under the then arbiter, U.S. President Grover Cleveland. Five years later he gained Brazil more than 100,000 square miles from French Guiana in the north. This victory was followed by others with Bolivia, settled in 1903, British Guyana and Ecuador in 1904, Venezuela in 1905, the Netherlands over the territory now called Suriname in 1906, and Colombia in 1907. By 1909, Rio Branco had successfully settled all of Brazil's boundaries after a long and protracted agreement with Peru was finally established, and the Treaty of 1909 with Uruguay.[29] Brazil's South American neighbors did not doubt that Brazil was poising itself to become a power of the twentieth century.

But the euphoria and superficial celebration that accompanied the nascent nationalism was tempered by a continued pessimism, if not degradation associated with a perceived cultural backwardness. Central to this pessimism were questions of race and their role of blacks in Brazil's future.   But its treatment was far from central to national discourse. Pessimism was fueled by regionalist, oligarchic rule, coupled by the lack of clearly marked national boundaries, while lack of internal communication remained a critical challenge to national consciousness, as did the deplorable conditions of the working class rendered in works such as Aluisio Azevedo's *O Cortiço*.[30] Other writers, such as Oliveira Viana and Nina Rodriques, clothed their whitening ideal in vestments of science, particularly psychology and psychiatry, based on European racist ideas from the end of the nineteenth century.[31]

'Blacks' never disappeared as objects within Brazilian texts, but race relations never became important enough to merit serious sociological or historical attention before the late 1920s. Indeed, Rodriques' pioneering studies in Bahia which relied on psychiatry indicated that Brazilians treated blackness as a disease or an ugly spirit from the past that somehow needed to be exorcised from the national psyche. Black perspectives often emerged through mulattos such as Rodrigues or intellectuals such as the poets António Cândido Gonçalves Crespo (1846-1883), and João da Cruz e Souza (1862-1893), and through one of Brazil's greatest writers of the period, Joaquim María Machado de Assis (1839-1908). But these writers could hardly represent the black voice. Indeed as a letter by Gonçalves Crespo to Machado de Assis indicated, many mulattos who had come to national prominence avoided the discussion of race as well, thereby adopting the values of the dominant intellectuals.[32]

At the same time, it is helpful to recall that the politics of individual identity was as complicated as they are today. Mulattos also faced extreme prejudice. Assis himself was not immune to this, as his works were often undermined because he was mulatto.[33] Another writer João do Rio, *a pardo*, was attacked by the *Correio da Manhã* for 'immoral acts with a soldier'.[34]

It is clear, however, that blacks and mulattos continued to play important roles in Brazil's cultural production despite their absence from the official cultural construct. That the fruits of their labor were not always officially recognized attests to the fact that both marginalization and integration were fiercely at work. In the minds of many whites the absorption of African influences would signal progress. Only where their contribution was indispensable were blacks referred to with frequency, particularly in popular culture. But even then, Brazilians would try to order and gentrify black influences when it came to national representation.

Nowhere was black support more indispensable than in the Brazilian military which relied on slaves and freedmen to defend their borders and maintain order. It is not surprising that the military had long been an integrating force in Brazilian society, particularly beginning with the Paraguayan War (1865-1970). The military was also responsible for creating the first black national heroes, the majority of them dying unknown and unidentified on the battlefields. While the military support of abolition was strong, the official position on blacks in society after abolition is less clear. Nonetheless, it is from the work of military journalist Euclides da Cunha from whom we glean our most salient vision of the relationship between race and nationhood prior to World War I.

Da Cunha's work reflects the contemporary struggle between patriotic euphoria and national pessimism.

Born on January 20 1866 in the provinces of Rio de Janeiro, Da Cunha studied both at the *Politécnica* and at Brazilian military schools. Fully aware of the positivist ideas, he practiced as an engineer both in and out of the army, which he entered and left several times. Da Cunha's positivism is seen in his commitment to technological and scientific designs to improve his government and his society.[35]

Euclides da Cunha's pessimism is far less interesting, however, than his authoritative vision of Brazil which he brings forth in his classic *Os Sertões*. Influenced by the pervading positivistic philosophy which dominated Brazilian society at the turn of the century in general, and the military in particular, da Cunha looked towards a future Brazil where order would rule.[36] Indeed Brazilians embraced positivism precisely because of its conservatism and emphasis on order. Yet Brazilian positivist rhetoric was paternalistic at best, calling for the integration of the ex-slave and protection of the Indian. With regards to the Indian, for example, the Positivists in the government spearheaded the drive for the creation of Brazil's Indian Service 1889-1910 which aimed to preserve the Indian culture and land.[37] By and large, positivists were macrosociologists who saw the world, as Comte did, in universal terms, in which man was capable of evolving from an 'inferior position' to a 'superior one'. Euclides da Cunha attempted to optimistically guide Brazilians towards a superior position that he himself could not envision. Along his journey he created another ethnographic text which spoke directly to the nation. His classic *Os Sertões*,[38] centered on the creation and destruction of Canudos, a symbol of hope and failure.[39] Like the author of *Canaan*, da Cunha's main objective is to explore manifestation of Brazilian identity. In the tradition of Sarmiento, da Cunha attempted to define Brazil in terms of 'civilization and barbarism', forging a discourse on race, culture, and national identity. Pessimistic about race mixture since he adhered to the theories of biological determinism prevalent at the time, his work is filled with patriotic tensions, monologues, and incongruent passages which vacillate between national pride and racist rhetoric. That both he and Rodrigues were biological mestizos attests to the extent to which mestizos and mulattos ascribed to the dominant national ideology.[40] That his work was well-received illustrates the contradictions of Brazilian Aryanism.

Da Cunha defined what he called 'The Brazilian Man', while idealizing the Portuguese influence and denigrating the African: 'the Portuguese gens link us to the intellect of the Celt; while [t]he Negro Race has brought with him the attributes of the Negro *afer*, son of those parched and barbarous regions where, more than anywhere else, natural selection is effected through an intense exercise of force and ferocity'.[41] Both Darwin and Spencer had a profound influence on da Cunha allowing him to conclude that biological evolution demanded the guarantee of social evolution. Yet on this very issue he himself is unclear. Despite his assertion that there was no 'Brazilian type', he saw the evolution of the races towards the *pardo*. Other Brazilian writers of mixed ancestry such as Nina Rodriques and Oliveira Viana predicted the eventual disappearance of blacks from Brazilian reality.[42] Despite the inconsistency of his thoughts, many of his stereotypes of blacks and Indians were inherited by the generation that followed: he black as 'humble and docile', the Indian, a 'roaming nomad, not adapted to toil'.[43]

His praise for the man of the interior anticipates the more nationalist verde amarela movement and the celebration of the heroism of the caboclo.

> The *sertanejo* s above all else a strong individual. He does not exhibit the debilitating racist tendencies of the neurasthenic mestiços of the seaboard. His appearance, it is true, at a first glance, would lead to think that this was not the case. He does not have the flawless features, the graceful bearing, the correct build of the athlete. He is ugly, awkward, stooped.[44]

Indeed *Os Sertões* established a reference point of national discourse, while illustrating a national ethos that would subsequently be modified with a more positive outlook on miscegenation. Like Sarmiento's work in Argentina, in the Brazilian canon, it set the stage for the modern debate of progress and national identity. As a military man, da Cunha was in favor of the destruction of Canudos, yet before retelling the story he is compelled to explain Civilization's (the City along European line's) defeat of Barbarism (the backlands). At the same time, however, he opposed violence: 'The strong race does not destroy the weak by force of arms, it crushes it with civilization'. This is crucial to understanding the co-optation of the masses, and the absorption of blacks into 'the national' through cultural populism. For da Cunha, the promotion of Brazilian civilization necessarily meant a gradual absorption of blacks.[45] Da Cunha's characterization is the Brazilian equivalent of Sarmiento's *Civilization and Barbarism*.

Da Cunha's 'civilization and barbarism' were distinctly Brazilian, eclectic, contradictory and intensely regionalist. He asserted the civility of the Portuguese, '...the Portuguese *gens* link us to the intellect of the Celt', and the barbarity of the black who 'has brought with him the attributes of the Negro, son of those parched and barbarous region where, more than anywhere else, natural selection is effected through an intense exercise of force and ferocity', although he himself was of mixed ancestry.[46] Herein lies a crucial element to understanding the Brazilian discourse on race: mestizos and mulattos very often validated the racial hierarchy originally enforced by the Portuguese which espoused the natural inferiority of their African forebears.

Da Cunha further divided Brazilians regionally from the backlands to the coasts. The former he called degenerate while the latter he categorized as 'stable' due to their isolation. This was a blatant indictment of coastal societies which had become multiethnic societies of citizens.[47] He echoed the sentiment of his generation, focusing on the need for assimilation. But assimilation was often synonymous with obliteration: 'The strong race does not destroy the weak by force of arms, it crushes it with civilization'.[48] Little social legislation had been introduced to ensure that the ex-slave be integrated into mainstream society. That Brazilians wished to avoid discussion of slaves and slavery was evidenced by Rui Barbosa's decree that ordered the destruction of all records of slavery, to avoid any lingering stigma.[49] Even though all records were not destroyed, census and other types of demographic information on ex-slaves was difficult to come by after the decline of the institution of slavery.

Several important issues should also be mentioned. Da Cunha was a transitional figure, between the racist theories of the liberals to the nationalists of the 1920s. He desired a more progressive ideal as a symbol of the Brazilian type. Although, he displays a marked apathy towards the Indian, the *mestiço* of the Indian and the European represented Brazilian identity for him. After the author's trip into the backlands, he developed a nascent pride for the interior and the native *mestiço*. Despite the overall negative attitude towards miscegenation, he wished to see the *pardo* become the national type. This contradiction can perhaps be seen in the inability of da Cunha to consolidate his own nationalist feelings, with the external reality and the popular racist theories of the time which saw the hybrid as a degenerate.[50]

Alberto Torres[51] refuted many of da Cunha's ideas while examining history and social habitats to study the nation's problems. Torres believed that there were no superior or inferior races only advanced and retarded ones. As Skidmore eludes, this implied that Brazil was behind and could still 'catch up'.[52] Torres, unlike Sarmiento, Nabuco, or Da Cunha opposed the immigration of whites as it would prejudice the already existing national institutions.[53] Still, Brazilian elites feared the popular masses of the coasts, but believed that blacks would, like the Canudos of 1896, become victims of progress. They would eventually be absorbed by the larger population.[54]   What united Torres and da Cunha, however, was not so much the content of their ideas but the framework which they used to discuss their subject--the Brazilian nation.   Torres represented another voice responding to the cultural matrix which questioned the future of Brazil within a context of national consolidation influenced by patriotism.

Born in 1865, Alberto Torres, who entered the Faculty of Medicine at the age of fifteen, founded the Centro Abolicionista in São Paulo and the Clube Republicano in Niteroi, served as a member of the Federal Congress and from 1897-1900, and also as President of Rio de Janeiro.   Before 1914, Torres published two major studies; *Vers la Paix* (1909), and *La problème mundial* (1913).   Unlike da Cunha, Torres' major work *O Problema nacional brasileiro*, published in 1914, had the benefit of anti-racist theoreticians such as Franz Boas.[55]   Torres, the foremost sociologist of his time, refuted the racist ideas that were anti-Brazilian. He had the benefit of the positivist generation ahead of him and the fervor of the nationalists that would follow.   Torres shifted the arguments from biology to culture, which was dependent on history and social habitats. His insistence that there were no superior or inferior races but only advanced and retarded ones places him squarely in the tradition of Sarmiento's civilization-barbarism dichotomy.   Like the modernists that followed, he saw miscegenation as a tool to advance national culture.[56] The concept of 'the national' is much more succinct in Torres' world, hence his more pointed criticism of Darwin, and other racists from Nietzsche to Gobineu.[57]

The 1920s

We have seen that prior to World War I, would-be nationalists utilized racist ideologies to promote a positive image of Brazil, while marginalizing, if not denigrating, the contribution of blacks to national culture.   Only in excluding blacks, indeed making them invisible could optimism prevail.   It is often said that change emerges from within radicals ranks, but before 1930, neither the communists nor the anarchists had effectively addressed the question of race.   The anarchists had refused to divide society into *any* classes, whereas the communists *only* divided society into economic classes.[58]   The period following World War I brought an introspection which would encourage Latin Americans to examine their Eurocentric constructions of nationhood. Intellectuals responded to three phobias that had prohibited Brazilian national consolidation: the 'Fear of the Negro', the 'Fear of the Indian' and the 'Dependency of Brazil'. Many struggled to forge new symbols for a new century. Out of the battle emerged a series of ideas about 'the national'; texts, essays and art which provided responses and counter-responses to the question 'Who are we?'

World War I signaled in many ways the failure of European cultural models for the Brazilian reality. In Latin America, a new generation of intellectuals, who experienced the crisis in the world order, saw the possibility of their cultural development due to European writers who began to predict the downfall of Western civilization. Osvald Spengler, for example, saw culture as a living organism. Every culture grew, rose to its level of great civilization, and eventually declined.[59] Spengler's influence became prominent among many intellectuals in a post-positivist era when the nation-state became the primary unit of international relations. This was particularly evident in the period leading up to the stock-market crash of 1929 when pessimism about Western culture directly influenced the construction of nationalism throughout Latin America. European intellectuals such as Osvald Spengler would write of the decay of Western culture.[60]

The modernist writers of the 1920s would borrow from diverse ideologies from anarchism to fascism, creating Brazilian texts that succeeded in forging a Brazilian national family, or at least creating a framework within which the notion of a Brazilian national family was conceivable. A decade later these texts would already become canonical. The literary and aesthetic revolution promoted by the modernists succeeded in introducing the popular masses to the question of 'the national', although they adopted a traditional framework of construction that was greatly influenced by Catholic values.

The Catholic church's belief in a Christian family played a major role in nationalist language even though prior to the 1920s, the Church concerned itself with its own political and economic position first, and then the interests of its followers, while at the same time providing lip service to the notion of a Brazilian family.[61] Still, Catholic forums such as *Ordem* promoted *brasilidade* as a national tradition which in essence meant Catholicism, corporatism, and conservative values.[62] Jackson de Figueiredo, the major interpreter of Catholic thought, for example, claimed that the Church was the nation's only hope of salvation--a cry that would be reiterated by Brazilian cultural nationalists.[63] Missing from the debate on religion as a unifying force were references to Afro-Brazilian religions despite the fact that the Yoruba-based religion of *candomblé* had a long tradition, and that the urban based *umbanda* emerged in the 1920s.

For Figueiredo, Brazil's heritage was always Catholic. It was religion that bound Brazilians together regardless of race. Figueiredo was always concerned with the political role that the Catholic church would play in national politics, but it was the integralists, who embraced the ideas of the Church in the construction of their own nationalistic secular projections.[64]   Catholicism affected and influenced other nationalist tendencies.[65] While most nationalist intellectuals dismissed Catholicism's spirituality, many adopted its corporatist and hierarchical structure in their construction of national culture. This assured blacks a role for the first time, but not at the top of the hierarchy.[66]

The cultural revolution dubbed modernism was a profoundly nationalistic movement influenced by a variety of tendencies, not all of which were reconcilable. Along with Catholic corporatist values, many modernists embraced anarchist and positivist influences as well as fascism to help them create a Brazilian language, and a new identity through *brasilidade*.[67]   The modernist manifestos called for a futuristic vision, spontaneity, optimism and a discovery of the historical roots of Brazil.[68] To be sure, modernism was a general spirit and not a single school. In fact, there were several schools within the Modernist movement which can be compared to their Spanish American counterparts of the *avant garde* who sought new ethical and aesthetic ways of expression.[69]

The modernists promoted *brasilidade* with unprecedented fervor, cultivating Brazilian texts with Brazilian heroes, and protagonists from the popular classes. Modernists formed distinct intellectual units, influenced mostly by region, but many writers from different regions of Brazil wrote from their own local perspective, employing local symbols as national ones. 'National Culture' became the panacea for the country's woes. Brazilians searched for the 'new Brazil', placing attention on areas undiscovered by the upper classes.[70] While race was central to all of these tenets, 'race relations' or 'racial discrimination', was downplayed in favor of inclusion. This was a small change from the marginalization of the decade before, but it was a change.

Patriotic tendencies emphasized the contribution of different ethnic groups to the construction of the nation, rather than to their ethnic communities, thereby relegating non-whites to the realm of history while imagining national utopias. The two major tendencies of modernism (the *Pau Brazil* or Brazilwood movement and *Verdeamerilsmo*, or the Green and Yellow movement) focused on national consolidation through essentialist rhetoric that reduced Brazilians to national essences which in its theoretical conceptualization homogenized both the black, and the white, but which in actuality marginalized black images in favor of whitened forms of the mestizo or mulatto. The 'Indian' received much more attention, albeit in a romantic fashion characteristic of nationalism. As Gilberto Mendonça Teles has indicated, the modernists were little interested in blacks since they believed that there was no prejudice in Brazil.[71]

Inclusion of blacks indicated the level of integration that had been attained, and modernists discussed blacks because of their focus on popular culture. On closer analysis, however, less attention is given to black-white social and political representation or blacks outside the context of assimilation and integration. Indeed, the focus on integration served to make blacks and their concerns invisible in national discourse. Only forty years after abolition, modernists were not fully prepared to grapple with the political and economic problems of the underclass created as a result of slavery.[72]

Verdeamerelismo took its symbols, (verde) green and (amarelo) yellow, from the Brazilian flag. Green represented the vast natural resources of Brazil, symbolized by the Amazon forests, and yellow, was an allusion to the sun and by extension to the tropicalism of the Brazilian culture. Cassiano Ricardo, Plínio Salgado, Menotti del Picchia and Candido Mota Filho helped support this tendency which was akin to a Brazilian type of Indianism, following in the tradition of José de Alencar, who in 1857 wrote *O Guarani*, in which he romanticized the Indian life and created the Athenian type youth Peri.[73] Indeed, for many modernists, it was the Tupi-Guarani who symbolized *brasilidade*. Like the indigenistas in Peru or Mexico, they looked to the indigenous past as a source of national inspiration, the point from which Brazilian civilization emerged.

In his classic text, *Martim Cerreré* (1928), Cassiano Ricardo related the stories of the interior of Brazil which he considered the cradle of the nation. The Brazilian 'race' emerged from an indigenous base followed by an amalgamation with the African and Portuguese.[74] Ricardo's text indicated, essentialist as it was, several important changes in regard to race: miscegenation was now considered a symbol of the new Brazil, which made Brazil unique among nations. Modernist writers attempted to order its cultural influences, indicating which ethnic element had been most important to the national soul. For Ricardo, it was the Indian and the mestizo. But in *Marcha para oeste*, Ricardo's paulista biases surface. Due to the long history of regionalism, regional heroes were often embellished for the national level. In this account of the expeditions of the *paulista bandeirantes* to penetrate the interior, put down rebellions, and colonize new lands, Ricardo portrays the *bandeirantes* as Brazilian pathfinders with great *paulista* pride. On the other hand he attributed many of their characteristics to their *mestiço* origins. It is difficult to forget that the bandeirantes, though mostly of mestiço influences, were responsible for the enslavement and extermination of thousands of natives.

Indianistas in Brazil shared much in common with the anarchists, at least rhetorically, in that they advocated a return to nature and armed themselves with an anti-industrialized rhetoric. Although at this time, the interior of Brazil remained un-colonized, for many intellectuals, the heart of Brazil was to be found in the national region that was unknown, rather than in the rapid industrialization, coupled with the high immigration of the city. Yet it was in the city, as Angel Rama tells us, where the modern intellectual emerged.[75]

Raul Bopp, despite being from Rio Grande de Sul, at the southern extreme of Brazil, associated the interior and the *caboclo* with *brasilidade*. In *Cobra Norato*, written in 1931, Bopp contributed to the search for identity with a Tupi fable represented by the heroic serpent. The serpent roamed the interior lands of splendor, which the author described in idyllic terms.[76] His theme, 'Let's Go Hunt Parrots', underscored the search for the ideal within 'the national', parrots symbolizing everything that was foreign to him.[77]

Paulo Prado, son of an elite Brazilian family, published his historical essay *Retrato do Brasil: Ensaio Sôbre a Tristeza Brasileira* before the Revolution of 1930. Although more pessimistic if not negative, *Retrato do Brasil*, which also focused on the Brazilian interior, classified the Brazilian people as sad and despondent. Yet, this must be understood in the political backwardness, and lack of coherency that Prado perceived prior to 1930. Prado's pessimism results largely from his assessment, not of race-relations, per se, but of the slave influence on Brazilian society, an influence which he regarded as 'terrible elements of corruption'.[78]

Mario de Andrade's seminal work, *Macunaíma* (1928), also turned national eyes towards the interior, promoting a modified rhetoric of Indianism while including the black influence within the context of cultural and racial mixing.[79] *Macunaíma*, tells the story of the black Tapanhumas Indian from the interior of Brazil who migrates to the booming city of São Paulo. The protagonist of the same name is an anti-hero who succeeds through the use of magical powers, wizardry, and sense of independence, combined magnificently with modern technology. Macunaíma indeed represented Brazil on many fronts. The text itself was a combination of many regional legends and some foreign, synthesized to express 'the national'. Furthermore, the protagonist is the self-sufficient independent hero who relies on both magic and technology to fight off the exogenous oppressors, and to retain his identity, depicting what Andrade called 'a revolt against the traditional national intelligence'.[80]

The issues of national identity and the national family are treated directly in the text, albeit in a satirical manner. Before Macunaíma and his brothers, Maanape and Jigue, set off to discover the city (São Paulo), they come upon a magical spring, where they are baptized as Brazilians by the purifying waters. Macunaíma, the first to emerge from the waters, is turned into a white man with blue eyes and blond hair--a direct reference to whitening in Brazil. Jigue, the second to enter, emerges with a skin complexion the color of bronze. The 'unfortunate' Maanape, however, arrives too late and only is able to lighten the soles of his feet and the palms of his hands. Despite the satire, from the sub-text emerges a powerful national myth: this is the projection of a racially diverse but united Brazilian family, the perfect national symbol. Yet *embranqueamento* is clearly evident. The narrator's comment that 'half a loaf is better than none' gives an insight into a national desire.[81]

Blacks had been transformed. Indeed with the abolition of slavery and the *senzala* came a desire for the abolition of blackness. *Mulatismo*, or the celebration of the mulatto as an idyllic cooperative step among blacks and whites, nonetheless was framed within the context in which whiteness was privileged, and blackness denigrated. Indeed the idea of being half-baked, not quite complete, underscored the national desire to move away from blackness, i.e., backwardness. On the other hand, it is no surprise that the mulatto becomes an important national symbol. Andrade joined in with other modernists involved in a movement called 'Movimento antropofágo', which aimed, according to the *Revista antropófago* (1929) to synthesize, that is, devour all foreign and regional influences in order to create an autonomous national culture. It is only later that Oswald de Andrade himself recognized the elitist role of many of the modernist texts.[82] Still, while Paulista modernists recreated Brazil as a new nation which was capable of eating up all foreign influences and creating a cultural (if not a biologically) *mestiço* people, modernists around the country devised national symbols that informed the nation-state that was in the process of formation.

Modernism was an important expression of 1920s nationalism. In Rio, for example, Graça Aranha staged the conference dedicated to 'The Modernist Spirit', in Rio's sanctuary of culture, The Academy of Brazilian Letters. Interest in blacks heightened largely because of European influences, as the visit of French poet Blaise Cedras, among others, clearly indicated.[83] One of the few forums that explicitly discussed the role of blacks within modernism was a lesser known magazine from Minas Gerais called *Leite Crioulo*. On May 13, 1929, João Dornas Filho, Atilo Vaivaquo, and Guilhermino César founded the magazine, which will be discussed in chapter three. Five years earlier in 1924 Guilherme de Almeida's poem, 'Raça', which he recited in the Teatro Santa Isabel had created a mild scandal which surely influenced the emergence of *Tropilha Crioulo* by Vargas Neto in 1925.

The strongest black components to Brazilian cultural heterogeneity came from the Northeast who reproduced national history in idyllic terms, and often with *saudade*, or longing, for a way of life that had long passed. Many argued that the Northeast represented the cradle of Brazilian civilization for it was there that the Portuguese first settled. Northeasterners tried to capture the Brazilian spirit in which the mulatto symbolized the historical relationship between the African and the Portuguese. Unlike other modernists who were connected to urban literary circles, the northeasterners included diverse writers such as Gilberto Freyre, José María Belo, and Jorge de Lima, and historian Sergio Buarque de Holanda.[84]

Of all the intellectuals, Gilberto Freyre received the most international and national attention. Freyre's contribution to national social sciences and psychohistory paralleled Mario Andrade's work in fiction. More than any single scholar, Freyre wrote of Portuguese miscegenation and adaptation to the tropics. For Freyre, mulatto was the symbol and hero of the 'New Brazil'. He challenged in international circles the theories of the inferiority of peoples of mixed stock and pointed to the contribution of both Africans and Indians to the development of modern Brazil. The search for national explanation and identity, coupled with his love for Brazil led him to attack the myth of the inferiority of the 'mixed-blood', which represented, to a large extent, modern Brazil.

It was Freyre who we now associate with the ideology of 'racial democracy' which became widely popularized in the 1930s. Indeed 'racial democracy', was a 1920s modernist construct which found its most successful expression in Freyre's work. Responding to the concerns of his generation, Gilberto Freyre institutionalized the classic ideas of racial democracy with his nationalistic writings. As Frank Tannenbaum aptly indicated: 'Many Brazilians will tell you that, in the future, the history of their country will be chronicled in two parts; that before and after Gilberto Freyre. The dividing line is *Casa Grande e Senzala*...first published in 1933'.[85]

According to Freyre, his desire to write about Brazil occurred when he was in New York and he saw a group of mulatto Brazilian soldiers who '...seemed to him like caricatures of men and he remembers with bitterness the disrespectful phrase from two Anglo-Saxon tourists that spoke of the fearful Mongrel aspect of the Brazilian population'.[86] Freyre's scholastic and personal experience abroad had, as Jeffrey E. Needell has succinctly shown, a profound effect on his conceptualization of Brazilian identity. After Freyre studied the colonization of Brazil, he saw patterns which reinforced his nationalist sentiments. His tutelage under Franz Boas undoubtedly aided him in dispelling the negative image of Brazil as a country of 'fearful mongrels'. The rapid miscegenation which he saw gave credit to the theory of racial democracy. At the center of Freyre's myth was the Brazilian hero, the mulatto.[87]

Freyre, like his fellow modernists, failed to recognize Brazil's gradual social definition of race and the victimization of blacks due to the preference for the mulatto, and at the same time the limited social mobility of the mulattos in a society still run by whites. Furthermore, his 'Casa Grande' paradigm was too static to account for whitening in which even the 'biological' mulattos who had participated in elite positions, such as the famous novelist Machado de Assis, were often considered 'white'.[88] Moreover, his views had a damaging effect on black Brazilian mobilization, and stymied discussions of racial conflict by dismissing it as a legitimate issue for discussion. While promoting racial democracy, he apparently justified his lack of support for an anti-discrimination bill, claiming that it was not needed in Brazil.[89]

Other writers and politicians would reiterate Freyre's ideas. José María Belo from Pernambuco, for example, shared his fervor. Belo, who served as governor of the Northeastern state of Pernambuco from 1930-1934 defended the representation of classes on the Constituent Assembly. Belo believed that the rapid industrialization and urbanization threatened the rural aristocracy that ruled Brazil prior to 1930. He called for Brazilians to realize their historical roots and the three great ethnicities that had contributed to the development of Brazil: the African, the Portuguese, and the indigenous. Yet in an effort to determine their psychological contribution to the nation, he classified the former as complacent, and the latter as economical. According to Freyre, Brazil had inherited the Indians' fatalism and resistance to social transformation. As in Freyre's interpretation, the Portuguese are the major heroes since they provided a cultural umbrella of integration through a common language and religion.[90]

The Portuguese were endowed with a certain cultural ability which allowed them to easily mingle among peoples of other races and cultures. These ideas would later develop into the nationalist ideology called *lusotropicalism,* a Portuguese prediposition to the tropics which included a natural ability to peacefully coexist with people from different cultures. Historian Sergio Buarque de Holanda would further argue that Brazil was still linked to the peninsula through tradition.[91] Buarque acknowledged an American dimension of Brazil, but one entrenched in the Portuguese tradition that had kept all of the diverse elements of Brazil together. Indeed this Creole Brazilian identity was how Brazilians would imagine themselves.

Writers of the 1920s were no less familiar with racist writers of the turn of the century than their compatriots a decade earlier.[92] In an effort to promote national pride, modernists forged a positive identification towards race mixing while combating the nineteenth century myth that tropicalism and geographical determinism had led to degeneracy. In the process, they shook off the psychological shackles of colonialism. Mestizaje and miscegenation had become central to Brazilian history. While Brazilians lauded their indigenous and African pasts, they ignored their continual presence.[93]

Important to the acceptance of the classic view of racial democracy was not only local propagation, but the fact that the ideas of internationally acclaimed writers such as Freyre and later Jorge Amado were endorsed by many foreign writers, historians, and artists. The nationalism of the corporate and populist type was anti-imperialistic and many American leftist intellectuals, in particular, saw the Brazilian model as an alternative to race relations in the U.S. In this regard, the modernists had succeeded in changing their national image, and indeed their identity.[94]

National Identity, Blackness, and Other Media

While this discussion has focused primarily on written national texts, nationalism and the idea of a national family in which miscegenation played a primordial role was evident in national painting and both the emerging film and music industry.

Modernist painters in search of national roots were influenced by European currents, particular cubism, as well as by muralism which had come in vogue in Mexico. Emiliano Cavalcanti (1897-1976) and Vicente do Rego Monteiro (1899-1970) and Tarsila do Amaral were three better known. But many of the images of 'the people' in general and of blacks and mulattos in particular were stereotypical and one-dimensional. Rego Monteiro's 'Mulata with parrot', is an exotic portrait unifying the mulatta with the animal in bright colors. Ironically, Mario de Andrade would later criticize the state for not allowing paintings with black subjects to be sent to expositions abroad.[95]

Cinema came to Brazil when the Spanish-born Enrique Moya installed the 'Cinematógrafo Edison' in the city of Rio de Janeiro in 1897. A decade would pass before cinema became a craze of the elite and the small middle classes. By the 1920s, popular images had already begun to emerge on the silver screen, although Brazil would see a more strident development of race in national cinema with the dawn of *cinema novo* in the late 1950s. Films such as *O Guarani*, *Aitaré da Praia*, and *Barro Humano* brought forth some of the first images of non-white Brazil, although North American cinema dominated almost 90 percent of the film market. The *belle époque* assured viewers that images such as the *melindrosas,* the delicate and often prudish woman with exaggerated manners, would last for a long time, and black images would only appear in primitive forms.

'Blackness' was much more of an integral part of Brazil's national music--that music that received promotion through national (and international forums) through the existing means of communication. It is difficult to speak of popular music without mentioning blacks at the turn of the century. But in order for what was perceived as black music to represent the nation it would have to be modified. The introduction of the gramophone to Brazil in 1904 would provide Brazilians with a new media of influence, as would the radio later introduced by Roquette Pinto. European aesthetics in music largely dominated the airways and the recording studios. Classical composers and performers such as Hector Vila Lobos and Franciso Mignone did not hesitate to create Brazilian scores in which they included Brazilian (non-white) elements. This was certainly the case of Vila Lobo's *Alma Brasileira* (1926) and Mignone's, *No Sertão* (1925), the later clearly influenced by the work of da Cunha.

By 1906 the mulatta had already become the object of attention of many composers and performers, symbol of the decadence and joy of the *belle époque*. Arquemedes de Oliveira, for example, popularized the verse of Bastos Tigres' 'Vem Cá , Mulata', ('Come Here Mulatta') in that year. But three years earlier 'Quem Inventou a Mulata' by Ernesto de Souza was already a carnival success. The first samba was not registered at the Biblioteca Nacional in Rio de Janeiro until Nov 27, 1916. Then, a timid Ernesto Santos registered 'Pelo Telefone' (roticeiro no. 3295 composition) which would later became the carnival hit of 1917.

While black images appeared frequently in popular lyrics, popular black musicians received little or no official national attention from critics, newspapers, or intellectuals. Of course neither did popular

white musicians who insisted on appealing to the popular taste.   One
obvious exception was the auto-didactic Ernesto Nazareth, better known as
Pixinguinha.   Born in 1898 to a musical family, by 1919 Pixinguinha had
put together his first band, *Os Oito Batutas*, who soon began touring in
places such as Argentina and Paris, becoming one of the first Brazilian
bands to perform in Europe.   But even success in Paris would not halt
criticism and complaints.   According to Claus Schreiner, *cariocas*, for
example, lamented that Brazil's first cultural mission was composed of a
band of blacks.[96]

Conclusions

Before Brazil would enter into the second republic, create a new political
climate, and institutionalize the positive national identity of a multi-ethnic
identity, it suffered the questioning phase of post-abolitionism which
culminated in the modernist revolution at the end of the 1920s.
Intellectuals were in the midst of cultivating patriotism, as nationalists
such as Elysio Caravalho adamantly preached the importance of patriotic
feelings, contending that Brazil would grow in proportion to the pride that
Brazilians felt for Brazil.[97]   History was at the disposition of nationalism.
As late as 1936, the historian Sérgio Buarque de Holanda also used history
as a means of national consolidation in his *Raizes do Brasil*.   De Holanda
attempted to understand Brazil from its rural heritage, but more
importantly he examined the Portuguese tradition which allowed for the
consolidation of Brazilian culture, *brasilidade* and racial democracy.
Freyre goes one step further by associating the Spanish character with that
of the Portuguese.   Spain and Portugal, he reported were not orthodox
Europeans in their vision of life.   They were a people formed from the
influences of European Christianity and African Islam.[98]
        The promotion of the Portuguese tradition and its union with the
black population rose as a response to a generation's search for national
identity.   This interpretation surfaced in the face of extensive non-
Portuguese immigration.   In addition, the rise of North American cultural
imperialism constituted another force with which the nationalists would
reckon.   It was not of little significance that both Buarque and Freyre were
of Portuguese stock, and that both were instrumental in promoting the idea
of Portuguese adaptation to the tropics which would later become known
as *lusotropicalism*.   Paulista nationalists, especially Mario de Andrade did
not support the notion of *lusotropicalism*.   Nonetheless, the union of races

in the formation of an ethnically democratic Brazilian family was a popular belief.

Many intellectuals have been omitted from this study,[99] nonetheless this chapter has provided a panorama of ideas and their interpretations and relationship with race and culture in the modern period. The concepts of culture were directly dependent on the ideological leaning or agenda of the intellectual units. Whatever their political persuasion, Brazilians saw their particular view of national culture in the context of progress for Brazil. Nabuco was a liberal spokesman before abolition who was concerned not directly with race relations but liberal development. That there were inferior and superior races was the basic tenet for his drive against slavery. Slavery inhibited European migration which would enable Brazil to progress.

The positivists and the liberals in Brazil shared a desire for development. Da Cunha attempted to construct an ideal Brazilian type based on the common liberal racist rhetoric in the *sertanejo*. His regard for the blacks and mulattos are less than positive, even though as other records show, it would have been almost impossible to distinguish many of these racial types. Torres, on the other hand, shifted the argument from inferior and superior races to advanced and retarded, and in this sense was a more coherent mainstream positivist. These shifts in cultural perceptions allowed for the development of the Brazilian race from a more backward stage to a nationally sound and stable one. Torres, however, as a precursor to the modernists, called for a new Brazilian independence, which had not occurred in 1822![100]

The modernists directly addressed Brazil's past and synthesized a cultural direction for the nation's future. From the modernists, the myth of racial democracy was solidified in a highly nationalistic spirit. The effects of the modernists are still very strong today. Nonetheless, many revisionists have come along attempting to discredit these national myths which, rather than serve as metaphor of reality, tend to obscure it. Yet the modernists must be understood in a historical light as pathfinders who were motivated by the fundamental desire to ameliorate conditions which made it unfavorable for those of non-European background. Most of the studies centered on regional analysis which was then extended to the national framework, providing a basis for the cultural nationalism promoted by Getúlio Vargas.[101]

It would be erroneous to suggest that all of the intellectuals of the 1920s and 1930s generation supported Vargas' goals and methods. Many did. Many did not. Martins de Almeida was one critical writer.[102] Nationalist thinkers agreed, however, on their cultural and moral authority within the national milieu. In their own nationalistic way, each intellectual unit attempted to describe *brasilidade*, not in elitist terms but with a desire to include all sectors. While some saw Brazil's essence in the indigenous past, others saw it in the mulatto. Racial democracy became the dominant symbol of *brasilidade* of this generation, both locally and abroad. This meant that there was no prejudice or discrimination in Brazil. Brazilians defined themselves as inherently having no racial prejudice.

Intellectuals saw the importance of education in creating national consciousness. Three great races had contributed to the formation of the Brazilian nation. In the forging process, these ideas were institutionalized through the publication of books and articles which were distributed through the state-controlled education system. Education meant inculcation of culture to avoid disintegration of community. Culture, as we have seen, was to be defined by the few. Brazil's participation in international (Western) circles also allowed these myths to flourish. Modernism had promoted a radically different vision of race, heralding miscegenation as a national phenomenon not in a positive light. Nationalism had special appeal to politicians, and was sometimes carried to extremes, as we have seen in the case of the integralists.

The ideas of Afonso Arinos de Melo Franco, a native *mineiro* from Belo Horizonte had inspired this generation. His approach to the creation of the nation can best be described as humanist.[103] Arinos believed that the spiritual force was the only energy that would guide Brazil into the future. He rejected both communism and integralism and called upon the intellectual to wake the masses with their ideas. Arinos wanted the national intellectuals to come together to guide the Brazilian culture, civilization for him could only be constructed by spiritually inclined intellectuals. He warned Brazilians to avoid the decadent materialism of the United States which he viewed as lacking in culture.[104]

Arinos saw disorganization, but he himself was a member of a generation that was forging a national consciousness based on order.

> This undeniable disorder in the realm of the spirit is the preponderant factor of the anarchic state in which our national forces are developing. Without intellectual order, social organization is a myth and strides inevitably towards violence or disillusion.[105]

He emphasized that before action there had to be an ideological agenda. Successful revolutions only succeeded when they were ideologically sound. At the same time, Arinos saw the imperative of overcoming regionalism and orienting the *patria* along national lines. He rejected the materialist nation of the nation state and preferred a humanist approach. Arinos was in agreement with the other writers of his generation when it came to racial unity. Three elements had contributed to the formation of the nation: the Portuguese language, religion and miscegenation. Although he saw disorder, he made it clear that miscegenation had no part in it. Miscegenation in Brazil had been of a special character and had created the Brazilian mulatto who had influenced all other ethnic groups, even the white.[106]

Thus Brazil emerged as a new modern symbol, as an example of what Europe and the United States had not attained. It was the basis for Brazilian national superiority at a time when religious intolerance and racial segregation were major obstacles of consolidation of the Western European republics. The Brazilian intelligentsia, at the opportune and triumphant moment of national political consolidation defined their national culture in praiseworthy terms. This brings us to the major issue of the second part of this dissertation: the issue of cultures and subcultures. As T. S. Elliot noted, if a national culture is to flourish, the constellation of sub-cultures which make up the whole must develop in a dynamic way so that they mutually benefit one another. But this version of national consciousness in Brazil was a top-down process in which the state played a significant role. To test Elliot's assertion it is imperative to look at the other popular and not so fortunate intellectual units and their responses to the institutionalization of national mythology.[107] Before this is possible, however, it is crucial to examine the state's role in institutionalizing the Brazilian national identity.

Notes

[1]
 Leonard Doob, *Patriotism and Nationalism: Their Psychological Foundations* (New Haven and London: Yale University Press, 1964), introduction.

[2]
 Thomas E. Skidmore, *Race and Nationality in Brazilian Thought* (New York: Oxford University Press, 1974), 17. See also pages 3-37 for an elaboration of the abolitionist movement. Joaquim Nabuco (1849-1910) was a diplomat, parliamentarian and a writer. A graduate of the elite Colégio Pedro II, Nabuco later studied law in Recife, traveled to both Europe and to the United States. In London, he wrote his masterpiece *O Abolicionismo* (*Abolitionism*) in 1883 while a member of the Anti-Slavery Society there.

[3]
 Roger Bastide, *A Poesia Afro-Brasileira* (São Paulo: Martins, 1943), 24.

[4]
 Gonçalves Crespo, *Obras Completas* (Rio de Janeiro: Livros de Portugal, 1942), 5-30. In the preface, Peixoto quotes a letter by Crespo, also a mulatto to

Machado de Assis, referring to a common 'secret' that the two writers share: that of being mulattos.

[5] Elisa Larkin Nascimento, *Dois Negros Libertários: Luis Gama e Abdias do Nascimento*, 4. Sílvio Romero, *Historia da Literatura Brasileira* vol. IV (6th Ed. (Rio de Janeiro: Editora José Olympio, 1960), 1165.

[6] *Constituições Brasileiras*, 517. Deodoro created a commission of five members to elaborate the Constitution. Tom Holloway, *Policing Rio de Janeiro: Repression and Resistance in a 19th Century City*, 43-63.

[7] Much of this information comes from Carlos Hasenbalg who, in addition to the above mentioned reasons for the lack of Civil Rights, states that the rapid increase in population, especially through immigration diminished the likelihood that natives construct an authentic Civil Rights movement. In fact, many parliamentarians began to propose anti-immigrant attitudes and legislation. Social movements such as communism and anarchism, and anarcho-syndicalism were blamed on immigrants. See Hasenbalg, *Discriminação e Desigualdade Racial no Brasil* (Rio de Janeiro: Graal, 1979), 256-259.

[8] 'Revolta de Marinheiros: A Sua Terminação', *Jornal do Brasil*, November 27, 1910, 9-10. 'Revolta de Marinheiros: O Dia de Hontem', (Sic) *Jornal do Brasil*, November 28, 1910, 5-6.

[9] Morel, 129-145. Ricardo de Morais, 39-40. Morél reproduces a list of ex-sailors who had been given amnesty during the November revolt, but who were listed as members of the ship by the police.

[10] Jose Feliciano, 'A Anistia- Uma Nota Civilista e Cívica', *O Estado de São Paulo*, Sunday November 27, 1910, n.p.

[11] *Careta*, (No. 132) Saturday, December 10, 1910, cover.

[12] *O Malho*, No. 429 December 3, 1910, see also No. 428, November 26, 1910. da Silva, 62-69.

[13] *O Estado de São Paulo*, November 24, 1910, (paper clipping, n.p.)

[14] Ibid, 4-12.

[15] E. Bradford Burns, 'Ideology in Nineteenth-Century Latin American Historiography' in *Hispanic American Historic Review* 58, (3): 409-431.

[16] *Novo Diccionario de Historia do Brasil* (São Paulo: Indústrias de Papel, 1970), 349. In Brazil, however, the journalistic tradition began in Great Britain with the establishment of the *Correio Brasiliense ou Armazén Literário* in 1808 by Costa Pereiera Furtado de Mondonça. This newspaper was an instrumental forum of the events of 1822. Between 1808 and 1822, inspired by the accomplishments of Mendonça, many newspapers and journals appeared. Local writers and thinkers were supported by the *Impressão Régia* founded in Rio de Janeiro by the Portuguese Royal family who had fled the peninsula due to the Napoleonic wars. Although the Impressão Régia allowed for the expansion of the press, the ideas which came from its quarters were monitored by the Crown. In 1815, censorship was 'softened' and the press was allowed to

print invitations, announcements and the like. In 1821, official censorship was abolished, resulting in the emergence of several newspapers, including the *Réverbero Constitucional Fluminense*. Newspapers were the major forum for the dissemination of ideas throughout the nineteenth century, followed by magazines and journals which did not develop until the latter part of the nineteenth century. Illiteracy and the lack of a bourgeoisie were two factors which did not allow for the development of more matured genres until the early part of the twentieth century. The 1920s marked the commencement of what could be called the Brazilian 'Golden Age'.

[17] Raymond Williams, *Key Words: A Vocabulary of Culture and Society* (New York: Oxford University Press, 1966).

[18] Mario de Andrade, an important modernist writer and nationalist, began the column 'Taxi' in the *Diario Nacional* in 1929. Many of the important articles from the column have been organized by Tele Porto Ancona Lopez, *Mario de Andrade: Taxi e Crónicas no Diario Nacional* (Sao Paulo, 1976).

[19] T.S. Elliot, *What is a Classic?* (London: Faber and Faber Ltd, 1946), 15. See also Frank Kermode, *The Classic: Literary Images of permanence and Change.* (New York: Viking Press, 1975) which is a further elaboration of the Elliot text. The definition of a classic comes from Julio Ramos, *Desencuentros de la modernidad en America Latina* (Mexico: Fondo de Cultura Económica, 1989), 229. Ramos also best describes the relationship between myth and classic in another work: 'un clásico es un evento discutivo que, institucionalizado en diferentes coyunturas históricas, asumen un enorme poder referential. Un texto que en la historia de sus lecturas pierde su cáracter de acontecimeinto discusivo y se lee en función de la presencia del mundo representante y immediate del mundo representativo'.

[20] Domingo Faustino Sarmiento, *Facundo* (Mexico: Nuestros Clásicos, Universidad Nacional Autónoma de México, 1972), 1. Mitre founded the Junta Historia y Numismática American in 1893. Born in Buenos Aires in 1821, Mitre served in various cabinet positions after the fall of Rosas, but he is best known as one of Argentina's foremost writers of the nineteenth century.

[21] Maria Elena Rodriquez-Castro, 'La escritura de lo nacional y los intelectuales puertorriqueños'. Ph.D. Diss. Princeton University, 1988.

[22] Antonio Gramsci, *Los intelectuales y la organization de la cultura* (México: Juan Pablos Ed, 1975), 11-28.

[23] Nabuco, p. 121.

[24] Benedict Anderson, *Imagined Communities*, 46.

[25] Skidmore, *Black into White*, 222.

[26] Anderson, 45 and 71.

[27] Skidmore, 11.

[28] Graça Aranha, *Canaan* Mariano Joaquim Lorente trans. (Boston: The Four Seas Company, 1920), 240.

[29]   E. Bradford Burns, *History of Brazil.* Third Edition (New York: Columbia University Press, 1993), 276-278.

[30]   Alúzio Azevedo, *O cortiço* (1880).

[31]   See Skidmore, 200-202 and 57-62.

[32]   In the preface of António Cândido Gonçalves Crespo, *Obras Completas* (Rio de Janeiro, 1942), 6, Afrânio Peixoto comments on the letter from 1871 where Gonçalves writes 'A V. Exa conhecia eu de nome ha muito tempo. De nome e por uma secreta simpatia que eu para si me levou quando me disseram que era de cor como eu. Sera?'

[33]   (Vol. 3, no. 72).

[34]   The 'immoral acts' refer to Rio's homosexuality. Public humiliation was more likely precisely because he was a man 'of color'. The inter-connection between race and sexual orientation during this time period has yet to be systematically studied.

[35]   Jack Ray Thomas, *Biographical Dictionary of Latin American Historians and Historiography* (Westport, Conn. and London: Greenwood Press, 1984): 45. See also *Novo Dicionário*, 222.

[36]   Robert G. Nachman, 'Positivism, Modernization and the Middle Class in Brazil', *Hispanic American Historical Review* 57, no. 7 (Feb 1977): 1-23. *Rebellion in the Backlands* Samuel Putnam trans. (Chicago: University of Chicago Press, 1944).

[37]   David Hall Stauffer, 'The Origins and Establishment of Brazil's Indian Service: 1889-1910'. Ph.D. Diss. (University of Texas, 1956).

[38]   The English edition used for this study is *Rebellion in the Backlands* Samuel Putnam trans. (Chicago: University of Chicago Press, 1944).

[39]   In this sense, I disagree with Skidmore (113) when he stated that neither Aranha nor Da Cunha thought much of the patriotic rhetoric.

[40]   Ibid, 84. I make this comment to point out the problems of *embranqueamento*. It is thought that money, power, education and fame also whiten. Miscegenation is defined, in this sense, not only as a biological function but as a social one as well.

[41]   *Rebellion in the Backlands*, 54.

[42]   In other parts of Latin America similar arguments about the eventual disappearance of blacks were not uncommon. In Cuba, for example, see Gustavo Enrique Mustelier, *La Extinción del Negro* (Habana: Imprenta de Rambla, 1912). See chapter 2. For an excellent assessment of Oliviera Viana's *oeuvre* see Jeffrey D. Needell, 'History, Race, and the State in the Thought of Oliviera Viana', *Hispanic American Historical Review* Vol. 75, No. 1 (1995): 1-30.

[43]   *Rebellion in the Backlands*, 72-82.

[44]   Ibid, 89.

[45]   Ibid, 87. As E. Bradford Burns points out, Canudos was the victim of progress. In the eyes of the new positivist republic, the people of Canudos (barbarism)

was a threat, jeopardizing progress; 'all the native beliefs from barbarous fetishism to aberrations of Catholicism, all the impulsive tendencies of lower races given free outlet in the undisciplined life of the backlands, were condensed in his fierce and extravagant mysticism'. This brings us to our third conclusion; the fear of the urban classes clinging to the Atlantic shores. The Brazilian elite was uneasy, and aware of its perilous and racist policies towards the masses, and had feared rebellion of all kinds for some time. See E. Bradford Burns, 'The Destruction of a Folk Past: Euclides Da Cunha and Cataclysmic Cultural Clash', *Review of Latin American Studies* 3, no. 1, (1990): 16-35.

[46]   Ibid, 54 and 84.

[47]   Ibid, 72-82.

[48]   Ibid, 87.

[49]   This decree which attempted to destroy all records, from ownership papers, ship logs, religious documents. See Robert W. Slenes, 'O que Rui Barbosa não queimou: Novas fontes para o estudo da escravidão no século XIX', *Revista de Estudos Econômicos* Vol 13, no. 1: 117-50.

[50]   For some of the theoreticians who espoused the degeneracy of mixed stocks see G.R. Gliddon and J.C. Nott, *Types of Mankind or Ethnological Researches* (Philadelphia, Lippincoatt and London: Trubner, 1884). Also see Artur de Gobineau. *The Inequality of Human Races* Vol. I 1853-1855 (London: Heinemann, 1915).

[51]   *Novo Dicionário*, 574-575. Born in 1865, Alberto Torres entered the Faculty of Medicine at the age of fifteen. He was the founder of the Centro Abolicionista in São Paulo and the Clube Republicano in Niteroi. In 1893, he served as a member of the Federal Congress and from 1897-1900. Before 1914, Torres published two major studies; *Vers la Paix* (1909) and *La probleme mundial* (1913). Unlike da Cunha's masterpiece, Torres' major work *O problema nacional brasileiro,* published in 1914, had the benefit of anti-racist theoreticians such as Franz Boas. Franz Boas did his research at Columbia University in the 1910s. See *Race, Language and Culture* (New York: Free Press, 1940).

[52]   Skidmore, 17. Alberto Torres, *O problema nacional brasileiro* (Rio de Janeiro, Impresa Nacional Brasileiro, 1914), 129.

[53]   Ibid, 131.

[54]   E. Bradford Burns, 'The Destruction of a Folk Past: Euclides Da Cunha and Cataclysmic Cultural Clash', *Review of Latin American Studies* Vol. 3 No 1, (1990): 16-35.

[55]   *Novo Dicionário*, 574-575. Franz Boas did his research at Columbia University in the 1910s. See *Race, Language and Culture* (New York; Free Press, 1940).

[56]   Skidmore, *Politics in Brazil*, 17. Alberto Torres, *O problema nacional brasileiro* (Rio de Janeiro, Imprensa Nacional Brasileiro, 1914), 129. It is

interesting to point out that Torres is one of the few intellectuals who opposed extensive immigration of whites as it would prejudice the already existing national institutions.

[57]   He was especially critical of Gobineau's racist ideas. In the nineteen thirties a group of followers created a society in his honor promoting his nationalistic ideas. It was called Sociedade de Amigos de Alberto Torres.

[58]   Despite the influence of the heavy migrations, anarchists reacted to dehumanizing conditions of workers in Brazil. The theory and reality were closely related. Nonetheless, the authorities used the allegations that anarchists came from outside to attack 'foreign agitators'. One can convincingly argue that the creation of Vargas' Ministry of Labour was a direct response to both anarchist-syndicalist and communist led labour unrest. How did the anarchists attempt to forge a national ideology? Clearly they were outside the mainstream. The answer to this question must be understood in the context of what the anarchist stood for: abolition of the state. To the anarchist, the state tended to preserve the class and caste privileges of the few. The anarchists attempted to create 'social schools' for all, men and women of all races. The women's participation was also important as they did not attain suffrage in Brazil until 1932. Other than these broad statements frequently voiced by followers of anarchism, it is difficult to ascertain clearly the anarchist view on national culture, although they were theoretically opposed to the very notion. Because of the lack of institutionalization of the philosophy in Brazil, the anarchists had a syncretic type of existence; especially with the syndicalists. Many writers published under pseudonyms or wrote most frequently in newspapers. Despite the absence of seminal works, many literary works document and reflect racial thoughts and patterns through the eyes of the anarchist. One such writer that supported anarchist thought was António Avelino Fóscolo (1864-1944) who wrote *O caboclo* in 1902 and *O mestiço* in 1903. Both novels deal with the racial control and fatalism of family traditions in the rural environment. These novels were used not to address the question of the nation directly, but to attack the traditions which the elites used to exploit the other members of society. In *O mestiço*, for example, the drama takes place on a plantation in the Rio das Velhas valley, near Sabará, Minas Gerais prior to abolition. Fóscolo was clearly not satisfied with the bourgeois republic. He was a talented *mineiro* of modest background, and not connected to state interests, who detested, above all, the oppression of the *fazendeiros*. The anarchist rhetoric was anti-elite. Yet their ideas were so far removed from main stream culture that they had little or no effect on national consciousness. a good study of anarchism in Brazil is Eric Gordon, 'Anarchism in Brazil: Theory and Practice, 1890-1920' Diss., (Tulane 1978), 144-149.

[59]   Oswald Spengler, *Decline of the West* Vol I (New York: Alfred A. Knopf, 1926), 104-113. Spengler was an affront to the Darwinian-Spencerian ideas of

the nineteenth century. He saw the development of the world in terms of the rise and fall of cultures.

[60] Oswald Spengler, *The Decline of the West* Vol I (New York: Alfred A. Knopf, 1926), 96-97.

[61] This is also the position taken by Ralph Della Cava in his article 'Catholicism and Society in the Twentieth Century', *Latin American Research Review* vol. 11 no. 2 (1976): 7-50.

[62] Mônica Pimenta Velloso, 'A Ordem: uma revista de doutrina, política e cultura católica', *Revista de Ciencia Política* Vol 21 no. 3 (1978): 127-128.

[63] Jackson de Figueiredo, *Pascal e a Inquietacão Moderna* (Rio de Janeiro: Anuario do Brasil, 1922), 8-10. In his early years, he lived in Bahia and was somewhat of a bohemian and very anti-Catholic. His move to Rio de Janeiro in 1914 marked an important change in his lifestyle.

[64] Jackson de Figueiredo, *In Memoriam* (Rio de Janeiro: Centro D. Vidal), 8. As João Cruz Costa mentions in *A History of Ideas in Brazil* Suzette Macedo trans. (Berkeley and Los Angeles: University of California Press), 261. Figueiredo was well aware of the 'lukewarm character' of Catholicism in Brazil.

[65] Eloy Martins da Silva has written an illuminating article which shows the commonality in demands of Communists and Catholics. 'D. Vicente Scherer, os operários e os comunistas'. *Novos Rumbos* 144 (November 10-16, 1961): 4.

[66] Alceu Amoroso Lima, 'Catolicismo e Integralismo-I', *A Ordem* (January 1935): 412-413. The information about the archbishop is taken from Margaret Todaro Williams, 'Integralism and the Brazilian Church' *Hispanic American Historical Review* 53, no. 3 (1974): 431-452.

[67] Wilson Martins, *The Modernist Idea*. Jach E. Tomlin trans. (West Port, Conn: Greenwood Press Publishers, 1971), 71 and 142.

[68] The most important modernist manifestos include Oswald de Andrade 'Pau Brasil and 'Manifesto Antropófago', *Obras Completas* Vol 6 (Rio de Janeiro: Civilizacão Brasileira, 1970), 3-20.

[69] According to Nist, five of the major Modernist schools were the hallucinists, the spiritualists, the nationalists, the dynamists and the regionalists. I have modified this to fit a broader analysis than the literary one given by Nist. In Spanish America two of the most dominant schools were *creacionismo* and *ultraísmo*. See glossary for definitions. See also John Nist, *The Modernist Movement in Brazil* (Austin and London: University of Austin Press, 1967), 96-97.

[70] It is important to point out that even though the majority of the modernists wrote about a 'New Brasil' and were indeed interested in society's needs, not all were politically involved. In addition, a number of them wrote more on aesthetics than ethics.

[71] Gilberto Mendonça Teles, *Vanguardia européia e modernismo brasileiro* second ed. (Petropiolis, Vozes, 1971), 233-236.

[72]   Mario de Andrade, *A Escrava que não e Isaura*, (São Paulo, Lealdade, 1925), 24.

[73]   Jose de Alencar, *O Guaraní* (Rio de Janeiro, 1857) and *Iracema* (Rio de Janeiro, 1857).

[74]   Cassiano Ricardo, *Martim Cereré* (São Paulo: Revista de Tribunais, 1928).

[75]   See Angel Rama, *La ciudad letrada en cultura urbana latinoamericana* (Buenos Aires, 1985).

[76]   Raul Bopp, *Antología Poética* (Rio de Janeiro, Editôra Leitura, S.A., 1947), 8-60. The poet refers to Brazil, and more specifically the interior of Brazil as 'as terras do sem-fim', (the never-ending land).

[77]   Nist, 11. Originally quoted in an interview with the newspaper *A Noite*, January 18, 1952. In concluding it should be mentioned that Plínio Salgado, the integralist, also was a supporter of this tendency and even learned to speak and write Tupí.

[78]   Paulo Prado, *Retrato de Brasil* (São Paulo; Duprat, 1928), 8, and 158-60.

[79]   Francisco de Assis Barbosa, *Testamento de Mario de Andrade e Outros Reportagens* (Rio de Janeiro, 1954).

[80]   Mario de Andrade, *O movimento modernista* (Rio de Janeiro, 1942), 24-25.

[81]   Mario de Andrade, *Macunaíma* (São Paulo: Livraria Martins, 1968). Many critics have attested that Andrade was actually satirizing *embranqueamento* and the racism of Brazil. Andrade's views on black consciousness and its role in Brazil, however, is entirely unclear.

[82]   Oswald de Andrade, *Obras Completas*, (Rio de Janeiro: Editora Civilização Brasileira, 1971) vol II, 131-133.

[83]   Martha Rossetti et al, *Brasil: Primeiro Tempo Modernista (1917-1929)*. São Paulo: Instituto de Estudos Brasileiros, USP, 1972), 235.

[84]   Jorge de Lima (1895-1953) a mulatto born in União, Alagoas in 1893 (died 1953) was the chief poet of the North Eastern regionalist movement. Lima wrote of the 'African Soul' of Brazil, celebrating its contribution to Brazilian society, despite socioeconomic hardships in 'That Negress Fulô'(1928). Beside his poetry Bandeira, born in 1886, wrote an account of his childhood memories in Recife evoking a *saudade* found also in Freyre. He also evoked a sense of teh Brazilian spoken language.

[85]   See Frank Tannenbaum's introduction to Gilberto Freyre, *The Mansions and the Shanties: Making of Modern Brazil* (New York: Alfred A. Knopf, 1963).

[86]   This is taken from Lewis Hanke, *Gilberto Freyre. Vida y Obra. Bibliografía Antología* (New York: Instituto de las Españas en los Estados Unidos, 1939), 8.

[87]   Gilberto Freyre. 'Social Life in Brazil in the Middle of the Nineteenth Century', *Hispanic American Historical Review*. 5 (1922): 597-630. Flora Edwards Mancuso, *The Theater of Black Diaspora; A comparative Study of Drama in Brazil, Cuba and the United State'* Ph.D. Diss. (New York University, 1975), 16. Jeffrey Needell, 'Identity, Race, Gender and Modernity

in the Origins of Gilberto Freyre's Oeuvre', *American Historical Review* vol. 100 no. 1 (February 1995): 51-77.

[88] Emilia Viotti da Costa, *The Brazilian Empire: Myths and Histories* (Belmont, California: Wadsworth Publishing Company, 1985), chapter nine.

[89] Gilberto Freyre, *Alem do apenas moderno* (Rio de Janeiro: José Olympico Editora, 1973).

[90] José María Bello, *Panorama do Brasil* (Rio de Janeiro: Imprensa Nacional, 1936).

[91] Sergio Buarque de Holanda, *Raízes do Brasil* (Rio de Janeiro 2nd ed., 1948), 15. The first edition was published in 1936.

[92] In Clovis Bevilaqua, 'Gustave Le Bon e a psicologia dos povos', *Revista Brasileira*, 5 (1896) reported in *Esbocos e fragmentos* (Rio de Janeiro, 1899), 253-274. This deals with the Escola da Recife.

[93] In 1938, even in the southern Florianópolis, Oswaldo R. Cabral investigated the influence of blacks in that region of Brazil. Oswaldo R. Cabral. 'Os grupos negros em Santa Catarina', *Laguna e outros ensaios* (Florionópolis: Imprensa Oficial, 1939). In São Paulo, 'Tipos de povamente de São Paulo' and *A aculturação negra no Brasil* (1924) appeared attempting to show interest in race relations and understanding other dimensions of a new national culture. Renato Mendonça did a very interesting piece on the African influence to Brazilian culture from a linguistic point of view. Artur Ramos, *A aculturação negra no Brasil* (São Paulo: Companhia Editora Nacional, 1942). Also see *As culturas negras.* (Rio de Janeiro: Casa de Estudante do Brasil, 1972), which analyzes the African contribution to Brazilian civilization. Dácio Aranha de A. Campos, 'Tipos de povamento de São Paulo' *Revista do Arquivo Municipal* (São Paulo) 54, no. 139: 5-34. Renato Mendonça. *A influencia africana do portugues do Brasil* 3rd ed. (São Paulo: Companhia Editora Nacional, 1935).

[94] Anti-Americanism will be treated extensively in chapter five. See for example Eugene Gordon. *An Essay on Race Amalgamation* (Rio de Janeiro: Serviço de Publicacões, 1951). Donald Pierson, *Negroes in Brazil: A study of race Contact at Bahia* (Chicago: University of Chicago Press, 1942).

[95] Copy of article by Mario de Andrade that appeared in *O Estado de São Paulo* in February 7, 1939.

[96] Claus Schreiner, 93.

[97] Elysio Caravalho de, *A realidade brasileira.* (Rio de Janeiro: Anuario do Brasil, 1922). See also Ronald de Caravalho y Elysio de Caravalho, *Affirmacões, um agapé de intellectuães* (Rio de Janeiro: Monitor Mercantil, 1921).

[98] Sergio Buarque do Holanda, *Raizes do Brazil* 2nd ed. (Rio de Janeiro: José Olympio, ed., 1948), 14-16. The quote is taken from Gilberto Freyre, *Interpretación del Brasil* (México: Fondo de Cultura Económica, 1945), 7-9.

[99] Important thinkers such as Nina Rodrigues who predated the modernist as well as modernists such as Alcântara Machado or the most important Oswald de

Andrade who wrote many of the modernist manifestos have been omitted. See Wilson Martins, *The Modernists Idea* for a complete study of these contributors.

[100] Alberto Torres, *A organizacão nacional* (Rio de Janeiro: Imprensa Nacional, 1912). See also *O problema nacional*. (São Paulo: Companhia Editora Nacional, 1938).

[101] Note that in the late 1980s, many studies appeared which deal with race, class and gender in Brazil. The majority of these have been done by foreigners. Recently, however, Brazilian scholars have increasingly begun to look at issues of race relations.

[102] Martins de Almeida, *Brasil errado*. (Rio de Janeiro: Schmidt), 1932.

[103] Humanist refers to a doctrine or attitude that espouses the interests of the human spirit. Perhaps a better term to use would be a spiritualist. However, Nist has used this term to define a group of literary writers of the same time who were religiously motivated and who wrote of spiritual conquests without references to secular humanism. The Jewish Brazilian writer Graça Aranha (1894-1931) can be considered a secular humanist as well. Arinos considered him a mentor. Before his death, Aranha wrote the novel *Canaan* about a German immigrant who settled in the backlands of Brazil.

[104] Afonso Arinos de Mello Franco, *Introdção á Realidade Brasileira* (Rio de Janeiro: Schmidt-Editor, 1933), 28-31.

[105] Ibid, 38.

[106] Ibid, 40-43. Arinos compares the mixing of races in several countries throughout the world. He defends the mulatto against racist 'American theories'.

[107] T. S. Elliot, *Notes Towards The Definition of Culture* (New York: Harcourt, Brace and Company, 1949), 58.

3. The Getúlio Vargas Regime and the Institutionalization of National Culture, 1930-1945

Qué es la historia sino la intervención de nuestra voluntad en las cosas.

Medardo Vitier, *La Enseñanza y La Cohesion Cubana*

To command is to fit people into their destiny.

José Ortega y Gassett, *Revolt of the Masses*

In a speech at the 1945 conference of Brazilian writers which centered on the theme of 'Democratization of Culture', Oswald de Andrade thanked his fellow-writers for their role in the creation of national culture:

> Because of your pains, the mute man of our nation, opened his mouth and spoke. He spoke with you, he told his history with you, he broke the secular silence of his exile and initiated a most joyous, a most profound debate with the universe.[1]

He also might have been thanking President Vargas who had painstakingly associated himself with the modernist writers of the 1920s and who, like them, had sought to give the popular sectors a voice rather than to encourage them to develop their own.

The revolution of 1930 represented a marriage of new political order with a new nationalist cultural mythology, constructed within the urban centers but purporting to represent Brazil in the spirit of *brasilidade*. Vargas' ascent to power not only validated the nationalist view of the modernist but ensured that Brazil would take a jealously right of center course while reinforcing the ideas of what it meant to be Brazilian. The cultural vision of the modernist was seen most noticeably in official institutions which centered around intellectual and cultural production within which blackness or any attempt to accentuate the authentic expression of blackness by blacks was discouraged as 'un-Brazilian'.

Despite the federalization policies of Vargas which culminated in the Estado Novo in 1937, the forgers of national culture came overwhelmingly from the urban areas of Brazil, particularly Rio and São Paulo. The Estado Novo helped institutionalize a national vision of Brazil that was urban and decidedly white.[2]

The cultural trajectory begun by the modernist saw its political culmination in the Estado Novo--dictatorial, Catholic, and populist. Azevedo Amaral, in his apologetic work, nonetheless claimed that the Estado Novo was a dynamic expression of the public's will, and that it was the state's duty to ensure that individual initiative developed within the broader framework of maintaining the system.[3] Thus laws that required workers to carry a mandatory professional (*carteira*) folder was not out of step with Vargas' broader need for order and progress.

This chapter examines the relationship between political institutions and cultural hegemony by focusing on the third phase of forging a national identity: institutionalization. How was the Vargas regime able to propagate a sense of Brazilian national family? And what effect did that identity have on the perception of blackness and black voices in Brazil? Moreover, this chapter seeks to show that Vargas' new cultural hegemony, aided by the nationalist-minded modernists (even those who did not support him) helped to create a climate of patriotic zeal which called for the representation of positive national values and order in the social realm. His populist stand prohibited the emergence of an effective challenge to the white middle class's cultural identity and its political, economic and cultural values.

The Vargas Revolution

Getúlio Vargas is undoubtedly the most prominent figure of twentieth-century Brazilian politics. From Rio Grande do Sul, Vargas emerged as an important leader at a time when Brazil was seeking a new political and cultural direction with its eyes towards modernity. Vargas ascended to national prominence on the wings of the Aliança Liberal, (Liberal Alliance) essentially a middle class coalition against the traditional politics that governed Brazil until 1930. Its platform was popular but cautious in nature, and called for improved health care and better social legislation on the one hand and control of labor unions and measures to protect local industry on the other.[4] Much like Juan Perón in Argentina, Vargas used a populist approach to build alliances among the middle and popular classes of Brazil in order to oppose the ruling oligarchy of the Old Republic.

Ruled by the pressures of the agricultural elite, especially from the coffee valley between São Paulo and Rio de Janeiro, the Old Republic was shattered by the 1930 revolution which ousted President Washington Luíz who had gained the presidency through fraudulent means. Once in power, Vargas began the most nationalist political process that Brazilian had seen in its history while balancing the power of the old regime with the rising uncertainty of the growing urban masses. Writer and Vargas supporter Amaral Azevedo recognized this, and in 1936, advocated the use of corporatism to overcome the problems of the 'greedy elite' and the 'lethargic masses'.[5] Even before Amaral however, a national commission was held in 1925 to revise the outdated 1891 Constitution. At this congress many members, tired of the elitist politics, called for the integration of states into a national unity.

Surprsingly, no civilian national university existed until 1930. The consolidation of a generation of nationalist intellectuals coincided with the creation of the new Brazilian state in 1930, and the institutionalization of a legitimate federal state structure based on corporatism.[6] The corporate state was instrumental to the modernizing process in Brazil as it assigned to each working individual a role important to the construction of a New Brazil. This political process, which began in 1930, emerged through a series of national watersheds until it was successfully embodied in the Estado Novo in 1937. The Estado Novo stood for change and development, but this could not take place without order, which relied heavily on paternalistic coercion, dominated by an elite, albeit a new emerging elite of technocrats, bureaucrats and military men. *Tenentismo,* one of the impetuses of the new generation, played an important part in Vargas' corporate state, even though the military's role was not clearly defined until 1964.[7]

Much research has been conducted on the role of corporatism in the political arena, but the role of 'cultural corporatism' as well as cultural populism in the forging of the Brazilian nation has been relatively ignored. Vargas attempted to please as many of his constituents as possible: the military, the growing urban working classes, and the middle class employers. Fond of presidential decrees, Vargas also used this presidential prerogative to appease the many Brazilian constituents, always maintaining a balance between patriotic rhetoric and authoritarianism.[8] In *Father of the Poor: Vargas and His Era* Robert Levine indicates that even though Vargas maintained a distance between himself and the popular classes, they supported him nonetheless.[9] Furthermore, Vargas hardly appointed blacks or other minorities to important political positions. The lone exception was Gregório Fortunato, his chief bodyguard!

In 1932, Vargas set into motion various forces which would change forever the traditional social system under the Republic. At the same time, he was carefully increasing his popularity among the masses without putting into operation a strong legislature or judicial system to enforce the reforms. By theoretically including the masses, Vargas was able to sell his image as a 'man of the people'. His reform of the electoral code in the same year was crucial to this process. On April 18, 1932 Vargas proposed that employers, employees and professional groups be represented directly in the new Constitutional Assembly. Organized to maintain what Vargas called 'class representation', the assembly was comprised of eighteen labor union delegates; seventeen employers, two bureaucrats, and three association representatives for a total of forty seats.[10]

The class-based composition was important since the President would be chosen by the Assembly, and not by popular vote. Thus Vargas, assured of a majority, became President in the elections of May 3, 1933. Once in power 'legitimately', he combined populism and nationalism to fit his political aims. Not surprisingly, in the period 1934-1937, most working-class Brazilians did not see an amelioration of their position vis-a-vis the upper classes, despite the intense industrialization and growth of infrastructure. Many of the upwardly mobile members of the middle sector fared well, by fitting into the expanded bureaucracy, but the urban elites remained intact.[11] The *tenentes* who had rebelled against the system in the 1920s were, by and large, satisfied with the revolution of 1930, and were eventually co-opted by the political developments that promised political change and democracy.[12]

At the same time, Vargas' Second Republic provided forums for political and cultural expressions of groups previously marginalized by the system, particularly women and blacks. In May 1932 Vargas passed a law that prohibited work by pregnant women one day before and one day after birth, as women were encouraged to participate in the construction of the new Brazil.[13] Retiring and pension arrangements were expanded and reasons for dismissals restricted. In 1932, suffrage was extended to women and the voting age was reduced from twenty-one to eighteen. In this same year, Vargas appointed a new labor chief, Joaquim Pedro Salgado Filho, from Rio Grande do Sul. Salgado also fond of decrees, convinced Vargas to institutionalize a forty-eight-hour week and to press for better conditions for women in the workplace.[14] Blacks were likewise encouraged to support the emerging nationalist agenda rather than through ethnic nationalism, as Carlos Drummond de Andrade forcibly indicated.[15]

Vargas also initially received support from the more conservative elements of society. Moreover, from 1930-1937, right-wing movements also proliferated seeing their most organized presence in the Integralist Party, led by the modernist Plínio Salgado. The ideas of the integralists, however, ranged from anti-imperialism to anti-Semitism to the construction of a Brazilian national family along Christian lines. The official integralist philosophy was the promotion of a national unity in which all members of different classes and races were to participate in a corporate state. Salgado called for the integration of all members of a diverse society to promote unity under a Luso-Brazilian rubric with clear aversion to foreign elements.[16]

Vargas' Machiavellian style called for the right of the state to monitor and if necessary control public opinion, a measure that nationalist José Maria Bello claimed as necessary to promote a positive image of a new Brazil.[17] Essential to the regime's tactics was a populist image which had long originated in the dominant political and intellectual circles as a response to the masses.[18] Indeed Vargas could not succeed without the support of many Brazilian intellectuals who supported the country's cultural nationalism. In literature, the arts and popular culture, cultural nationalism essentially promoted the idea that Brazil was home of a 'cosmic race', created from the union of the Indian, the African and the Portuguese. Racial democracy fit quite well into the ideology of the corporate national family. The intellectuals who sought to explain what it meant to be Brazilian, created a harmonious image of a country trying to heal the scars of the legacy of slavery. Brazil was in search, not only of a viable economic and political system, but of a cultural identity worthy of projection.

Vargas' approach was undoubtedly utilitarian--appeasing the greatest number of people at any given time. Indeed the regime's propensity to please and to justify its action on behalf of the imagined entity that he called the 'Brazilian people'. Institutionalization of the notion of a unified Brazilian family based largely on *brasilidade* and racial democracy occurred through three specific forums: by law, (constitutional, decrees or other), through censorship (implicit and explicit) directed by the Department of Press and Propaganda (Imprensa e Propaganda), and through institutions such as the Ministry of Education and Culture responsible for divulging national culture and promoting civic pride. Thus, Heloisa Paulo has correctly asserted that the Vargas state's institutionalization of propaganda and censorship were the most effective means of maintaining a consensus. But Vargas himself united and gave all of these forums meaning. His personal charm, conviction, and his role in the 1930 revolution which Brazilians believed was largely responsible for dismantling the old republic made him a central character in the national web he helped to spin.

Even before Vargas became president, André Filho had sought to immortalize him as the true heir to the National Palace in Catete in the *marcha* 'Seu Getúlio Vem' with its refrain that signaled a new relationship between the popular classes and the state:

> Sir Gertuli is bam bam bam (sic)
> in the palace he should be
> he is ready for every-thing (sic)
> Even ready to fight
> Let the people say what they want
> all of this is trick-er-y
> In the (presidential) chair should be
> only the winner of the election.[19]

Brazil's nationalism, based on a patriotic zeal and a pride in Brazil's uniqueness, was propagated thanks to a convenient marriage of intellectuals and the state. By promoting a populist model of nationhood, the state also created a partnership with the popular sectors by ensuring their representation, albeit rhetorically, but nonetheless successfully prohibiting any attacks on Brazilian construct of identity. Where the intellectuals of the 1920s had ordered national culture, the Vargas administrations were largely responsible for institutionalizing that organization and the propagation of a cultural memory. Brazil constructed a populist cultural nationalism based on two major factors: the notion of *brasilidade*, and cultural unity based on racial democracy in which political and ethnic dissident voices, would be silenced for the good of the whole. From 1933-1945, Vargas' 'contract with Brazil' increased political, economic and cultural awareness of the individual's role (economically, politically and culturally) in 'the national', forging a personal alliance with his and the (mythical people) reminiscent of the Nazi's motto 'Ein Volk, ein Reich, ein Fuhrer' (One People. One Regime, One Ruler).

The pursuit of a sense of Brazilian-ness motivated the Vargas regime to ban all foreign language instruction, and to establish a national infrastructure for mass communication, largely through the radio and the press, and later through the establishment of the Department of Press and Propaganda. Re-educating the Brazilian population through all the means of communication was tantamount to the regime's vision in promoting pride among Brazilians. Thus, in November 1933, Vargas proclaimed to the national assembly that 'primary education is the basis of public salvation', and he would use every possible opportunity to educate the masses, in a primary school educational style.[20]

This sense of nationhood conflicts with the ideas of contemporary thinkers such as Clifford Geertz who hold that personal identification should be publicly acknowledged rather than suppressed to guarantee a democratic association with the goals of the nation-state.[21] Indeed Vargas' respect for the popular classes and their ability to participate in the democratic process was illusory. His dictatorial style, even before the Estado Novo, indicated that the popular classes would be included through co-optation alone. His method of organization, which included commissions, institutes and special committees, indicated an unprecedented interest in Brazilian popular culture, although they were guided mostly by white intellectuals who did not come from the popular sectors. Moreover, laws and decrees helped keep the popular sectors in line.

Not coincidentally, economic class emerged for the first time as a viable paradigm for explaining Brazilian reality, and writers such as Gilberto Freyre and Sergio Buarque de Holanda produced their classic texts in the 1930s re-interpreting Brazilian reality as a mecca of social and racial interaction.[22] As Carlos Guilherme Motta so aptly concluded, 'the crisis in the oligarchy with the Revolution of 1930 provoked an elaboration of an ensemble of reflections which found their highest expressions in the work of Gilberto Freyre and Sérgio Buarque de Holanda'.[23] The emergence of a neo-republic headed by Vargas occurred simultaneously with the ascendance of a new vision, a new image, a new way of imagining Brazil. The Revolution of 1930 facilitated the birth of a new intellectual order which in turn facilitated the establishment of an anti-oligarchic state and the eventual establishment of the Estado Novo. Gilberto Freyre and Sergio Buarque de Holanda were as much products of the post-abolition era gazing back on Brazilian history with what has come to be called *saudismo*, as Vargas and Gustavo Capanema, Oswaldo Aranha and Francisco Campos were visionaries attempting to reclaim an imagined glory of an entity they called 'the Brazilian family'.

The paternalism inherent in the vision meant that both the state and its self-proclaimed national intellectuals would implement a top-down approach of inclusion. Indeed the erudite bias essential to Oswaldo de Andrade's' discourse in 1945 had emerged out of the modernist search for *brasilidade* which mirrored, and developed along-side the new political order. An apparent belief in the decadence of national culture necessitated a concerted organization responsible for transforming, propagating and establishing the new order.

Brazilian intellectual scholar Sergio Miceli confirmed that a select group of intellectuals were invited to assume positions in the most important branches of the executive, state and federal sectors of the Brazilian government. These positions gave like-minded intellectuals direct power in transforming and institutionalizing bureaucratic changes that would have important ramifications for decades to come. With reason Miceli refers to this group as a cultural elite who very often adapted their intellectual production to the goals of the state.[24] Moreover, the marriage of nationalist intellectuals, particularly those influenced by modernism, and the state guaranteed that a more or less unified sense of 'national culture' would be propagated though cultural institutions under Vargas.

In addition to placing nationalist intellectuals in important positions in established traditional institutions such as the National Historical Museum, the National Library, and the National Museum, the Vargas administration formed new institutions that heralded the participation of men such as Sergio Buarque de Holanda, (director of the Divisão de Consultas of the National Library), Edgar Roquette Pinto, (director of the National Institute for Educational Cinema), and Genolino Amado and Helio Vianna (the Department of Propaganda and Cultural Diffusion of the Federal District), among others. Ad hoc committees and councils flourished to discuss and recommend policy to a host of government agencies, among them the Consulting Council for the Preservation of the National Historical Artistic Patrimony (Conselho do Serviço do Patrimonio Hístorico e Artístico Nacional), and the National Education Council (Conselho Nacional de Educação).

In 1930, Vargas affirmed the messianic nature of his government as the salvation of the people in uncompromising paternalistic rhetoric in 'The Manifesto to the Nation', while underscoring the new state's desire to forge a sense of a unified nationality. 'All of the social categories', he wrote 'without difference to age or gender, partook of an identical fraternal and dominating thought: the construction of a new homeland'. Vargas promised to 'resume the central ideas of national reconstruction for the curing of the moral and physical woes of the nation', in a rhetoric analogous to the romanticism of modernists such as Gilberto Freyre.[25]

Inherent to this discourse was a longing for an idealized past (which never existed) but nonetheless served as a basis for forging a nationalist alliance against those forces that were 'un-Brazilian'. But Vargas did not rely on rhetoric alone. He used the law both to fulfill his promises to the people and to provide a basis for faith in nationhood.

The passion with which the divergent political philosophies emerged after 1932 helped Vargas define a centrist position to preserve the status quo which would celebrate national culture. Vargas must be seen as the mainstream political spokesman of a Zeitgeist with its various interpretations of Brazilian-ness. Independent of the different interpretations of *brasilidade* that intellectuals or other Brazilians might have held, the Vargas administration adhered to a public policy that a 'Brazilian essence', did in fact exist, and that miscegenation under Portuguese tutelage had played crucial parts in its creation.[26]

The state assumed a national cultural construct and utilized both corporatism and populism to propagate it. In the process of consolidating the national identity, Brazil would officially promote pride in a bright future, while eradicating the fears and pessimism of the past. Naturally there were critics of the state, but the 1935 National Security Law ('Lei de Segurança Nacional' de 1935) gave the government broad powers to pursue its enemies. Ilha Grande became a famed prison for dissidents opposed to the regime. Thus Vargas began a new political era as if he had a *tabula rasa*.[27]

Forging Nationhood by Decree

It is not surprising that Vargas prohibited the distribution of Charley Chaplin's, *The Dictator* in Brazil. Political satire surely represents one of the most powerful forms of criticism, and Chaplin's film, although a parody of Germany's *führer* certainly, was an indictment of dictatorship in general, which Brazilians close to Vargas would have easily noticed.[28] Vargas, moreover, was painfully aware of his un-democratic policies which he nonetheless pursued in the name of the salvation of the people. One of Vargas' closest allies, Francisco Campos, the first Minister of Education and Culture and later the Minister of Justice, conceded to a journalist at the *Correio da Manhã* that the Estado Novo was imperative to national survival.[29] The authoritarian model provided a framework within which dissident voices could be justifiably extinguished, and in which like-minded voices from differing power positions could be integrated into the status quo. Thus conceived, the regime saw its role as saving the nation and protecting its people.

Messianic conceptualization of nationhood assured Brazilians that they needed a savior, and once imagined, the Vargas regime instituted itself through law and rhetoric as such. National survival was defined by the state through a number of sacred civilian texts which governed the land and played a singular role in setting the stage for the institutionalization of a national view. They included the Constitution of 1934 and 1938, and the presidential decrees, which Vargas sporadically issued for the apparent benefit of the popular classes. Among the social legislation which initially pleased workers, both black and white, and helped to consolidate a sense of Brazilian family was the state's new restricted immigration policy directed by the Council for Immigration and Colonization (Conselho de Imigracão e Colonizacão), theoretically allowing workers to better organize and to bargain with employers without the interference of non-unionized expatriates. Another decree mandated that all companies have at least a two-thirds Brazilian working force. Retiring and pension arrangements were expanded and reasons for dismissals restricted.[30]

Restriction on immigration represented a xenophobic, anti-foreign gesture on the part of the Vargas administration, but coupled with the two-thirds law, the state's propaganda machine promoted it as a triumph for the popular class and the consolidation of the nation. The government's ban on all foreign language clubs as well as foreign newspapers meant that the state valued its national culture and language and would ensure that it be adopted. It was no coincidence that in 1939 schools in São Paulo suspected of instructing students in Japanese were denounced by Nuno da Gama Lobo d'Eça representing the Legião Cívica Nacional Pro-Bandeira Brasileira (The National Civic League for the Brazilian Flag).[31]

Portuguese immigrants were also hit by the renewed nationalism indicating the extent to which the cultural nationalism transcended language, and the historical links between the two peoples. Vargas' concern in forging a unified front based on *brasilidade* was particularly aimed at urban centers overflowing with workers and other members of the popular class. The Ministry of Labor encouraged single Portuguese male agricultural workers to migrate to Brazil, but expressed concern about those who migrated to rural areas only to 'mock the law and travel to the urban centers to compete with national workers, causing problems in the political order, and aggravating the problems related to unemployment'.[32]

Brazilians affirmed their sense of loyalty to their nation by joining institutions such as Eça's or the Instituto de Nacionalisação which aimed to 'help foreigners, and Brazilian sons and daughters of foreigners to integrate into Brazilian society, teaching them the national language, history and geography'. Moreover, it was important for the state to stress that patriotism was an obligation which citizens forged because they were 'Brazilian promoters and defenders of *brasilidade* and the New State, without personal interests', who acted only out of love for the homeland.[33] The explicit patriarchal vision of the new nationalism was highlighted by Clemete Quaglio's non-governmental publication which declared that the first obligation of a good citizen was to 'be a man and follow with determined virility'.[34] The explicit focus on integration and assimilation implied a dissolution of one's individual identity in a manner proposed by the *antropófagos*. That male immigrants were particularly targeted for this immigration, and that citizenship was conceived as a male right emphasized the patriarchal nature of the Vargas' regime. But integration into what? The answer implied a unified Brazilian culture, remarkably static, not a dynamic culture in evolution.

Constitutions

The Constitution, the sacred text of the republic provided both a framework for citizen participation and a vision of the nation's ethos. The new federal constitution of 1934 helped forge a new way of thinking about a citizen's participation in a 'new Brazil'.[35] Promulgated in 1934, one day before Getúlio Vargas was officially elected by the Constituent Assembly that he helped organize, the Federal Constitution officially validated the new government. That same year, Dr. António Marques dos Reis, Professor of Law in Bahia, and promoter of military justice affirmed: 'The Constitution of 1934 honors our Brazilian culture. It reaffirms the greatness of our people, and the perseverance of the luminous trajectory of Brazil'.[36] This was the most centralist constitution to date, and Article 2 attempted to underscore the sense of democracy by purporting that 'all power emanates from the People, and in the name of the People it is used'. Article 12, however, described the relationship between the federal government and the states, setting down the conditions under which the federal government may exercise its control in state matters.[37]

The 1934 Constitution was also the most nationalistic constitutional document in Brazilian history. It legislated mass participation in the political process, while securing for the state the right to intervene in an individual's affairs. Among other national reforms, the vote becomes obligatory, and 'privilege' was ambiguously outlawed (although not discrimination), allowing for equal access to national resources, and the promotion of national culture.[38] According to Title III, Chapter II:

> There will be no privileges, nor distinctions because of birth, sex, race, personal professions or professions of parents, social class, wealth, religious beliefs or political ideas.[39]

The Constitution also mandated that the Nation, state and *municipio* develop art, science and culture through a national plan organized through the recently created National Education Council.[40]

Intellectuals, politicians and artists understood the historical importance of the Second Republic, while Civil Rights, and grass roots movements took a decidedly non-confrontational dialogue with the state throughout this period. As in the pre-abolition period, two types of Civil Rights supporters emerged: activists and moderates, both proclaiming the rights of Brazilian citizens. The principal objective of both these groups was integration, and they requested that rights be allocated to a sector of society that had been deprived of them, although interested advocates in Congress had, by this time, begun to realize the importance of legislation to guard against discrimination.

Afonso Arinos de Melo Franco, from Belo Horizonte inspired this Brazilian generation. Arinos saw disorganization and conflict in Brazilian society and encouraged a state framework that would encourage order: 'This undeniable disorder in the realm of the spirit is the preponderant factor of the anarchic state in which our national forces are developing. Without intellectual order, social organization is a myth and strides inevitably towards violence or disillusion'.[41] He emphasized that before action there had to be an ideological agenda based on racial unity.[42] This period also saw the first mass-based Civil Rights movement with its own generation's activists: the Frente Negra Brasileira.[43] Civil Rights for the Frente meant equal treatment under the law, and the right to work free of discrimination and full integration of blacks in national life, issues to be examined in detail in chapter five.[44]

The institutionalization of national culture, promoting to Brazilians a vision of a national family also began in the Constitution. Articles 152 under the general heading 'On the Family, on Education, and on Culture', the 1934 Constitution established the National Council on Education to advise the state on how to improve the educational standards (Brazil' was still reportedly 70 percent illiterate), while article 149 reaffirmed the protection of historical objects, the cultural patrimony and intellectual property.[45]

As we have seen, education played a key role in forging a sense of Brazilian-ness. The state established education as 'a right', and a responsibility of the family and the state. While Article 149 guaranteed the nationalist intent of education in Brazil to promote 'a moral life, a national economy and the development of the Brazilian spirit of human solidarity', Article 150 effectively allowed for the creation of two types of educational systems; one 'based on intellectual pursuits' and another based on technical skills. The class and racial bias implicit in this division was hauntingly caste-like, and was as anti-working class as Article 9 which discouraged aspiration of social mobility, but allowed the state to use other 'extra methods for the repression of crime' particularly in the backlands.[46] Repression as a deterrence to crime however, meant that a disproportionate number of blacks in urban areas would suffer.

As Brazilians scrambled to adjust themselves to the new nationalist fervor, a new Constitution of the Estado Novo came into effect in 1937. While this constitution represented the culmination of his nationalist agenda to rid the country of socialism and fascism, it also legalized a dictatorship which would last until 1945. It was also one of the only two Constitutions not written by a Constituent Assembly.[47] The Constitution guaranteed individual freedoms so long as the end was to guarantee peace order and public security. Vargas relied on education to continue his nationalism with strict guidelines for education of culture included in the Constitution, mandating physical education for the promotion of a healthy nation and civic education for the promotion of patriotism.[48]

The Constitution of the Estado Novo promulgated in 1938 reaffirmed the state's role as educator, although in an interview with the *Correio da Manhã*, Education Minister Capanema underscored that the national educational aim was not to enhance critical thinking among the people but to guarantee that the less favored classes might acquire the technical knowledge necessary for the acquisition of useful and productive jobs (as defined by the state).[49]

Article 129 of the New Constitution makes explicit the state's relationship to the popular classes, and its intent to create a caste system which would allow little, if any chance for families to improve their social status:

> To those in infancy and youth who lack the necessary resources to study in private institutions, it is the duty of the nation, of municipal studies to guarantee, through the establishment of public institutions of learning for all grades, the possibility of receiving an adequate education according to their faculties, aptitudes and vocational tendencies...Pre-vocational and professional teaching destined for the less favored classes is, in terms of educational material, the first duty of the State.... It is the duty of industry and of economic labor unions to create, in the fields of their specialties, schools of apprentership for the children of workers and their associates...[50]

Despite the overarching charitable tone of this discourse, the state's static representation of the Brazilian nationhood based on an entrenched social structure indicated an unwavering conviction in the stability and impermutability of the class system.

A climate in which political challenges to national ideology were deterred, national black movements such as the Frente Negra Brasileira or the União Negra Brasileira were too weak to survive. To many blacks, however, the Constitution seemed to guarantee them education and possible employment.[51] Concomitantly blacks were co-opted into the national through the nationalization of popular culture, particularly music and the propagation of national values in popular sport, particularly football. In the schools' educational curriculum, the state stressed physical fitness, morality and national pride for all Brazilians. The rhetoric of equality symbolized by terms such as 'all' and 'the people' provided a convenient umbrella of inclusion that glossed over the gross historical inequalities that had led to pauperization and marginalization of blacks in Brazil.

The Estado Novo nonetheless relentlessly pursued an agenda of educating, and molding new citizens, both mentally and physically. Articles 131 and 132 of the 1937 Constitution mandated physical education, manual work and civics in primary, normal and secondary schools. Both Vargas and Capanema believed that the health of the Brazilian nation was closely related to its wealth, and that sports was a way in which students could build discipline, improve their health, and serve their nation. Article 132, in particular, required the state to construct buildings and institutions that would provide support for civic associations, physical fitness, and voluntary manual work such as the cleaning of buildings and parks.[52]

Vargas believed it necessary that Brazilian youth be 'educated' in moral and civic duties and in order that the individual be subjugated to the good of the nation.[53] Minister Capanema stressed the Estado Novo's role as educator in a more adamant fashion when he confirmed that 'now education in Brazil has to be placed decisively at the service of the nation'. Expressly corporatist in mentality, Capanema saw the Estado Novo not so much as a new state but as a state that was intended to preserve the hegemony of the status quo. This implied maintaining complex paternalist relationships which privileged the white upper classes. Capanema endorsed the notion that education was to prepare individuals for specific roles in order to preserve the 'moral, economic, and political unity of the Nation'.[54] The Ministry of Education and Public Health would thus play a critical role in the forging of a national consciousness.

Nationalist Intellectuals and the Ministry of Education and Public Health

Unlike the dictatorships of the post-1960 era, the Vargas administration was able to attract the support of the major intellectuals who saw in his actions a fulfillment of the national ideal, although many remained critical of the regime's power.[55] Still, the 'Decálogo do Escritor', published in the government official A Manhã indicated the intellectual-state link:

(1)   To love Brazil above all things

(2)   To honor the fraternal expression of our *brasilidade* within our sense of Americanism.

(3)   To contribute to the educational formation of the Brazilian people, created in harmony with national customs and tendencies.

(4)   To re-establish the Family as a moral synthesis of the *patria*, and the Flag as a symbol of its glory.

(5)   To honor the Christian and Civic tradition of 'the eternal' Brazil for our culture.

(6)   To serve with the same devotion arms and letters

(7)   To faithfully fulfill the duties of political life

(8)   To strive to improve primary education, the initial defense of our language and our race.

(9)   To learn from the great lessons of our forefathers.
(10) To sanctify with nationalist faith the heroic days of the
      patria and the useful days of work.[56]

The unequivocal faith in Brazilian nationhood coupled with a sense of duty informed the relationship between intellectuals and the state. Intellectuals played a crucial role in propagating the idea of a national culture through government sponsored forums such as *conselhos* and *palestras*. In conjunction with the all-important Ministry of Education and Public Health. Many had found prominent positions in key government agencies, although others pledged independent support.[57] While ministries that cater to the education and health or national populations are today common place in the 1930s the Brazilian state's involvement in public health was crucial to the forging of Brazilian nationalism which, as we have seen, was a response to modernization. At the same time, the turn-of-the- century notions of eugenics, although largely refuted, had played a crucial role in shaping the nation's views about degeneracy and backwardness, linking them to poor health and bad hygiene.

Nancy Ley Stephans has indicated that eugenics in Brazil was already associated with the health and medical profession, and that the adoption of eugenics was certainly associated with modernity. Moreover public health was associated with material wealth, and therefore it seemed highly appropriate to create an institution which would link the nation's public health policy with education.[58] While eugenic societies such as the one created in São Paulo in 1918 (which formed in an effort to legalize inter-familial marriages) were never timid about airing their racist views, institutionalized public health and education programs were more subtly inclined towards the improvement of the nation through socialization, although some persisted with the idea that inherited traits would doom the country.[59] Public Health was conceived under a larger rubric of Public Education which as the legend of the entrance hall of the Ministry of Education and Culture in Rio de Janeiro read, 'Education is the Material of Public Salvation'.

Since national education was a priority under Vargas, his administration intended to build a national monument to house the new ministry and that would also become a symbol of the 'new Brazil'. National educational reform under Vargas began in the early 1930 before the building of the ministry however. Most notably in 1931, the Reforma Lourenço Filho emerged in São Paulo and the Reforma Aníso Texeira in Rio one year later. Indeed 1932 was a particularly important milestone in national education. In that year, the intellectuals of the Brazilian

Education Association presented their manifesto entitled 'The Educational Reconstruction of Brazil', to its main two constituents: 'the people' and 'the government'. Before the Estado Novo came into being this document became quickly known as 'The Manifesto of the Pioneers of the New School'. Intellectuals called for a greater union of the state and the people, and a critical participation of the state in the education of Brazil.[60] From 1934 to 1945, with the help of leading intellectuals, many of whom had participated in the modernist movement, Gustavo Capanema set out to reconstruct the relationship between state and people, making education, culture and public health important national issues for the Vargas regime.

Educational reform had been a long tradition in Brazilian history. In the early nineteenth century, educational duties fell under a general ministry called the Ministry of Brazil until 1822 when the Ministry of Justice was created. The Vargas regime was the first to create a separate ministry dedicated solely to national education and the diffusion of national culture and the promotion of public health. By 1942 the ministry had created a complex bureaucracy responsible for the micro management of a diversity of activities from museums and libraries to health campaigns for malaria and leprosy[61] (see Diagrams #1 and #2 below).

Ministry of Brazil (11/03/1808)

Ministry of the Kingdom (23/06/1817)

Ministry of the Kingdom and Ex-Patriots (02/05/1822)

Ministry of Justice (03/07/1822)

Ministry of Justice and Interior Affairs (30/10/1891)

Ministry of Education and Public Health (14/11/1930)

Ministry of Education and Health (13/01/1937)

Source: SPHAN

Figure 3.1 The Evolution of the Ministry of Education and Health

Table 3.1 The Organization of the Ministry of Education and Health (1942)

Efficiency Commission
Cabinet
National Security Section

Faculty of Law, Recife	Imperial Museum
Faculty of Medicine, Porto Alegre	National Historical and artistic Patrimony
Faculty of Medicine, Bahia	The House of Rui Brabosa
Federal Commission on Education	National Insitute of Educational Cinema
Museum of Fine Arts	National Institute of the Deaf and Mute
National Council of Sports	Insp Commission of Psychiatric Services
National Council for the Protection Didactic of Psychopaths	National Commission of Books
National Council for Culture	National Commission on Primary Education
National Council for Social Services	Pedro II College (Day School
National Council on Education	Pedro II (Boarding School)
Planning Commission of the	Educational Radio Diffusion Service
University of Brazil	National Theater Service
National Institute of the Book	National Museum
National Library	National Historical Museum
National Institute for Pedagogical Studies	National Observatory
National Department of the Child	University of Brazil
National Department of Health Health Service Statistics Documentation Service Department	Administration
	National Dept. of Education

Source: SPHAN

Although the populist rhetoric adopted the people's well-being as the state's raison d'être, and the target of the education and health campaign, the two-track system of educational reform, *escolas técnicas* and *escolas professionais* meant that the system left little room for social mobility. For blacks this meant that young students would overwhelmingly be ushered into the technical areas with little possibility for acquiring professional jobs. That the federal state would be responsible for financing the technical schools, and the state government in charge of the professional schools meant that more resources would be funneled into the latter, but that issues of patriotism championed by the national government would be much more evident in the former.[62]

Not surprisingly it was a military officer, General Gaspar Dutra, then Minster of War, who likened the state's educational goals to a military campaign. In a discourse in the Palacio Tiradentes in 1940, Dutra, a loyal Vargas supporter, saw education's major objective not as the elimination of illiteracy and illness or the creation of critical minds, but the forging of a national consciousness. Thus, at the First Education Conference of the Ministry of Education and Public Health held in 1941, Major Euclides Sarmento, a representative of the Ministry of War, urged a continued intimate relationship between the military, educational and cultural institutions.[63]

While the implications of race in education never became a subject of discussion, blacks as part of the larger masses of the urban centers continued to be regarded suspiciously. In lending its support to the Ministry of Education and Health, the Ministry of War assured Brazilians that a national conscience would be forged through education, indoctrination and force. It was significant that Major Sarmento suggested that the Brazilian soldier be presented as a national model because of his dedication to 'the invigoration of the Brazilian race', a concept that was ill-used by Hitler in his promotion of anti-semitism.[64] The Brazilian 'race' had to be purged because it was infested with disease from alcoholism to syphilis, and because illiteracy plagued a large portion of the population. The military's support of the eradication of these ills focused on the *malandro* factor of Brazilian society, largely associated with blacks and slavery, rather than amelioration of deeper causes of the malaise.[65]

Education from primary schools up to universities encouraged identification with national myths. The educational system clearly favored the upper and middle classes, although in theory all Brazilians had access to formal education. The government did not organize any special campaigns to increase the formal education possibilities among the poor and disenfranchised popular sectors. As blacks and mulattos occupied the lower classes, they represented a small percentage of students within the school system. The equal access theory which apparently offered opportunities to all citizens tended to reinforce the stereotypes that blacks were not as capable as whites. Nonetheless, overall levels of literacy climbed steadily and rapidly from 1930 to 1950. By 1950, the total enrollment in secondary schools and universities had grown from 90,000 to 493,000 and 17,000 to 45,000 respectively, but this increase still did not meet the demands of the expanding population calculated at approximately 51,722,000 million.[66] [Assumed racial equality and fraternity, one of the powerful national myths essentially molded a national paradigm which bound Brazilians in a corporatist static manner in which both blacks and whites occupied predetermined place in the national hierarchy.[67] This myth allowed the directors of the Brazilian educational system to avoid addressing the special needs of the black and mulatto populations who had been historically marginalized and discouraged from pursuing social change. Moreover, schools had little autonomy, and where there was no perceived problem there was no need to mend the system to address issues of race./ Since 1805, all education had been financed and directed by the state. Each state had a department of education which had special guidelines for *normal school*, primary school, secondary school, the *vestibular*, pre-university, and for universities in general. In the republican period, the secondary schools were seen as a medium for the upper classes to carry on the leadership role in society and thus maintain the status quo. This period maintained a secular humanistic approach which carried into the post-1930 period. Following the ideas of the French educational system (*escola nova*), schools were seen as a means to affect social and political inculcation by attempting to focus attention on the individual.[68]

That schools were utilized as means of forging a national consciousness is seen by looking at required texts such as Afonso Celso's *Right or Wrong My Country*. In the primary school, the history curriculum followed strict guidelines. In the fifth grade, for example, students were introduced to the history of the formation of the Brazilian people. According to one guide, primary school teachers were to explain the formation of the Brazilian people as such:

> The formation of Brazilian people: the white, contributing with the language, the customs, the religion; the black bequeathing us gentleness and the spirit of sacrifice of the African; the environment (and by extension the indigenous population) transmitting the use of the characteristics of love for liberty and

attachment to the earth, which are innate feelings of the Brazilian.[69]

The program stressed that the progress of the *patria* depended on the work of the children. The presentation of such vivid and determined stereotypes would plant the seeds for the growth and acceptability of the classic texts such as *Casa Grande e Senzala* in high school and the university. Thus, the educational system promoted *brasilidade* at a very early age.[70]

Indeed *brasilidade* became such an important concept that many Brazilians became increasingly xenophobic, as they rallied behind the nationalist cry 'Let us restore the Nation'. In turn, the fear that one's *brasilidade* could be negated was like accusing one of treason. Foreign influences, for example, which encouraged non-national identification were thus regarded as anti-Brazilian. This was particularly true of North American influences. Not only did economic and political dislocation alone stymie the emergence of political and cultural expressions of blackness, but so did an overwhelming coercion/desire to identify with the nation. The idea of a Brazilian race forged as a result of miscegenation was crucial to the notion of *brasilidade*.

In this way white Brazilians also discouraged any possibilities of pan-Africanism, particularly of black American collaboration. Indeed at the turn of the century, Joaquim Nabuco had already argued that blacks in Brazil were better than their counterparts in the United States.[71] Black activism was regarded with outright suspicion and branded anti-Brazilian, comparable to the way in much the way that racist attitudes in the United States were condoned as part of the 'American way'.[72] In 1949, one Brazilian senator went so far as to say that any racism present in Brazil was a direct result of North American style democracy's filtering into Brazil.

When the black social and political organization, the Brazilian Black Front, informed the Ministry of Education of its desire to serve and defend the nation's interests, Carlos Andrade, Ministry of Education's Cabinet Chief, remarked that the group's social concepts were based on ideas contrary to 'the civil and constitutional order of Brazil'. Under no circumstances could the Ministry condone, much less support, a movement it perceived as being governed by what Andrade called a 'racial social politics'. Indeed because of the Black Front's emphasis on racial concerns, all of its suggestions, including important educational ones were considered invalid.[74]

On the other hand, academic projects on racial and ethnic contributions to Brazil received a different reception. Conferences such as the 1934 Congresso Afro-Brasileiro organized by Gilberto Freyre in Recife, while profoundly important to the furthering of Brazilian research, did little to further appreciation of the importance of blacks to Brazilian nationhood within the population at large. Topics such as 'Blacks in Brazilian folklore and literature', (Renato Mendonça) 'Nago Vocabulary', (Rodolfo García) 'Blacks in the history of Alagoas' (Alfredo Brandão), 'Mental illness among blacks in Pernambuco' (Ulysses Pernambuco), among others, focused on blacks in history, the arts and health issues, but did not broach the political aspect of race relations in the contemporary era. While the topics discussed helped to fill the lucanae of information about blacks in Brazil, little discussion of the power dynamics inherent to Brazilian race relations emerged.[75]

There were two exceptions at the 1934 Congress. In his discourse 'Situacão do negro no Brasil', Edison Carneiro underscored the fact that abolition was not a black solution but a white one. Indeed, Carneiro's defiant voice emphasized the fact that blacks had been and continued to be marginalized by forces over which they had little control.[76] At the same time, Miguel Barros, the Frente Negra Pelotense's representative, gave a short discourse which supported black cultural pride within a broader nationalist campaign. Barros ensured white Brazilians that blacks desired to stand tall together with their white counterparts in support of their nation. He underscored the fact that the black movement must arise within the framework of 'Unity, Culture, and Equality' his organization's motto.[77]

The vision of the united Brazilian family comprised of three races but creating one national race had cultural, economic and political ramifications both at home and abroad. Official documents such as the Constitution of the *Estado Novo* further exploited the vision of a unified Brazilian family. In addition to laying down the base for the economic phase of Brazilian nationalism, the Constitution called for the nationalization of mines, all sources of energy, insurance companies. These circumstances set the stage for the Brazilian model of peaceful racial coexistence under a state-run economy. With help from their European counterparts dazzled by the resistance of 'non-Western cultures', Brazil projected itself in positive terms, eradicating the image of a nation of shiftless half-breeds.[78]

The presence of modernists in the Ministry of Education and Culture would mean that the modernist *welthanshuung*, which would promote a nationalism based on integrating populist factors, would necessarily predominate in federal institutions responsible for promoting 'national culture' and setting standards for national education and health. The desire to control and direct the symbols of national representation with a hidden European aesthetic bias, although not explicit indicated a lack of faith in the emergence of popular Brazilian symbols or those created by Brazilians themselves. This was vividly seen in the competition to choose a design for the headquarters of the Ministry of Education and Culture.[79]

After having held a national competition, modernist advisors[80] to Capanema convinced the minister not to use the leading Brazilian design but instead to invite the French architect Le Corbusier to create a completely new design. Important Brazilian architects and artists in search of a symbol of 'national affirmation and modernity' illustrated their continued cultural attachment to Paris, to which they looked for direction. Francophile bias aside, the building nonetheless did represent a collective national work which saw the collaboration of a number of Brazilian architects including Oscar Niemeyer, Ernani Vasconcelos, Afonso Reidy, Jorge Moreiera and Carlos Leão, among others.[81]

Construction began in 1937 and terminated in 1945 at the end of Vargas' Estado Novo. Today this building bears the name 'The Capanema Palace', in tribute to the legendary Minister of Education and Public Health, and continues to house the original pieces of art and sculptors by leading Brazilian artists, and the famed gardens of Burle Marx. Located on the Esplanade do Castello in the Center of Rio de Janeiro, the building represents only one facet of an important nationalist process guided by the new Brazilian state under Getúlio Vargas. The selection of art icons and sculptures contained within this national space served to immortalize the Brazilian conceptualization of nation which continues to represent *brasilidade* today. At the time of its completion, the edifice contained twenty-one works by Cândido Torquato Portinari, twelve by Bruno Giorgi, three by Celso Antônio and two by Luiz Goulart---all symbols of a modern Brazil imagined as unified in all its greatness.

The Ministry's essentialist anti-black sentiments were seen most vividly in its construction of 'O Homen Brasileiro' (The Brazilian Man) which, according to Minister Gustavo Capanema, would be the building's defining statue since the ministry was built to prepare, mold and shape the Brazilian man. Made of granite and modeled after Rodin's *Penseur*, the statue would rest in a wide open space in front of the Ministry. Its figure was to evoke a tranquillity and strength nascent in the Brazilian people. Capanema regarded the construction of this national symbol seriously, and compared it to the Colossos of Menon en Tebas and the statues of Amon in Karnak.[82]

In creating a national ideal---a male sculpture---that would represent Brazilians, Capanema relied on the advice of his respected friends and intellectuals who constitued part of the new patriachal order. In October 1937, he wrote letters to prominent Brazilian thinkers Oliveira Viana, Rocha Vaz, Roquette Pinto and Fróis da Fonseca, requesting their advice on how the ideal Brazilian should be represented.   In his letters, Capanema wrote:

> It is clear the work...will not simply be a work of art. There is an important scientific side in it, which is to establish now, I wouldn't say the Brazilian type (that doesn't exist yet), but the ideal figure that we can clearly imagine as a representative of the Brazilian man of the future. In order to complete this work I request your valuable opinion. How should the body of the Brazilian man be, of the future Brazilian man, not of the vulgar and inferior man, but of the most exemplary (man) of our race? What is his height? His color? What is his head like? The shape of his face? His physiognomy?...[83]

It is telling that Capanema wrote to Oliviana Vianna, particularly since he must have known Viana's views as expressed in *Populações meriodionais do Brasil* (1920).   A historian and sociologist, Viana was a member of the Brazilian Academy of Letters, his views as Jeffrey D. Needell forcibly argues 'was fundamental to his condemnation of liberal democracy and his call for nationalist statism'.[84]

The most powerful precedent in the search for a Brazilian type, essentialist in its very nature, was to be found in Euclides da Cunha's *Rebellion in the Backlands*, but Da Cunha's and other written theoretical musing never arrived at a precise physical representation.   That Capanema imagined the creation of a statue representing 'the Brazilian' required specific physical, naturally essentiaist attributes, and brought into question issues of race and nationhood.   Despite the celebration of the Brazilian racial and cultural mestizaje, Capanema and his colleagues seemed to have agreed that the best aesthetic representation of the Brazilian was a type of white, preferably the *moreno*, according to Pinto,[85] or the white with 'straight hair and dark eyes' according to Rocha Vaz.[86]

The Ministry again prepared to hold a nation-wide competition in which it would seek the design of the statue that would 'represent the Brazilian racial type of the best physical and mental qualities' in 1938, but as in the case of the architectural design, they opted for the familiar. Capanema   commissioned   sculptor   Celso   Antonio,   personally

recommended by Le Corbusier.   Celso Antonio, in defiance of the
Minster's wishes, opted for a sculpture of the Brazilian Indian as the ideal
type, since in his opinion, 'the (white) immigrant did not represent Brazil'.
This squabble between the Minister and the artist meant that the statue
would never be completed, but nonetheless illustrated three important
truths: the prevalence of the whitening ideal within the Vargas
administration, the Brazilian intellectual's propensity towards the
romanticization of the Indian contribution to nationhood, and an aversion
to blackness.[87]

This aversion to blackness is implicit in the choices of a white or
Indian male as a representation of the Brazilian people predominantly
black and mulatto.   For Brazilians, the white ideal remained a public
aspiration.   At the same time nationalists could celebrate the idealized
Indian, *the noble savage*'s past while indigenous populations continued to
be marginalized.   No consultant suggested that the sculpture be black or
even mulatto or mestizo-looking.   Roquette Pinto remarked that blacks
merely constituted 14 percent of the population, and thus would be an
unjustifiable selection.   But what about the mulatto or mestizo?   As late as
the 1940s, and despite the rhetorical celebration of their multi-racial
heritage, Brazilians considered mulattos and mestizos 'evolving types' that
would eventually be absorbed by whites.   A static representation of a
Brazilian race necessitated an ideal: naturally male and white.[88]

Racial discourses and debates such as these, carried out with
what seemed frankness, were not dismissed as racist but rather as a
disagreement among men over the best representation of the Brazilian
type.   The journalist Jaime Aroldo criticized the sculptor Antonio for
committing a crass historical and ethnographic error in choosing the
Brazilian Indian.   Instead Aroldo chose to praise Capanema for rejecting
the artist's vision, underscoring the Brazilian elite and middle classes'
fusion of class and racial characteristics.   In his 1938 article, Aroldo
affirmed that the Brazilian type was neither the immigrant, nor was it the
Indian, (not Camarão, not Henrique Dias nor Araribóia), but he proposes
other choices such as 'various *bandeirantes* from the South and the North,
all of them as close to the Aryan as equidistant to the Black and the
Indian'.[89]   This compromise so crucial to the Brazilian concept of
whitening illustrated yet another lesson: that on the one hand the new
cultural elite could celebrate their biological *mestiço* or mulatto roots, but
that the socially constructed themselves as white.   Indeed 'whiteness' by
definition implied full citizenship and power defined in opposition to
'blackness', which meant poverty and marginalization.

The choice of a representation of the national aesthetic, necessarily a political process everywhere, takes on a racial dimension in a multi-ethnic society which reflects how people feel about color or race. The *gaucha* Yolanda Pereira who became Ms. Universe in 1930 was white, and her whiteness was as important for the international community as it was for Brazil. Likewise, the entire government project to find an ideal representation of Brazil to be erected as a statue was of vast symbolic importance. Brazil wanted to project itself in ways that would earn it international attention as a modern nation. The Ministry of Culture was to exude a sense of history, and to promote pride and progress. Thus the headquarters of the Ministry and all of its art became crucial to the state's propaganda. Mulattos and blacks were often included as symbols of national talent, but not as representatives of *brasilidade* as was the case of the second floor waiting room of the Ministry which contained Portinari's murals (frescos), 'Meninos de Brododósqui', and a replica of a statute of the prophet Isaiah, originally by the mulatto sculptor from Minas Gerais, Aleijadinho.[90]

In the Ministry's 'Salão Nobre', twelve of Portinari's panels poetically interpret the major economic cycles of Brazil. These panels, reminiscent of the nationalist icons of Mexican muralists such as Diego Rivera and José Orozco y Berra, represented a romantic vision of Brazilian history which saw the participation of strong and healthy manual laborers rendered in earthy colors. The twelve cycles represented: cutting of brazilwood; harvesting of sugar cane; the rearing of cattle; the extraction of gold; the harvesting and collecting of tobacco; the harvesting of cotton; the cultivation of mate tea; the cultivation of coffee; the harvesting of cacao; the founding of casting iron, the extraction of rubber; and exploiting palm wax: certainly an idealized essentialist view focusing on the fruits of labor rather than the laborers. This choice allowed the artist to center on the rich Brazilian resources as modern representation without reference to the system of labor, slavery, or indentured servitude. The ahistorical beauty that the panels elicited was in keeping with a nationalist reinterpretation of the Brazilian past for the construction of a harmonious future.

The focus on the future and concomitant escape from the past were vividly noted in Bruno Giorgi's sculpture 'Youth'. Recalling José Rodo's magnus obra *Ariel*, a call to the youth of Latin America, 'Youth' presented a young male, with his left hand across his chest in a reverent, patriotic stance, and a young female with her left hand raised and her right hand touching her elbow.[91] Dedicated to the Brazilian youth, the statute indicated a hope in a stronger future for Brazilian nation that would be built by that youth. The Ministry of Education and Public Health had already mandated the creation of civic centers in schools, sports clubs and had created a special youth organization, the Organization of Brazilian Youth (Juventude Brasileira).[92]

Giorgi's sculptures captured the praises of the Ministry, the Brazilian Youth Brigade, and of the critics, which Celso Antônio's 'The Brazilian Man 'could not. Mario Andrade praised Giorgi's sculptures for their dignity, while the *Correio da Manha* described the work as a triumph that represented the youth 'in agile and harmonious movement', while being accessible to 'the public mentality'.[93] Controversy did not surround the representation of the Brazilian youth, as it did in the creation of the 'Brazilian Man'. Antonio was not commissioned, and Giorgi was eventually chosen from the group of artists invited to compete.   It was also 1944.   The *moreno* continued to symbolize *brasilidade* de facto. The *moreno* as the architypical Brazilian became crucial, not as an 'escape hatch', but as a model to which the nation could aspire. Neither a mulatto nor a black model of 'Juventude' would be appropriate, for much the same reason that a male model, rather than a female model was chosen. Given the gross discrepancies between the national image emerging and demographic reality, a strong system of propaganda and censorship would be required to disseminate the ideas of the status quo. The Department of Press and Propaganda served this purpose.

The Department of Press and Propaganda

Created in December 1939 by Federal Decree (Decreto Lei 1.915), the Department of Press and Propaganda (Departamento de Imprensa e Propaganda or DIP) performed many functions of censorship and propaganda from maintaining order and security to promoting outright nationalism in the political, social and cultural spheres. While such agencies existed prior to the 1930s,[94] and Vargas had already created the Delegaçia Especial de Segurança Política e Social (DESPS) in 1933, DIP would have a more pervasive effect in cultural matters.[95] Indeed the organization virtually served as an agency responsible for the co-optation of citizens through pacific and not so pacific means until May 1945.[96]

Its two main objectives were simple: to propagate the government's nationalist propaganda, and to censor criticism against the government.   Thus the DIP was divided into five main branches: propagation, radio diffusion, cinema and theater,[97] tourism, and the press.

Through conferences, radio programs and publications, the regime created a nationalist offensive strategy. Manipulation, suppression and alteration of songs, newspaper articles, theater and cinema production, constituted the regime's defensive strategy against criticism and dissidence. In addition to the official DIP publications, the state relied on private publishing houses such as the famed Editora José Olympico to disseminate information, often in exchange for financial support.[98]

The tourism division was particularly important in forging an image of Brazil for the exterior, editing calendars, organizing special expositions abroad, and publishing the magazine *Travel in Brazil*. The depression and later the war meant that tourism had declined, and DIP was partly responsible for maintaining international interest in Brazil. Despite Brazil's support to the Allies during the war, DIP maintained exchanges with Argentina, and despite its ban on foreign languages within the national boundaries, it broadcast programs in English, French, German, Spanish and Italian on a weekly basis (although the German and French ones were discontinued in April 1941).[99]

It is important to recall Benedict Anderson's focus on the role of the means of communication in propagating the sense of an (imagined) community. Official regime publications such as *Cultura Política* and *Ciéncia Política* forged a sense of national order, and were supplemented by more than one hundred propaganda pamphlets and books focusing on social order, politics and administration. While newspapers and the newly created publishing houses of the 1920s helped give birth to a renaissance in Brazilian letters, the improvement in printing technology in the hands of private enterprise allied with the state made for a process of modernization which assured unequivocal control of the major means of communication, particularly the printing industry. This centralization of 'intellectual capital' facilitated DIP's successfully completing its mandate through widely circulated publications which praised the new regime. These publications also explained to the middle classes for the first time how their government operated and focused on promoting the government as an institution of the people, and Getúlio Vargas as a man of the people. The government's focus was aptly reflected in titles such as 'The Carioca Shantytowns in the New Regime', 'Getúlio Vargas, Social Reformer', 'What Brazilians Should Know', 'Love of Country', 'Moral Unity and Economic Unity in Nationality', 'The Pedagogy of the New State', 'Everyone is Necessary to One Another', all published in 1941. Concomitantly DIP had censored several publications and had prohibited others.[100]

Still more revealing are the responses to requests for Brazilian publications from other Latin American nations, which necessarily carried an element of propaganda. In response to the librarian of the Circular of Bellas Artes in Havana, Cuba for books that would be used to familiarize associates with Brazil, the Ministry of Education sent nine publications: João Riberio, *Historia do Brasil*; Oliveira Viana, *A Evolução do Povo Brasileiro*; Mario Viega Cabral, *Compendio de Corografia do Brasil*; J. Capistrano de Abreu, *O Descobrimento do Brasil*; Gilberto Freyre, *Sobrados e Mocambos*; Basilio de Magalhães, *Expansão Geografica do Brasil Colonial*; Luiz Edmundo, *O Rio de Janeiro no Tempo dos Vice Reis*; Sergio Buarque de Holanda, *Raizes do Brasil*; and P. Gerlado José Pauwels, *Atlas Geográfico Geral.*[101]

Angela Maria de Castro has forcibly argued that the state's desire to control the nation's internal and external image was justified on grounds that the state was protecting the interest of the common man. Indeed this paternalistic stand taken by intellectuals of the 1930s was pervasive among all of the major institutions of propaganda. The DIP became one of the most powerful agencies for maintaining public order as it sought to impose its view of Brazilian culture by employing a paternalistic rhetoric which illustrated exactly how little faith the regime had in the common people they proposed to defend.[102]

Vargas' hand-picked pro-Hitler director of the DIP, Lourival Fontes, who assumed control over all facilities and public communication would have a chilling affect over the entire department until 1943 when DIP received a new military director in the person of Major Amilcar Dutra Menezes. While Fontes could hardly impose an Aryanist view of Brazil, he did sanction the publication and dissemination of materials that defended the 'Brazilian race' in rather Aryan rhetoric. Indeed, DIP was largely instrumental in promoting the idea of a 'Brazilian Race', an idea largely negated by Brazilian anthropologists who hastened to add that Brazilians were not yet a race, but a sub-race. Eloi Pontes' 1940 subsidized publication, *In Defense of the Race,* was one such example. Pontes praised the Vargas administration for its labor laws which protected maternity, children and adolescence because it was done 'in defense of the Brazilian race'. Vargas' administration was a crucial turning point, claimed the author, in the consolidation of the Brazilian race, since it cultivated a creative and fertile nationalism, distinct from 'the promising but disorderly degenerate nativism'.[103]

Vargas utilized the press, and other popular media to endear himself to the public, and the DIP succeeded in forging an image for him as a national consolidator and father of the nation. While decrees such as the two thirds law which required that the labor force of national companies be made up of two thirds Brazilians, and the restrictions on immigration potentially benefited black workers, these government actions took on a nationalist rhetoric. Limits on immigration would benefit and consolidate *brasilidade*, and avoid ethnic antagonism with non-Brazilians.

DIP's celebration of the Brazilian melting pot or 'the amalgamation of races' given the paternalistic relationship of the state to the popular classes, particularly blacks and other economic minorities, constituted exactly what Eloi Pontes criticized. Pontes provided a nativist and nationalistic rhetoric not accompanied by conviction. Indeed Vargas' state was not only intent on national organization and administration through authoritarian rule, but on the careful construction of a 'national race' devoid of ethnic connotations which preserved a largely white status quo. Eloi Pontes best explained the state's position when he attempts to console minorities under the Estado Novo:

> The present situation only constitutes a tyrannical axiom in reference to the future. The American countries cannot put the phenomenon of the amalgamation of races on the margin. The principle of these phenomena is sovereign because of the force of doctrines that prevail among European peoples. Racial minorities should not be alarmed, not now, not in the future. They should not because the government's vigilance is permanent and every day greater. 'Defense of the Race' dominates all of the projects of the present nation.[104]

Indeed Vargas' state was just as interested in the moral health of the 'national race', which necessitated policies which would eradicate class, racial and gender conflict. With the help of intellectual paradigms from writers such as Oliviera Viana, Cassiano Ricardo, Gilberto Freyre, and others, the state set out to recreate itself and its relation to the nation whom it sought to represent legitimately.[105]

The new ways of communicating, particularly the radio, photography and to a lesser extent cinema combined with the perfected use of the press allowed the nationalist to exert its model of Brazil to the masses. The attention to and inclusion of popular cultural forms, albeit modified to the aesthetic taste of the white middle class, nonetheless ensured a mass market. Music was particularly important owing to its ability to rapidly forge consciousness and deliver messages. Thus the state's vigilance of both was not unwarranted. But popular music became a much more powerful tune for nationalist rhythm. Once radio provided the foium for a non-confrontational passive reception of national musical forms, as in the case of what Benedict Anderson calls print capitalism, those models could be imitated and 'where expedient, consciously exploited in a Machiavellian spirit. Indeed the convergence of 'the Vargas revolution' with the technological advances of mass media created the possibility of re-creating and re-imagining the new nation. For many who were still illiterate, radio played an essential role in their connection to *brasilidade*.[106] It is important to remember that many of Vargas' nationalist policies, while directed to the popular classes in general, had the potential for benefiting Brazilian blacks.

Conclusion

In 1937, the government formed its Public Relations Service, which served as a sort of undercover police service. The Press Information Service was responsible for a variety of propaganda, including a one-hour radio program, *A Hora do Brasil*, which broadcast speeches, Brazilian music and drama. By and large, the growing middle sector, professionals and intellectuals who shared similar nationalist sentiments praised these developments adding to the nationalist euphoria.[107] As Heloisa Paulo correctly asserted, 'any individual ready to speak the language of the regime was a potential collaborator'.[108] The language of the regime had been appropriated and molded from the modernist's discourse of the 1920s which asserted that there was a definable essence called *brasilidade* which helped forge a 'Brazilian race'.[109]

The writers of the period understood the importance of propaganda to forging a national identity. Modernist writers such as Monteiro Lobato, for example, understood the power of the media and began to advertise books in newspapers, and selling them in barber shops and drugstores.[110] This generation of writer from a privileged background responded to the *povo* for the first time in the history of Brazil.[111] Responding to the popular masses did not mean accepting them as equal participants in creating a national culture however. Intellectuals and politicians during the Vargas era sought to symbolically represent blacks just as the Constitution of 1934, extremely popular and nationalist in nature, allowed for the theoretical citizenship of all Brazilians.

In his classic work on black social movements in Brazil, Florestan Fernandes confirmed that black revolution had a 'clearly and expressly integrationist's stamp'.[112] The integrationist stamp was a historical phenomenon that swept through the major corners of Brazilian life in the 1930s. The mechanism through which integration was to be achieved, however, would differ substantially among the various sectors of Brazilian society. The political generation allowed for the appearance and acceptance of the national myths of Brazil, while the state constructed new economic alliances. The creation of the government bureaucracy, the crisis of the traditional landed elite and the expansion due to industrialization, created new opportunities for the largely black and mulatto working class, but they did not afford them much social mobility. Culture was owned by the elite, and the system of propagation of ideas in Brazil guaranteed that the 'new elite' would determine how national culture would be defined. Blacks surveyed their options and responded to the political, economic and cultural factors. Institutionalized nationalism was a force with which to reckon and ultimately stymied social mobilization and protest.[113]

Not surprisingly, the popular sector which included black movements and social organization outside the state structure shared the nationalist goals. Thus Brazil personified for Europe and the United States a national community without apparent racial and social tensions which became a basis for Brazilian national superiority. The Brazilian intelligentsia, at the opportune moment of national political consolidation defined their national culture in praise-worthy terms. The forging of national consciousness in Brazil was a top-down process in which the state played a significant role.

But if a national culture is to flourish, the constellation of sub-cultures which make up the whole must develop in a dynamic way so that they mutually benefit one another. It is imperative to examine the ways in which popular culture responded to the nationalist *Zeitgeist*. Given the importance of the new radio and record industries, *música popular brasileira* in the 1930s provides us with an important forum for the analysis of the relationship between the institutionalization of national culture and the emergence of a national popular culture.[114]

Blending both populism and corporatism, Vargas appealed to the working classes. He attempted to promote both order and progress, while stifling extremists of the far right such as Plínio Salgado's 'Green Shirts', as well as the leftist agitators from the Communist Party. Vargas had learned many of his populist tactics from Pedro Ernesto, Rio's populist mayor in the 1920s. Both these leaders adopted campaign images of a familial, rural traditional patriarch. Ernesto had portrayed himself as a 'kindhearted doctor', while Vargas was 'the father of the poor'.[115] While

Vargas did not single-handedly create Brazilian nationalism, he was the national figure who best articulated those aspirations in the political arena. He included forgotten sectors of the Brazilian milieu: women, blacks and the masses in general. Immigration was also curbed in the hopes of boosting national support. Once in power, however, Vargas began his slow movement towards support of the status quo in the name of nationalism.[116]

Notes

[1] Carlos Guilherme Mota, *Ideologia da cultura brasileira, 1933-1974* (São Paulo: Editora Ática, 1990), 137.

[2] For an excellent précis of the Vargas regime see Robert M. Levine, *Father of the Poor? Vargas and His Era* (Cambridge, United Kingdom: Cambridge University Press, 1998).

[3] Azevedo Amaral, *O estado autoritário e a realidade nacional* (Rio de Janeiro: José Olympico, 1938), 308-310.

[4] Virgilio A. Melo Franco, *Outubre 1930* (Rio de Janeiro: Nova Fronteira, 1980), 282. See also João Neves da Fontoura, *A Aliança Liberal e a revolução de 1930* Memorias II (Porto Alegre: Editora Globo, 1963).

[5] Antonio José Amaral Azevedo *Ensaios brasileiros* 2nd ed. (Rio de Janeiro: Omena e Barreto, 1930). See also *Renovação nacional*, in which the author lashed out at the agricultural interests which placed severe restrictions on Brazil's capacity to integrate prior to the 1930s. Amaral was an apologist of the revolution. He also saw the revolution as the instinct of the Brazilian not to be complacent.

[6] For a good discussion on corporatism see Howard J. Wiarda, 'Towards a Framework for the Study of Political Change: The Iberic-Latin Tradition. The Corporate Model', *World Politics* XXV (January 1973): 206-235. The arguments elaborated upon here are a slight modification of Wiarda's arguments found in Howard J. Wiarda, 'Corporatism and Development in the Iberic-Latin World: Persistent Strains and Variations', *The New Corporatism*, Fredrick Pike and Thomas Strich eds. (Notre Dame: Notre Dame University Press, 1974), 3-51.

[7] Neuma Agiar Walker, 'Corporativismo y Clase Trabajadora', *Desarrollo Económico* VII (July-Dec, 1968): 313-348. Tenentism is the term applied to the rise of the military tenentes who led the revolution against the republican elite government in the 1920s.

[8] Dulles, 88-95.

[9] Robert Levine, *Father of the Poor*, p. 101.

[10] Dulles, 131. Alfonso Henriques, *Vargas o Maquiavelico* (São Paulo: Palácio do Livro, 1961), 223-226.

[11]   Thomas Skidmore, *Politics in Brazil: Experiments in Democracy, 1930-1964* (New York: Oxford University Press, 1967), 28-30. Such a broad statement as 'working class Brazilians did not see an amelioration of their poor position' has to be qualified. This statement refers back to the fact that Vargas did not attempt to revolutionize the system, but to revise it.

[12]   Virginio Santa Rosa *Que foi o tenetismo?* (Rio de Janiero: Civilizacão Brasileira, 1963), 23-28. Members of the Club 3 de Outubro, nontheless, provided a critical forum from 1931-1935.

[13]   Ilan Rachun, 'Feminism, Woman Suffrage and National Politics in Brazil: 1922-1937', *Luso Brazilian Review* 14 (1977): 118-134. Also see Rachun, 'Nationalism and Revolution in Brazil, 1922-1930' Diss., Columbia University, 1970.

[14]   Levine, 88-95. See also Departamento de Imprensa e Propaganda, *O nome tutelar das massas trabalhadoras no Brasil; benefícios assegurados pelo Presidente Vargas ao proletariado nacional.* (Rio de Janeiro: D.I.P., 1942). Lowenthal, *Brazil Under Vargas*, 285.

[15]   'Carlos D. Andrade to the Secretary of the Presidency' April 2, 1936, Folder 31, Ministry of Education and Health 1936, ANRJ, Rio.

[16]   *Dicionário Histórico Brasileiro*, 3053-3057. Plínio Salgado, 'Manifesto de Outubro de 1932', *O integralismo perante a nação* 2nd Edição (Rio de Janeiro: Livraria Clássica Brasileira, S.A., 1950), 19. Translation of 'o homem vale pelo trabalho........': 'Man is valued for his work and for the sacrifice in favor of the family, of the patria and of the society'. In his manifesto of 1943, published after the Estado Novo had abolished all political organizations, he became much more rhetorical, writing of the need to fight against the ruling of one race over another. In his 'Manifesto Diretivo', he called for the equality of all races, yet the only group singled out for praise was his 'Luso-Portuguese ancestors'. For Salgado, in order that society function in an orderly fashion, each member had to follow his destiny, and respect authority. He viewed the Japanese colonies of São Paulo, for example, in a positive light, precisely because of their work ethic and their contribution to the society at large without 'mixing'. Salgado's nationalist rhetoric camaflouged his racist ideas and his attitude toward Jews remained ambiguous, despite the anti-Jew stand of the fascists.

[17]   José María Bello, *A questão social e a solução Brasileira* (Rio de Janeiro: Imprensa Nacional, 1936).

[18]   Francisco Weffort, *O populismo na política brasileira* (Rio de Janeiro: Paz e Terra, 1978), 61-76.

[19]   Translation mine.

'Seu Geuli é bam-bam-bam
No Palácio ele ha de estar

Para tudo está disposto
Diposto até para lutar
Fale o povo que quiser
Tudo isso é tapeação
Na cadeira ha de sentar
Só quem vencer na eleição'.

[20] 'Primeiro Congresso de Educação' (Rio de Janeiro: MEC, Serviço de Documentação, 1946), 102. Vargas' original quote, 'O ensino primario é matéria de salvação publica', was a prominent slogan of the 1930s.

[21] See Clifford Geertz, 'The Integrative Revolution: Primordial Sentiments and Civil Politics in New States', Old Societies and New States: The Quest for Modernity in Asia and Africa ed. Clifford Geertz (Glencoe, Illinois: Free Press, 1963): 105-57.

[22] See Gilberto Freyre, Casa Grande e Senzala (1933) and Sérgio Buarque de Holanda, Raízes do Brasil (1936).

[23] Carlos Guilherme Motta, Ideologia da Cultura Brasileira 1933-1974 (São Paulo: Editora Atica, 1990), 31.

[24] Sergio Miceli, Intelletuais e Classe Dirigente no Brasil, 1920-1945 (São Paulo and Rio de Janeiro: Difusão Editorial S.A., 1979), 146-147.

[25] Hélio Silva, 1930: A Revolucão traída (Rio de Janeiro: Editora Civilização), 413-416.

[26] Leonard W. Doob, Patriotism and Nationalism: Their Psychological Foundations (New Haven and London: Yale University Press, 1964), 4. Doob points out other definitions of nationalism such as that given by Fallers: 'An ideological commitment to the pursuit of unity, independence and interests of people who conceive of themselves as forming a community'.

[27] For a powerful personal account of the prison on Ilha Grande see Graciliano Ramos, an intellectual opposed to Vargas' regime who wrote, Memórias do Cárcare. (1953).

[28] Robert Levine, The Vargas Regime. The Critical Years 1934-1938 (New York and London: Columbia University Press, 1970), 167.

[29] 'Interview with Sr. Francisco Campos', Correio da Manhã (December 1, 1938), clippings folder CPDOC Fundação Getúlio Vargas, Rio de Janeiro.

[30] Levine, 88-95. See also Departamento de Imprensa e Propaganda, O nome tutelar das massas trabalhadoras no Brasil; benefícios assegurados pelo Presidente Vargas ao proletariado nacional (Rio de Janeiro, D.I.P., 1942). Lowenthal, Brazil Under Vargas, 285.

[31] Nuno da Gama Lobo d'Eça to Gertulio Vargas, November 13, 1939 (Folder 188), Ministry of Education and Health 1940 doc 29/27, ANRJ, Rio.

[32] S. Pinheiro Machado, Secretary of the Ministry of Work, Industry and Commerce to D. Vergera, March 27, 1937, Folder 124, Secretaria da

Presidência (1933), ANRJ, Rio. The Brazilian government allowed single male workers to migrate not only because of needed labor, but also because of the ability of single males who traveled without partners to integrate more rapidly into the Brazilian culture.

[33] Nuno da Gama Lobo d'Eça to Getúlio Vargas, November 13, 1939 (Folder 188), Ministry of Education and Health 1940 doc 29/27, ANRJ, Rio.

[34] 'Capanema to Vargas', January 25, 1940, Folder 188, Ministry of Education and Health 1940, ANRJ, Rio. Capanema is requesting that Vargas send a thank you letter to the author for sending his publication, *Nova Orientação do Pensamento do Estado Novo*.

[35] John Foster Dulles, *Vargas of Brazil*, 30-34.

[36] António Marques dos Reis, *A Constituição Federal Brasileira de 1934* (Rio de Janeiro: A. Coelho Branco F. Editor, 1934), introduction.

[37] Dos Reis, 85 and 109-110.

[38] João Gilberto Lucas Coelho, 'Breves Anotações Sobre a Constituição de 1934', *Constituição e Constituinte*, 27. National education was still an embarrassment, however, owing to its blatant disregard for the understanding of the Afro-Brazilian reality. Abdias do Nascimento, *Povo Negro: A Sucessão e a Nova República*, 25.

[39] *Constituições Brasileiras* 447. Amendment No. 3 later added that any civil servant could be dismissed for participation in subversive activities of a social or political nature (December 18, 1935).

[40] *Constituições Brasileiras*, 447 (see Articles 148 and 152).

[41] Afonso Arinos de Mello Franco, *Introdução `a Realidade Brasileira* (Rio de Janeiro: Schmidt-Editor, 1933), 28-31.

[42] Ibid, 40-43.

[43] Most scholars seem to agree that the Frente Negra Brasileira was the first major movement to address the question of race and class in a national framework.

[44] 'A Lei do Lynch', *O Clarim D'Alvorada* September 28, 1930, n.p. See also the article, 'Destroe o Paternal Imperialismo Norteamericano', *O Clarim D'Alvorada* September 28, 1930, n.p.

[45] Dos Reis, 259-262.

[46] Dos Reis, 107, and 259-262. This clause, which allowed for the repression of crime in the backlands, was explicitly directed at the sertanejos, and he correctly reports that the embarrassment of including 'sertanejo crimes' would have been too much, and not in the spirit of modern nationhood.

[47] Francisco Yglesias, 'A Constituição de 1937', *Constituicão e Constituinte*, 28.

[48] *Constituições Brasileiras*, 375, Article 122.

[49] Augusto E. Estellita Lins, ed., *A Nova Constituição dos Estados Unidos do Brasil* (Rio: José Konfino, 1938), p. 367-369. See also *Correio da Manhã*, November 28, 1937.

[50]   Augusto E. Estellita Lins, 367-369. The Portuguese original reads: 'A infância e a juventude a que faltam os recursos necessários a eduaação em instituições particulares, é dever da Nação, dos Estados e dos Municípios assegurar, pela fundação de instituições públicas de ensino em todos os seus graus, a possibilidade de receber uma educação adequada as suas faculdades, aptidões e tendências vocacionais. O ensino prevocacional e profissional destinado ás classes menos favorecidas é, em matéria de educação, o primeiro dever do Estado... E dever das indústrias e dos sindicatos econômicos criar, na esfera de sua especialidade, escolas de aprendizes, destinados a os filhos de seus operários ou de seus associados'.

[51]   Levine, *The Vargas Regime. The Critical Years 1934-1938*, 161. Valdecir Mello, *1978-1988: 10 Anos De Luta Contra O Racismo* (Salvador: Movimento Negro Unificado, 1988), 64-79.

[52]   Augusto E. Estellita Lins, 367-369.

[53]   Ibid, 367-369.

[54]   Gustavo Capanema, 'Discourse given on December 2, 1938 during the commemoration of the 100 year anniversary of the Colégio Pedro II', reprinted in Augusto E. Estellita Lins, 379-380.

[55]   Otto Lara Resende, 'Um surto renascentista no Brasil dos anos 30', *Folha de São Paulo-Ilustrado* November 22, 1992, 6-3. Also cited in Alberto Ribeiro da Silva, *Sinal Fechado: A Música Popular Brasileira Sob Censura* (Rio de Janeiro: Obra Aberta, 1994), 43.

[56]   'O dever do escritor', *A Manha* April 4, 1943, reprinted in Alberto Rebeiro da Silva, *Sinal Fechado: A Música Popular Brasileira Sob Censura* (Rio de Janeiro: Obra Aberta, 1994), 46-47.

[57]   It is important to stress that intellectual support of the regime was not incumbent on political favors. Indeed Vargas represented the desires of many intellectuals, who supported him. Some such as João Minas, president of the National Academy of Letters, wrote to the Ministry of Education and Public Health suggesting that given their importance to the new regime, they should receive pensions from the government. (See Capanema to Getúlio Vargas, January 4, 1940, Folder 188, Ministry of Education and Health 1940, ANRJ, Rio.)

[58]   Nancy Ley Stephans, *The Hour of Eugenics: Race, Gender, and Nation in Latin America* (Ithaca and London: Cornell University Press, 1991), 40-46.

[59]   See, for example, Otavio Domingues, *A hereditareidade em face de educação* (São Paulo, Melhoramentos, 1929), 89-91. Also Karl Lowenstein, *Brazil Under Vargas* (New York: Macmillan, 1942), 193.

[60]   Secretaria do Patrimônio Histórico e Artístico Nacional (SPHAN, Rio de Janeiro) 679-42, photograph of organizational structure.

[61]   Law no. 4244 (April 9, 1942) 'Lei Orgânica do Ensino Secundario'. 'Letter to Getúlio Vargas from Gustavo Capanema', January 21, 1941, reprinted in

Ministério da Educação e Saúde, 'Primeiro Congresso de Educação' (Rio de Janeiro: MEC, Serviço de Documentação, 1946), 19. See also 'Projeto de Resolução, No. 5, Projeto da Commissão Especial Sôbre administração e disseminação do Ensino Profissional', 'Primeiro Congresso de Educação' (Rio de Janeiro: MEC, Serviço de Documentação, 1946), 70.

⁶² 'Primeiro Congresso de Educação' (Rio de Janeiro: MEC, 1946), 102. A host of other institutions were directly involved in MEC's mission including the Associacão Brasileira de Compositores e Autores (ABCA). Sociedade Brasileira de Autores, Compositores e Editores de Música (SBACEM).

⁶³ 'Primeiro Congresso de Educação' (Rio de Janeiro: MEC, 1946), 102. A host of other institutions were directly involved in MEC's mission including SBAT, Associação Brasileira de Compositores e Autores (ABCA). Sociedade Brasileira de Autores, Compositores e Editores de Música (SBACEM).

⁶⁴ 'Primeiro Congresso de Educação' (Rio de Janeiro: MEC, Serviço de Documentação, 1946), 104.

⁶⁵ Edison Carneiro, 'Situacão do Negro no Brasil', *Estudos Afro-Brasileiros* vol. I (Rio de Janeiro: Ariel, Editora Ltd, 1935): 240.

⁶⁶ Robert J. Havighurts and J. Roberto Moreira, *Society and Education in Brazil.* (University of Pittsburgh Press, 1965), 187. See also *Anuário Estatístico do Brasil* (1953).

⁶⁷ Emilia Viotta da Costa, *The Brazilian Empire: Myths and Histories* (Chicago: University of Chicago Press, 1985), 236.

⁶⁸ Havighurts and Moreira, 91 and 188.

⁶⁹ Orbelino Geraldes Ferreira, *Brasil Pedagógico* (Lisboa: Edição da Acadêmica da Escola do Magistério Primário, 1953), 154.

⁷⁰ Ibid, 157. Meanwhile others, such as Orbelino Geraldes Ferreira, argued as late as 1953 that the mixture of races would make it difficult to create the patriotic mentality that the legislators desired. He underestimated the power of myth and symbolism that afforded the students a framework for viewing the world and Brazil in particular.

⁷¹ Joaquim Nabuco, *Abolitionism: The Brazilian Anti-Slavery Struggle* (Urbana, Chicago and London: University of Chicago Press, 1977), 21.

⁷² Mary L. Dudziak, 'Desegregation and the Cold War Imperative', *Stanford Law Review* (vol 41: 61): 61-120.

⁷³ 'O Racismo Ante O Parlamento', *Quilombo* I, no. II (May 1949): 6. In the same issue, João Conceição translated W. Hardin Hughes' article on the Klu Klux Klan from the 1947 *The Negro Yearbook*. In *Quilombo*, the article appeared as 'K.K K., organização terrorista dos Estados Unidos'.

⁷⁴ 'Carlos D. Andrade to the Secretary of the Presidency', April 2, 1936, Folder 31, Ministry of Education and Health 1936, ANRJ, Rio.

⁷⁵ For a complete list and reproduction of the presentations from the conference see *Estudos Afro-Brasileiros* Vol. I (Rio de Janeiro: Ariel Editora Ltd, 1935).

[76] Edison Carneiro, 'Situação do Negro no Brasil', 237-241. Carneiro, a communist, also argued that the struggle of blacks be part of a larger proletarian struggle, and the major cause of discrimination was economic exploitation by the Brazilian bourgeoisie.

[77] Carneiro, 269-271.

[78] By inferiority complex I refer to the idea that prevailed in some Brazilian quarters that Brazil's development was limited due to the presence of the Indian and African.

[79] MEC, Delegacia do MEC no Estado do Rio de Janeiro, *Palácio Gustavo Capanema 50 Anos. Rio de Janeiro*, 10. Archive MEC: Sec/SPHAN Processo No. 1.252.T.89.

[80] Which included Lúcio Costa, Rodrigo Melo Franco de Andrade, Mario de Andrade, Carlos Drummond de Andrade, and Manuel Bandeira.

[81] MEC, Delegacia do MEC no Estado do Rio de Janeiro, *Pálacio Gustavo Capanema 50 Anos. Rio de Janeiro*, 10. Archive MEC: Sec/SPHAN Processo No. 1.252.T.89.

[82] 'Gustavo Capanema to Getúlio Vargas' June 14, 1937, *Colunas da Educação* Maurício Lissovsky and Paulo Sergio Moraes de Sá organizers (Rio de Janeiro: Fundação Getúlio Vargas/ CPDOC, 1996), 224-225.

[83] 'Gustavo Capanema to Oliveira Viana' October 30, 1937. Reprinted in *Colunas da Educação* Mauricio Lissovsky and Paulo Sérgio Moraes de Sá organizers (Rio de Janeiro: Fundação Getúlio Vargas/ CPDOC, 1996), 225.

[84] Needell, 1.

[85] 'Roquette Pinto to Gustavo Capanema' October 30, 1937, *Colunas da Educação* Maurício Lissovsky and Paulo Sérgio Moraes de Sá organizers (Rio de Janeiro: Fundacão Getúlio Vargas/ CPDOC, 1996), 226.

[86] 'Rocha Vaz to Gustavo Capanema' November 14, 1937, *Colunas da Educação* Mauricio Lissovsky and Paulo Sérgio Moraes de Sá organizers (Rio de Janeiro: Fundacão Getúlio Vargas/ CPDOC, 1996), 226-228.

[87] 'Editorial de concurso' January 1938, 226-228. M. Paul Filho, 'Homem Brasileiro' *Correio da Manhã* September 23, 1938, *Colunas da Educação*, 235. 'Minuta de contrato entre Celso Antônio e o Ministério da Educação e Saúde (July 1938) reprinted in *Colunas da Educação*, 235. Jaime Aroldo 'O Tipo Brasileiro', *A Nota* (Rio de Janeiro) September 29, 1938, reprinted in *Colunas da Educação* Getúlio Vargas/ CPDOC, 1996), 237-238.

[88] 'Roquette Pinto to Gustavo Capanema'.

[89] Jaime Aroldo, 'O Tipo Brasileiro', *A Nota* (Rio de Janeiro) September 29, 1938 reprinted in *Colunas da Educação*, 237-238.

[90] MEC, Delegacia do MEC no Estado do Rio de Janeiro, *Palácio Gustavo Capanema 50 Anos. Rio de Janeiro*, p. 14. Archive MEC: Sec/SPHAN Processo No. 1.252.T.89.

[91]   Giorgi also created busts of Machado de Assis and Rui Barbosa for the second floor, Castro Alves and Gonçalves Dias for the auditorium, and a statue entitled 'Crioula in the grand salon of the minister'. The edifice would not be complete without a bust of the President of the Republic, Getúlio Vargas by Celso Antonio Menezes in the grand salon.

[92]   'Primeiro Congresso de Educação' (Rio de Janeiro: MEC, Serviço de Documentação, 1946), 77-80. The Organization of Youth was not uncommon for the time. Indeed Hitler's Youth Brigade performed similar functions in Germany's openly racist nationalist society.

[93]   Mário de Andrade to Gustavo Capanema, October 19, 1943 Reprinted in *Colunas da Educação* Mauricio Lissovsky and Paulo Sérgio Moraes de Sá organizers. (Rio de Janeiro: Fundação Getúlio Vargas/ CPDOC, 1996), p. 300. 'A Juventude', *Correio da Manhã* April 19, 1944 *Colunas da Educação* Mauricio Lissovsky and Paulo Sérgio Moraes de Sá organizers. (Rio de Janeiro: Fundação Getúlio Vargas/ CPDOC, 1996), p. 304-308.

[94]   The political police included agencies such as the Corpo de Investigação e Segurança, and the Inspetoria de Investigacão e Segurança Pública, both sections of the Polícia Civil of the Federal District of Rio de Janeiro.

[95]   'Decreto-Lei no 1.915 de 27 de dezembro de 1939', *Coleção das Leis do Brasil* (Rio de Janeiro, 1939), Vol. 6, 666-667.

[96]   'Cooperando para o desenvolvimento da cultura e da educação', *A Noite* January 7, 1945, 4. See Levine, *Father of the Poor?*, p. 59-61.

[97]   DIP also published a cinema journal, *Cinejornal Brasileiro* from 1938-1946, although foreign films dominated the Brazilain cinema houses.

[98]   Heloisa Paulo, 139-144. The Estado Novo maintained a series of official publications including the Diário Oficial, the English language tourist newspaper Travel in Brazil, Boletim de Informações and state-run newspapers such as *A Noite*, *O Estado de São Paulo* (after 1940), and *A Manhã*, in addition to scholarly magazines such as *Cultura Política* directed by Almir de Andrade.

[99]   Department of Print and Propaganda, *Written Report* (1941), Folder 510, Presidencia da Republica, ANRJ, Rio.

[100]   Department of Print and Propaganda, Written Report (1941).

[101]   Instituto Nacional do Livro to Cabinet Chief, Minsitry of Education and Public Health, May 2, 1939, Folder 109, Ministry of Education (1939), ANRJ, Rio. A similar request from Ecuador (for a small municipal library's Brazilian Section was fulfilled with E. Roquete Pinto's *Rondônia*; Pandiá Calogeras's, *O Marquês de Barbacena*, and Arthur Ramos's *O Negro Brasileiro*, while a primary school in Mexico received Affonso Arinos de Melo Franco's *Lendas e tradições brasileiras*; José de Alencar's *Iracema* and Euclides da Cunha's *Os Sertões*.

[102]   Angela Maria do Castro Gomes, 'A construção do homem novo, O trabalhador brasileiro', *Estado Novo - Ideologia e Poder* ed. Lúcia Lippi de Oliveira et al.

(Rio de Janeiro: Zahar, 1982), 159. Levine, *The Vargas Regime: The Critical Years, 1934-1938*, 152, 167 and 178.

[103] Elói Pontes, *Em defesa da raça* (Rio de Janeiro: D.I.P., 1940), 8 and 19.

[104] Elói Pontes, *Em Defesa da Raça*, 64-65.

[105] Elói Pontes, *Ação do Presidente Vargas No Governo Provísório na Fase Constitucional do Novo Regime* (Rio de Janeiro: Civilização Brasileira S/A, 1940), 178. Cassiano Ricardo, director of DEIP in São Paulo also wrote the modernist work *Marcha Pra O Oeste*. For more details on Ricardo's Role in DIEP see Silvano Goulart, *Sob A Verdade Oficial: Ideologia, Propaganda e Censura no Estado Novo* (São Paulo, 1990).

[106] Anderson, 45-46.

[107] Levine, Chapter 8.

[108] Levine, 150.

[109] The list of modernists who participated in the Vargas regime as directors, public servants, ambassadors, etc. is endless. The exact numbers are less important than the point that the Vargas regime institutionalized a modernist world view which relegated blackness to marginality, and encouraged a view of a 'Brazilian race' that was based on miscegenation. See Paulo, 151 for a list of intellectuals and their positions in government.

[110] Monteiro Lobato (1883-1948) was also a caboclista. He was a coffee planter, a novelist, and an important critic of the era.

[111] Symona Gropper, 'A geração que falou do povo', *Jornal do Brazil* October 11, 1980, (Caderno B): 1. Began with José Americo de Almeida's *A Bagaceira*. See also Nist, 43.

[112] Florestan Fernandes, *The Negro in Brazilian Society* (New York: Columbia University Press, 1969), 189.

[113] Not only does this type of nationalism stymie social mobilization but also any attempts to work outside of the system to achieve one's needs. International and regional integration are also viewed as an affront to the national family. Brazil's low level of participation in Pan-Africanism in the early years in one example. In addition, the term 'black' in English may have to be clarified according to color and not race.

[114] T. S. Elliot, *Notes Towards The Definition of Culture* (New York: Harcourt, Brace and Company, 1949), 58.

[115] Michael Lee Conniff, 'Rio de Janeiro During the Great Depression 1928-1937. Social Reform and Emergence of Populism in Brazil' Ph.D. Diss. (Stanford, 1976), 304.

[116] Ilan Rachun, 'Feminism, Women's Suffrage and National Politics in Brazil: 1922-1937', *Luso Brazilian Review* 14 (1977): 118-134. See also Rachun, 'Nationalism and Revolution in Brazil, 1922-1930' Ph.D. Diss., (Columbia University), 1970.

4. The Nationalization of Popular Culture

A vida não se resolve em festivais

Geraldo Vandré, at the Brazilian Song Festival at the Maracanazinho, February 10, 1968

Devouring foreign influence was a necessary precursor to creating a Brazilian mestizo or mulatto identity that could be governed by white aesthetic values. *Mulatismo*, the celebration of the syncretic intermingling of the Portuguese and the African intrinsic to this process, occurred in an uneven manner, however. Africans arrived in Brazil as slaves, and even after abolition, the inferior status associated with blackness would play a significant role in determining their contribution to Brazil. In order for the mulatto to ascend to the apex of national iconography, given the political, economic and general cultural dominance of European culture and aesthetic values in Brazil, he would have to become more white than black, rather than, as Carl Degler and others have put it, 'neither white nor black'.

The ideology of whitening was not applied solely to blacks, but to mulattos and mestizos as well. The ascendance of the mulatto occurred in both high culture and popular culture. But it was a mulatto made by whites for whites, paraded before the popular class as evidence of black inclusion in the nationalist framework. Not surprisingly, however, blacks never attained a visibility in the national imagery, and it was only through select mulattos that they were included at all. Far more than a physical transmutation, whitening was a national ideology, anti-black in the most insidious way. Black images represented *brasilidade* only in rare instances even within popular culture. State and upper-class control of the means of communication guaranteed this.

Within this framework, two national popular pastimes emerged as uniquely Brazilian: samba and soccer (*futebol*). The history of their development as a national pastime provides us with a window onto the dialectic between black culture and national culture. By the close of the 1930s, the Brazilian state had played a significant role in forging national pastimes utilizing elements of popular culture that had been carefully gentrified and sanitized. Vargas' Estado Novo, which heralded an invasive department of propaganda and censorship, insured that themes of patriotism would inform national taste. Media conglomerates in Rio and

120

São Paulo gave unprecedented attention to the urban popular classes, and aided in the propagation of national culture.

Music, dance, carnival and sports such as soccer emerged as possible forums around which Brazilians of all classes and ethnicities and regions could identify. In the words of Karl Mannheim, these activities became a means of uniting human beings and engendering emotional integration on a national scale.[1] Public displays of national solidarity were particularly welcomed by the Vargas regime. Brazilian popular music rose up the ranks from the popular masses to the middle class, suffering its necessary permutations to gain a place in the national pantheon. Football, in contrast, descended the ranks from an elite British phenomenon, and through a process of Brazilianization (aided by the attraction of the middle and popular classes became, by the late 1930s, a national pastime. In both cases, black influences were downplayed and black icons were marginalized.

This chapter examines the utilization of soccer and popular Brazilian music as forums for the promotion of *brasilidade* during the Vargas era. It examines the development of soccer and popular Brazilian music, while playing close attention to the relationship between popularization and nationalization. Finally, while paying close attention to the role of blacks and blackness within these two areas, it will be important to examine the ways in which soccer and popular music became important forums for celebrating 'the national'.

Race, Sport and Nation

Race played an important role in the dynamics which led to the popularization of soccer as a national sport and the nationalization of soccer as a popular sport under the Vargas regime. The Ministry of Education and Public Health with its proclivity towards the promotion of physical education, together with writers and journalists, played a significant role in celebrating soccer as a national expression, as a symbol of Brazil's racial democracy. Brazilian soccer was to be celebrated because Brazilians had conquered and perfected a British sport to which all Brazilians theoretically had access. Despite the democratic rhetoric on inclusion, incipient patriarchy and paternalism assured that black representation in national sports on the highest level would be kept at bay at least until the 1950s. The few mulattos who won national attention seemed indicative of an 'escape hatch' mentality, often promoted as evidence of Brazil's non-discriminatory attitude.

The development of Brazilian soccer as a national pastime manifests a marked difference from the growth of Brazilian popular music as a national passion, although they both became crucial to *brasilidade* and Brazilian national identity in the 1930s. *Musica popular brasileira* was essentially a symbol of blacks and mulattos from the popular classes, which gradually won acceptance among middle classes, leading to widespread national propagation. Popular Brazilian music rose to national attention in the classic process of gentrification seen with almost all musical forms that become national symbols from the *merengue* in the Dominican Republic to the tango in Argentina. With the help of a culturally populist censoring state, and growing consumer middle class that had a strong print and radio media at its disposal, popular music became national music in the 1930s.

The official development of Brazilian soccer on the other hand can be divided into four major periods: Introduction, 1890-1910, Propagation 1910-1920, Popularization, 1920-1933, the period in which amateur soccer prevailed, and Nationalization, 1933-1947, the first phase of Brazilian professionalism and government involvement when it took on a popular and national significance.[2] Football's development represents the prototype of *antropófagist* thought. Originally imported to Brazil from Great Britain, soccer was confined to the British expatriate communities and the Brazilian upper-classes who emulated the British in their quest to be perceived as 'modern'.[3] The development of national leagues, particularly in São Paulo and Rio, eventually led to the creation of a national league, and to the professionalization of the sport in 1933. As the state and more Brazilians from the popular and middle sectors became involved in the sport, soccer became Brazilianized as Brazilians eventually 'devoured' its foreign elements. The Brazilian popular sectors slowly conquered soccer, a process which coincided with the development of the nationalist Vargas regime bent on promoting sports and music as means of uniting the Brazilian family. The social history of this nationalization has been examined by several Brazilian sports historians, but few of them have systematically examined its relationship to race and nationhood within the context of the Vargas administration.[4]

Since the early nineteenth century, Brazilian men and women adopted British fashion, foods, tea time and a wide array of practices, including outdoor sports, which had become increasingly popular among the British middle and upper classes. The introduction of modern soccer into Brazilian territory came after other British sports such as tennis, rugby and cricket had been imported from Europe. Indeed it is important to recognize that soccer, which is today celebrated as the popular Brazilian past time *par excellence*, has its roots in the British bourgeoisie. While the

British origin of the sport was crucial to its attraction for the Brazilian upper classes, the passion and dedication of its British promoters ensured its acceptance and the eventual establishment of teams and leagues. That this process occurred at a time when the population of Brazil's urban centers were dramatically growing meant that the game was destined to be watched and then played by many more than it was originally intended. Football eventually filled the need for male cooperative recreation when other possibilities, such as *capoiera*, the Afro-Brazilian martial arts form, were being banned because they were thought to contribute to anti-social behavior.[5]

The optimism prevalent in Brazil at the turn of the century gave Brazilians a sense that they were entering a new century with a new attitude, and indeed a new *welthshauung*, thanks, in part, to the momentous changes of the 1880s. As we have seen, however, Brazil's political, economic and cultural identity remained in the hands of the few, nonetheless, and it was those few who decided the fate of Brazil during the *belle époque*. Culturally, Brazilians imitated the French, drank champagne and crowded newly created cafés in the urban centers. The journalist and *cronista* Luiz Edmundo remarked, for example, that anyone who was anyone was sure to be seen in Café Paris in Rio exuding a life of pure *chic*. Art and architecture inspired by the French *art nouveau* flourished in Brazil, as imports and other fine pieces sailed from Paris to remote parts of Brazil.[6] France's cultural importance was rivaled only by Great Britain's ideas on social and economic progress. Brazilian men in particular revered British customs and ideas. In addition to the *fin de siècle* British ideas of social and economic development which came from thinkers such as Herbert Spencer and Charles Darwin, the British emphasized the importance of physical exercise to health and hygiene, (or physical culture, as Brazilians called it). Once considered vulgar and for slaves, physical activity in the form of exercises and recreational sports slowly won appeal among Brazilians. Many British regarded their sports clubs as sanctuaries of British culture, and thus barred many Brazilians from entering and participating in sports events. While writers such as Lima Barreto criticized soccer as a non-Brazilian sport that discriminated against blacks and mulattos, it was precisely the class and racial exclusivity coupled with the perceived image of 'modernity' that attracted the upper classes to the sport at the turn-of-the-century.[7]

The first decade of soccer in Brazil reproduced this bourgeoisie taste with strict rules of behavior for both players and spectators. British economic imperialism in the nineteenth century was accompanied by a more surreptitious cultural imperialism, not precisely espoused by the British, but which made British practices desirable in undeveloped countries in search of modernity. The activities of the closely knit British colony in Brazil which dominated banking, transport and other industries became a fascination for Brazilians of all classes.[8]

Because of the lavish spectacle involved in attending a soccer match, spectators from the popular classes soon became witnesses to the games which they often saw while spying over the walls of the exclusive sports clubs. Soon soccer teams and leagues developed throughout São Paulo and Rio. Teams were naturally characterized and divided by their members, who they were and where they came from. The São Paulo Athletic Club was known as the *gran finos*, for example. From 1902-1904 they reigned as the state's all-English soccer champions under Charles Miller, who is credited as the founder of Brazilian soccer.[9] Other clubs, such as the Corinthians Paulistas, founded in Bom Retiro, were known as *clubes de esquina*, or corner clubs, a more middle class team of ex-patriots and Brazilians.[10]

Both leagues attempted to reproduce the 'high society' atmosphere of the British clubs, cultivated passionately by Brazilians. In Rio, even the more integrated clubs still had only a few Brazilians, and no blacks. The Bangú Athletic Club with a total of nine players, included seven English, one Italian, and one Brazilian. Other clubs such as Rio Cricket were exclusively for the British and children of British, creating what writer Mario Filho describes as two British communities, one more tolerant and open to Brazilians, the other jealously holding on to their British exclusivity. Given the small British population, almost every English man that landed in Brazil was guaranteed a spot on one of the prestigious soccer teams.[11]

Because of its sense of modernity, soccer was perceived as a privilege and therefore a pastime for whites. Blacks and mulattos literally had to whiten their 'faces' or drape themselves in white masks in order to participate. Moreover the Brazilian middle class, in its quest for modernity gravitated to soccer as a form of sports/entertainment that could replace *capoeira*, a Brazilian martial arts form typically associated with the black population. At the same time, police authorities restricted and, in some regions, banned *capoeira*.[12]

Few mestizos or mulattos could be found among the major soccer clubs. Football remained officially a white sport although members of the popular classes learned on the field and in practice with tolerant clubs like the Bangú, or as workers in one of the English companies such as the Progresso Industrial Company. When the upper classes did open up their ranks to Brazilians, as with exceptionalism the world over, Brazilians would have to prove that they were 'exceptionally' good players. Still no clubs admitted *pretos*, and even mulattos such as Carlos Alberto had to endure a physical *embranqueamento* which gained him the nickname *pó de arroz*.[13] Indeed it was widely known that Alberto, a mulatto, took baths in white rice to lighten his complexion before the matches.

In the 1920s one of the few non-white heroes that the sport had gained was Artur Freidrickson, who had a German father, green eyes, very light skin, and a mulatta mother. He had become a part of the first national team in 1914, and was apparently accepted by both the British and the Brazilian elite. By the late 1920s, clubs used stipends, and other perks to entice 'non-traditional' athletes to play for them. Still, mulattos were preferred to blacks, and few teams accepted blacks out rightly.[14] International competition prior to 1930 was limited to exhibition matches, South American championships and the occasional European tour. The broader economic and political change which shattered the traditional oligarchic rule ushered in Getúlio Vargas on the wings of both middle class and popular support. Football, previously relegated to the upper classes, became more popular, and accessible in the period after the Vargas revolution.

In 1933, soccer became a professional sport, entering another phase of national development. This was also the year that Gilberto Freyre published his classic, *Casa Grande e Senzala*. Five years later, Brazil was well on its way to becoming a soccer power. That same year the county saw its first major black soccer star, Leônidas da Silva. Still only exceptional black 'stars' were able to make the team. Vargas, however, was clear on his attitude towards sports in general and soccer in particular as a popular phenomenon. Far from seeing it as an idle form of recreation, he saw its potential for bringing Brazilians together.

By the mid 1930s, soccer had become a Brazilian sport in a manner that the *anthropófagos* of modernism (who celebrated the devouring of foreign influences in the creation of new Brazilian forms) would have enjoyed. Brazilians had taken an English sport and made it their own. In *Novo Mundo nos Tropicos*, Gilberto Freyre would show with pride that the national pastime had developed into a Brazilian dance, largely because of the African influences 'that reduce(s) everything to dance' in contrast to the 'British Apolinean spirit'.[15]

Despite the sweeping generalizations, the opening of the sport to the popular classes had dramatic influence on the game. J. O. Meira Penna, like Freyre, attributed this to the abilities that many Brazilian youth learned from dances such as the *capoeira*. Football had co-opted the national talent, and in so doing had become a phenomenon which connected the elite and the popular sectors. Sociological posturing aside, blacks had yet to be integrated into the top soccer clubs or into the national teams.

Blacks in National Soccer: The Issue of Representation

In his classic book, *O negro no futebol brasileiro*, Mario Filho explains that professionalization of soccer under Getúlio Vargas was an important act in eliminating the color barrier that prohibited many non-white players from entering the established soccer clubs.   From 1894-1933, soccer in Brazil underwent a dramatic transformation aided in part by the political and economic changes sweeping the nation.   By the mid 1930s, soccer, had emerged from the private clubs and was now practiced in sports stadiums around the country.   The amateur sportsmen gave way to professionalism, thus providing one of the most lucrative professions for members of the popular classes with little or no formal education. Concomitantly, soccer had ceased to be an all-white sport.[16]

Not coincidentally, writers such as Orlando Ferreira now criticized soccer for its violence and vulgarity.   According to Ferreira, soccer was 'stupid' and 'savage', and encouraged vice and degeneracy throughout the Brazilian population.   While expressing his concern that the excessive sweat and uncleanness would be harmful to muscles in septic biological terms, Ferriera added that soccer would have painful consequences for his generation, particularly because the 'latino is very different from the Anglo-Saxon'. Ferreira was one of the few critics who criticized not only the cultivation of professional sports, but of athleticism in general.[17]

The momentous changes which accompanied the Vargas Revolution had a direct impact on the promotion of sports throughout Brazil.   Michael Roberts has already indicated that the principal element of most spectator sports is to link the participant's destiny to that of the fans. While Roberts notes that links may occur around cities, races, religions, and institutions, under Vargas the health and wealth of the nation would be primary.   Exercise, practice, and competition among the various Brazilian clubs and schools allowed individuals to affirm regional identities which would later be tapped for national purposes.   This was not entirely a government controlled phenomenon.[18]

Sports were promoted in schools, along with manual work as a civic duty, essential to the state's emphasis on 'physical culture' (cultura física), side by side with 'mental culture'.[19]   The focus on physical education and sport, not unlike the policies pursued in Nazi Germany, made an explicit connection between strong healthy bodies and the glory of the Nation.   The Ministry of Education and Public Health played a key role in promoting sports as a healthy practice.   Sports in schools was deemed so important that they spurred debate about whether military education and discipline should be a mandatory part of the curriculum as well.

In his discourse to the National Council on Education, Americo Brazilio Silvado argued that everywhere in the world military discipline had become a basis of an orderly social life. While he believed that the physical and emotional stress inherent to military education were not appropriate for children under the age of 16, he argued that, military education should be mandatory for the last two years of secondary school, and that students from ages 10-14 should be trained in exercises compatible to their age. Although the Nacional Council had opposed the suggestion of the Minister of War who recommended obligatory military education, the council underscored the fact that physical education was for the betterment of the nation and that the state had an obligation to develop and finance such education.[20]

Throughout the 1930s and 1940s, the state took its obligation seriously. The 1940 law decree number 2,072, which obligated the state to instruct the country in civic, moral and physical education, also reinforced the vision of an ideal population, viewing physical exercise as protection against diseases. Laws also established a mechanism for funding sports institutions, and building recreation centers, and recreation centers around the country availed themselves of state funding.[21]

The professionalization of soccer in 1933 signaled a major watershed in the history of Brazilian sports. Professionalization, like abolition, was symbolically as well as psychologically important for the nation. On the one hand, it meant that the amateur era, during which men played for the love of the sport, had come to an abrupt end. On the other hand, teams had long defied the rules and had begun to give allowances to good players to attract them to their teams. Non-white players had already begun to infiltrate several teams in São Paulo and Rio. Professionalization made that practice widespread and legitimate, accelerating the integration of blacks into soccer clubs, although blacks rarely represented Brazil on the national level. The lack of integration on the national level, particularly Brazilian national representation in important competitions such as the World Cup and the South American Cup, attests to the fact that Brazilians were uncomfortable with blackness being associated with Brazilian-ness.

Football remained overwhelmingly a white national sport, despite its mass following. From 1933-1938, black and mulatto representation in major national competition was extremely low, despite professionalism and the unprecedented entrance of non-white players into the major soccer clubs. Racial exceptionalism guaranteed that only exceptional black players would be selected for international competition. As Joel Rufino dos Santos rightly explained, a conservative spirit forged by radio and newspapers kept the popular masses at bay. Despite the diversity among local teams, blacks were unofficially prohibited from important positions such as the goal keeper, and rarely participated as umpires or judges. Blacks were often blamed for the passing away of the amatuer period, and the carriers of a new era over-run by 'mercenaries'.[22]

At the same time, athletes became indicators of national health and vitality for many nations, and international competitions such as the Olympics, the World Cup, among others, allowed nations to showcase their talents. Hitler understood this during the 1936 Berlin Olympics, when the Nazis attempted to use the games as a forum for the display of Aryan virility. Brazil's relative underdevelopment of the sports industry was apparent save in the arena of soccer. Two major forums allowed for the showcase of national talent: the South American championship, and the World Cup, the latter being more prestigious than the former. Remarkably, Brazil is the only country in the world to have qualified for all World Cup championships, beginning with the first which took place in 1930 in neighboring Uruguay from July 13-30. Professionalism had not yet come to Brazilian soccer, and the Brazilian soccer team came from Brazilian clubs around Rio de Janeiro and São Paulo, indicating once again the monopolization of national culture and national representation by the southern sister cities.

Of the 23 players who represented Brazil, the clubs in Rio de Janeiro were best represented due to a last-minute, São Paulo boycott. Only one black player made the list.

**Table 4.1   List of Players From 1930 World Cup and Their Team
Affiliation**

Teams	Players
America:	Joel de Oliveira Monteiro (goalie), Hermogenes Fonseca
Vasco:	Moacir Siqueira de Queiros, Alfredo Brilhante da Costa, Luiz Gervazoni, Fausto dos Santos
Fluminense:	Fernando Giudicelli, João Coelho Netto, Osvaldo Velloso de Barros (goalie), Ivan Mariz, Agostinho Fortes Filho;
Botafogo:	Nilo Murtinho Braga, Benedicto Dantas, Carlos Colbert de Carvalho Leite, Estanislau Pamplona Rio's Sao Cristovão: Teophilo Bettencourt Pereira, Alfredo Almeida Rego, Jose Luiz de Oliveira
Flamengo:	Humberto de Araujo Benevenuto and Moderato Wissinteiner
Americano in Campos:	Policarpo Ribeiro de Oliveira
Santos, São Paulo state:	Araken Patuska da Silveira
Ypiranga (Niteroi):	Oscarino Costa Silva.

Fausto dos Santos, nicknamed 'The Black Marvel', was for Brazil exactly that: 'a black marvel' because he rose to national fame despite being black.   Originally from Codó, a small town in the northeastern state of Maranhão, Santos eventually moved to Europe to play professionally. Fausto had joined the Vasco soccer club in 1928, breaking with the previous class and racial taboos, leading the team to victory in the Carioca Championship of 1929. Although Brazil did not fare well in the first World Cup, Fausto's talent and skill earned him the name 'Maravilha Negra', making him one of the most popular players of the country. Fausto's battles with national notoriety were emblematic not only of race, but also of the Brazilian uneasiness with the professional athlete.

Before 1933, Brazil lost many great players to professional teams in Europe and in other parts of South America. Fausto was one of them. In June of 1931, Fausto left for Europe to take part in a series of tournaments with the Brazilian national selection. His performance in Spain eventually earned him a contract with the soccer team from Barcelona. Fausto was the most noticeable player on the Brazilian soccer team not only because he was the only black, but because he was the most versatile player on the team. It was a Spanish newspaper that provided the best insight into Fausto's position on the Brazilian team: 'Fausto works like a slave. Is it possible that all the Brazilian center-halves work like slaves. Is that the reason why all of them are black?'[23]

Brazil's organizational strategy was quite different from their European counterparts. The center-half, called the *eixo*, in Brazil was more of a central player responsible for covering the center of the field, from left to right, which required more running than any of the other players. Fausto's placement in this position attests to racial exceptionalism which required that blacks be exceptional players to merit a place on the team. At the same time, another foreign paper, the Portuguese *Os Sports* provides another window unto the racial dynamics. According to the paper, Fausto performed with 'such talent that he could be considered white'. Herein lies the deep ingrained Brazilian prejudice inherited from the Portuguese which necessarily equates blackness with backwardness and lack of class, thus when a black performs wells (through a variety of mechanisms) he ceases to be black.[24]

While Brazilians worked hard to improve their image in international events such as the World Cup, their attention to regional competition was less than enthusiastic. Brazil's appearance in the South American Championship was minimal. The championship was held seven times between 1929 and 1945, and Brazil never captured the crown: In 1929, 1937, 1941 and 1945 Argentina won in Buenos Aires, Buenos Aires and Santiago de Chile, and in Santiago de Chile respectively; in 1935 and 1942 Uruguay won in Lima, Peru and in Montevideo, the home capital respectively, and in 1937 Peru gained the highest honors in Lima. Brazil participated only three times, and despite its performance was quickly becoming one of the strongest players in the region, with bigger prizes in view. Because of the low Brazilian wages, the South American games also served to showcase Brazilian talent to Uruguayan and Argentine teams prepared to offer more lucrative contracts.

The Vargas Revolution occurred three months after the first World Cup. The Brazilian Sports Confederation (C.B.D.), which supported professionalization in 1933, slowly began its transformation as an independent organization to a national institution under the jurisdiction of the new nationalist government. By 1938, Vargas' Estado Novo had devised a system of federal legislation that would govern the growth of the Brazilian sport, and allowed private profits to be channeled into federal sports programs. Renato Pacheco, the C.B.D's president, illustrated the concern with blacks representing Brazil, as he attempted to prohibit the new black star, Leônidas da Silva from playing full time. Brazil's focus had moved from one exceptional black player to another, and the monikers that they received illustrated how racial exceptionalism only allowed space for few exceptional blacks. Leônidas, 'Black Diamond' replaced Fausto, the 'Black Marvel'.[25]

Robert Levine argues that in the 1920s, selected mulattos from the upper classes were allowed to join prestigious clubs due to a Brazilian tradition that excluded people based on class, not race. Levine is only partly right in citing mulatto (or mestizo) soccer giants such as Arthur Freidenreich and Antonio Prado Junior. Whereas class considerations played an important role, they were secondary to racial considerations and concerns about image, particularly if players were black rather than mulatto. In the 1930s, for the mulatto and mestizo populations, one's economic class could assist in acquiring certain white privileges only within limits. Blacks were an entirely different category to be avoided except in rare cases.[26] Even though he was an exceptional player, when Leônidas da Silva erred, the public often insulted him with racial slurs.[27]

The 1934 World Cup was an important stage for Brazil to exhibit its power, one year after professionalism. While players were fielded from both São Paulo and Rio, the Botafogo soccer club's dominance was clearly seen with a record nine players making the national team:

Table 4.2 List of Players From 1934 World Cup By Team

Teams	Players
Botafogo:	Roberto Gomes Pedrosa, Martim Mercio da Silveira, Heitor Canalli, Ariel Nogueira, Valdir Vicente, Carlos Colbert de Carvalho Leite, Atila de Carvalho, Germano Boettcher Sobrinho, Octacilio Pinheiro Guerra
S.P. da Floresta/CBD:	Silvio Hoffmann Mazzi, Luis Mesquita de Oliveira, Waldemar de Brito, Armando dos Santos
Vasco/CBD:	Alfredo Alves Tinoco, and Leônidas da Silva
Penarol-URU/CBD:	Luiz dos Santos Luz
Nacional-URU/CBD:	Rodolpho Bartezko Patesko

By the next World Cup (1938), Brazil had already installed the Estado Novo with a clear and decisive political, economic and cultural direction. The Ministry of Foreign Affairs, Oswald Aranha along with his brother Luís Aranha, president of the C.B.D. were intent on having the players be as prepared as possible to perform in the event to be held in France. The team, the most ethnically, regionally and team-wise diverse was closely watched by Brazil's ambassador to France, Souza Dantas.

Table 4.3 List of Players From 1938 World Cup By Team

Teams	Players
Fluminense:	Algisto Lorenzato (g), Romeu Pellicciari, Hercules de Miranda, and Elba de Padua Lima
Flamengo:	Domingos Antonio da Guia, Leonidas da Silva, Valter (g)
Botafogo:	José Procopio, Martim Mercio da Silveira, José Peracio, Alvaro Lopes Cancado, Rodolpho Bartezko Patesko
São Cristovão:	Affonso Guimaraes da Silva, Roberto Emilio da Cunha Corinthians: Jose dos Santos Lopes, Euclydes Barbosa, Jose Augusto Brandão
America:	Herminio de Brito
Portuguesa Santista:	Argemiro Pinheiro da Silva
Palestra Italia:	Luis Mesquita de Oliveira
Vasco:	Leonidio Fantoni.

Ironically, Fausto was barred from playing in the 1934 World Cup, purportedly because he played for a foreign professional team. Three players broke the color barrier, however: Leônidas, Elba Vargas Lima (Tim) and Domingos da Guia.[28] The first, Leônidas da Silva had become so popular that Marcos de Castro has called him the 'Getúlio Vargas of Football '. With professionalization in 1933, many sports clubs invited non-white players, and according to the director of Fluminese, one of the most elite clubs in Rio de Janeiro, 'the question of color' no longer existed. Leônidas became one of the most popular national idols to date.

With his fame came a host of commentary from journalists and scholars who celebrated the passing away of a British elite tradition. Gilberto Freyre, for example, remarked that 'the Brazilian mestizo, the Bahian, the Carioca, the mulatto... plays soccer, that is no longer the Apolinean game of the British, but almost a Dionysian dance'.[29] A host of other Brazilian nationalist writers embraced the new Brazilian sport, including Gilberto Amado and Coelho Neto. Still others were pessimistic about black participation, particularly when blacks did not perform particularly well, echoing Afrânio Peixoto's comment that 'to win in football, to win in sports, means discipline, cooperation and efficient solidarity',[30] qualities that many sports writers did not believe that blacks possessed.

At the highest levels, that of national teams, those who would represent Brazil abroad, blacks such as Domingos da Guia and Leônidas played important roles in claiming glory for the Brazilian nation. Still they remain exceptions. Historically soccer has played a potent force in unifying Brazilians of all walks of life through. Football heroes, regardless of their race, became national icons, celebrated by Brazilians at large, and often mentioned as another example of Brazil's racial democracy. Certainly in comparison with North American sports rudely divided along racial lines, Brazilian state and local team selections in the 1930s illustrate a high degree of integration. Still, the treatment of black players who officially represented Brazil as 'exceptional blacks', or as the Portuguese press reported 'almost white' also reflected the Luso-Brazilian uneasiness with blackness being associated with Brazilian-ness. A similar process was at work during the explosion of Brazilian popular music although, as indicated earlier, music played an all-important role in disseminating and forging ideas of 'the national'. As in the sacred texts of old, through music, Brazilians reaffirmed a national ethos.

Race, Nationhood and Brazilian Popular Music

As it is today, soccer's popularity in the 1930s was rivaled only by the popularity of what is often called *música popular brasileira*, which consists of a wide variety of musical forms with samba at its center. The images of both soccer and popular Brazilian music remained largely in white's hands, with few exceptional mulatto or black performers breaking the ranks. Whereas soccer had come from the British, the Afro-Brazilian influence on popular Brazilian music was unmistakable. Nonetheless, given the elite control of the record and radio industry, all 'official national music' that gained access to the public mind cultivated to downplay its popular black roots. The Vargas government pursued a number of venues to showcase a selected version of popular culture. Venues such as 'The Day of Brazilian Popular Music ' (officially January 3) provided for the national display of popular music, mainly from Rio, while radio programs and private institutions influenced by censorship aided in forging a musical aesthetic that reflected those intellectual and political currents that sanctioned *brasilidade*.

Rio de Janeiro had long been the center for cultural intermingling and musical creation even before it had become the capital in the 18th century. By the 1930s, Rio and São Paulo together housed the majority of the media for the creation and propagation of national culture including radio stations, publishing houses and later national universities. Similar to cities such as New York and Paris, Rio and to a lesser extent São Paulo, migrants from the north east, foreign immigrants, intellectuals, and entertainers. After abolition internal migration had swelled both cities, and migrants brought with them regional customs and music that would later coalesce into national rhythms. Capital investments in Rio and São Paulo allowed key communication industries to bloom, allowing these regional cities to create a monopoly over national cultural production.

Given the overwhelming association of blacks with the popular sectors and the rich African musical tradition, blacks played a significant role in the creation of popular Brazilian music. Black, mulattos and their lifestyles have provided material for many popular compositions. The production and propagation of Brazilian music involves power, however, and blacks were not among those with economic and political power who packaged and marketed the images of Brazilian popular music. Brazilian popular music, even today, remains one of the few professions where many blacks and mulattos are represented, although a careful analysis of who receives national attention, and why, might indicate that blacks remain under-represented. The co-optation and manipulation of black musical forms was not unique to Brazil, nor is it only an occurrence of periods gone by. In light of the modernist generations' celebration of miscegenation, Brazil's appropriation took a Latin American course that reveals the extent to which modernist ideas denigrated or marginalized blackness.

While some musical traditions in Latin American are clearly of African origin, many of them are widely performed, listened to and associated with non-blacks. Furthermore, Latin Americans often categorize music as 'black' or 'African-derived' based on a series of sociological and aesthetic characteristics based on long-held prejudices and stereotypes. While blacks and non-blacks share many of the same musical traditions, there are certain contexts in which black cultural patterns are distinctively and 'contextually' defined as such. In many contexts, non-blacks defined black music as erotic and virile which set it apart from other musical forms with clear black influences that were somehow perceived as mainstream and therefore not black.[31] In Brazil, black musical rhythms stripped of its black performers and performed outside their black context, ceased to be black. Indeed white performers have long served as vehicles for integrating black music into the mainstream.

Within the context of nation-formation, music played a crucial role in forging a sense of patriotism and encouraging identification with national values-- or those perceived by the elite as nationally shared. One of the most vivid examples of the use of music in the forging of national values can be gleaned from Brazil's national anthem. After the creation of the Brazilian republic in 1889, the state adopted as its National Anthem, a composition based on a poem by Osório Duque Estrada (1870-1927) and composed by Francisco Manuel da Silva (1795-1865) after the proclamation of independence.[32] In 1942 the Estado Novo reinforced the importance of the national anthem not only as an icon of national unity, but also as one that would serve a populist sense of order. Decree Number 4,545 not only mandated that the National Anthem be played during the raising of the national flag in public and private educational establishments at least once a week, but also prohibited any artistic or personal interpretations of the national hymn without permission of the Ministry of Education and Health. Furthermore, all public and private schools from the primary to the professional level were obliged to teach students the song.[33] Patriotism was not only an ideology that the government could cultivate, but one that the state was obliged to guide, if not control. Thus the anthem took on an all-important role in which Brazil, according to the anthem, was 'an intense dream/a living beam/of love and of hope that had descended to earth'.[34]

Leopoldo Miguez's (1852-1902) 'Hymn of the Proclamation of the Republic of the United States of Brazil', inspired by a poem by José Joaquim Medeiros e Albuquerque, which had almost become the national anthem, also implied a cultural unity of all Brazilians in search of liberty. This composition's official adoption as the song of the republic emphasized a new era for Brazilians, and encouraged optimism for the future. The second stanza makes a direct reference to a new attitude among Brazilians concerning slavery:

> We do not even believe that slaves existed
> In such a noble country...
> Today the rubious glittering of daybreak
> Finds a brother in the hostile tyrants.
>
> Equal we stand towards the future
> We will know, united, how to carry
> Our august banner that, purely shines
> Heeding the Fatherland at the altar.
>
> {Refrain} Liberty! Liberty!
> Open your wings over us
> From the battles in the tempest
> It is enough that we hear your voice.[35]

Public and private institutions of learning served as ideal places for the institutionalization of patriotic values, while public forums such as the radio halls, the cinema salons, carnival balls, together with newspapers and records helped in shaping both a national sensibility and aesthetic which informed popular culture. Creation of popular culture, to be sure, is a vibrant living process which is constantly changing. Indeed, it is the process of choosing various elements of popular culture at any particular moment and presenting that choice in a national forum at an appropriate time which succeeds in placing it with the pantheon of national culture---a seemingly timeless realm.

Music from the *haute culture*, such as classical music, was undoubtedly affected by the nationalist intent. Heitor Villa-Lobos, for example, utilized popular instruments, and injected popular rhythms and themes into his classical compositions. More importantly, however, the spirit of official music provided a rhetoric which both informed and was influenced by high culture and popular culture.

The ascent of a given musical form, icon, or style from popular culture to national culture necessarily implied a political relationship. In Brazil, it also implied a racial relationship for two basic reasons. First, black musicians and entertainers, with few exceptions, rarely received widespread coverage from any of the major media from the time of abolition to the beginning of World War II. Second, their musical creations did. Middle class musicians were not averse to entering the *favelas* or climbing the *morros* to listen to musical performances or secure musical compositions. Nor did they always hesitate to use black musicians in orchestras or as back-ups. Thus to enter the world of 'the national', black musicians relied on 'white figureheads' or sponsors, or significantly modified their performance for mainstream audiences. As Ramos Tinhorão affirms 'the people from the *morro* who took part in the recordings were the anonymous musicians who played the *surdos*, the *tambor*, the *tamborin*, the *reco reco* and the *cuica*'.[36]

This process of appropriation was not and still is not uncommon in other multi-ethnic societies, where cultural traditions from ethnic groups with creative genius are co-opted or appropriated by mainstream musicians. Given the historical prejudice and discrimination which officially or unofficially barred black musicians from attaining a living from performing in countries throughout the Americas, history is full of examples of whites who used the system to their advantage. Indeed in the same way, black performers and composers given their limited access often willingly sold or offered their compositions to white performers to attain visibility. It is helpful to examine the inter-relationship of race and power in the development of a national popular Brazilian music through music's most important record and radio industries.

Radios and Records

Oral communications proved to be an important form of forging a national community, particularly in a country whose illiteracy rate was almost 70 percent. Controlled by a small group of investors, the development of the Brazilian radi, like print journalism, was undoubtedly influenced by the growing nationalism of the times. Pioneer radio establishments did not commence merely as stations which broadcast to a national audience, but as self-financed societies or clubs that promoted national integration. The first radio stations began in 1922, but merely a year later there were many emissaries around the country.[37]

Radio Sociedade, the first and most important station of the time, began with a conference by Roquette Pinto, and would in 1936 become the Ministry of Culture's radio station. Pinto, a carioca medical doctor, anthropologist, and writer born in the 1880s, was a member of the Brazilian Academy of Sciences, the Brazilian Academy of Letters, and a friend and advisor to the Minster of Culture, Gustavo Capanema. After Radio Sociedade, Radio Club do Brasil, Radio Club de Pernambuco, Radio Educadora, Radio Mayrink, Viega Radio Guanabara, and others soon appeared on the air. In 1937, there were 65 radio stations, a figure that would grow to 117 by 1945. By the mid thirties, owning a radio became essential for both the middle and working classes, and from 1939 to 1942 the number of radio apparatus reached in the country reached 659,762.[38]

Radio Nacional, the federal emissary created in 1936 had, by 1938, become one of the leading radio stations creating a plethora of national programs. According to the Brazilian Institute for Public Opinion and Statistics, Radio Nacional had become the most listened to radio station in the region, followed by Tupi, Continental, Jornal do Brazil, Tamoio, Mayrink Viega, Globo, and the station run by the Ministry of Education. These stations filled the waves with the first national music programs, sketches, sports programs and exercises.[39]

A 1936 cartoon in the *Revista da Semana*[40] indicated that by the 1930s, radio had entered the home of a majority of Brazilians, and that broadcasting music was a central part of the radio's popularity. Before the 1930s, classical music and opera dominated the airwaves, but with the Vargas revolution and its focus on the popular sector, this would soon change. Indeed the Vargas government did not take long to realize the radio's capacity for promotion of 'the national', and for propaganda. On March 1, 1932, Vargas' government released Decree Number 21, 111 which essentially allowed the radio to be used officially for national advertisements.

Advertisers helped expand the radio audience through the introduction of more popular forms of music, variety shows, humor, and a host of other forms of entertainment. Through these channels, Brazilians began to hear, for the first time, a number of national celebrities who would then travel throughout the region to perform in radio salons and concert halls. The radio and record industry produced music and performers which would expand the national market while projecting a positive image of Brazil. The introduction of electrical recording to Brazil in 1927 greatly facilitated cooperation between the radio and the record companies. The result: a small group of celebrities was able to corner the national market for popular music. Important companies such as Radio Record, owned by São Paulo state governor, Altino Arantes (São Paulo); Radio Transmissora (Rio de Janeiro); Radio Tupy which had a stage, studios and a tea salon (São Paulo); Radio Cruzeiro do Sul (Rio de Janeiro and São Paulo); and later Radio Nacional (Rio de Janeiro), only proved to enhance Rio and São Paulo's hegemony in the production of national culture. By the late 1930s, many of the newspaper companies had expanded into the radio business, creating quasi-monopolies over the two major means of communication. In 1935, the *Jornal do Brasil* also developed a radio station, and *O Globo* had gained control over Radio Transmissora. By 1940, Radio Nacional had risen to its national zenith.[41]

Throughout this period the use of the radio as an undisputed tool of national education and propaganda was evident even within privately owned stations. While many lamented the widespread propagation of symbols of the masses, by the mid 1930s radio was the major medium of propagation of information of the Vargas regime. Genolino Amado and Roquette Pinto, among other radio pioneers, shared a sense of national commitment to this popular use of technology.[42] Meanwhile, the state's Department of Press and Propaganda (DIP) was carefully organizing the famed *A Hora do Brasil* which it used to divulge information on local national, and regional politics while cultivating a popular taste for Brazilian music, both popular and classical music, the latter created almost exclusively by Villa Lobos.

By censoring radio programs, DIP coordinated radio activities with a series of communication enterprises that made up the Union's Patrimony which included the newspapers *A Noite* (São Paulo), *A Manhã* (Rio de Janeiro) and *Radio Nacional*. Ten years earlier Decree number 20, 047 had already given the state the right to regulate not only radio programming but also *who* could be aired on the radio.[43] The struggle between the popularization of music from the *haute culture*, including so-called classical music and opera and the nationalization of the popular, represented a significant issue for state-sponsored radio programming. The state's desire to cultivate the taste of the general public was evident.

Julio Barata, director of the Radio Division of the Department of Print and Propaganda, justified the continuance of classical music recordings from Villa-Lobos, Mignone, Obradores, and others because he believed that the state's role was 'to elevate the public taste', without excluding popular music that encouraged an understanding of Brazilian life, and celebration. As a response to his critics, who accused him of hostility towards popular music, on the occasion of the celebration of the foundation of Rio de Janeiro in 1940, Barata organized a tribute to Noel Rosa, whom he regarded as 'the maximum representative of music that was genuinely Brazilian'.[44]

Rosa's widely hailed talent notwithstanding, the tribute indicated the ability of the state to impose a given aesthetic quality, rhythm, composer, and singer which would inevitably affect the public's taste, and its idea of who represented Brazil. Rosa's abilities were legendary in his time. What is illuminating, however, is that Rosa became an obvious choice to defend Barata against criticism because as Barata himself indicated, his music was not without civic importance. For Barata, Rosa represented *brasilidade* because 'he did not glorify *malandragem,* nor did he focus on the low elements of city life'. Talent aside, the fact that Rosa was white, and a legitimate representative of the voice of the popular class certainly influenced Barata's choice

Censorship was particularly acute during the Estado Novo, but patriotic encouragement if not control of the national taste had long been a trademark of the Vargas government. In 1941 alone, the DIP had cut more than forty-four radio programs because they did not share the state's 'moral and useful orientation'. In the same period, specific lyrics were censored from 9,363 songs, while 1,333 were prohibited from being broadcast. At the same time, efforts were made to increase musical and artistic production for air time both nationally and for export. The DIP maintained direct contact with the Coordinating Commission of Inter-American Affairs, and private broadcasting corporations such as NBC (National Broadcasting Company) to this end.[45]

The state was not alone in carefully choosing its songs and performers to represent Brazil. Indeed it was through the careful selection of performers that major celebrities emerged from private radio stations: Carmen Miranda, Mário Reis, Francisco Alves, Larmatine Babo, Noel Rosa, César Ladeira, Araci de Almeida, Dalva de Oliveira, Silvina Mello, Ary Barroso, Almirante, and only a handful of blacks among them. But few of them came from elite families. Indeed, the humble beginnings of popular music creators and performers such as Noel Rosa and Carmen

Miranda have been well established, both of whom made legitimate claims to represent the popular classes among whom they had lived.

As in many other post-slavery societies, entrance of blacks into visible national positions was slow in coming. Despite the enormous talent that flowed from many of the poor neighborhoods, blacks who appeared in the entertainment industry were the exception rather than the rule. Pixinguinha was both an exception and a genius. But as Claus Schreiner reports, Brazilians objected to a black man representing Brazil, particularly in Europe.[46] Black composers such as Donga (Ernesto do Santos) and Sinhô (José Barbosa da Silva), Sinval Silva, and Oswaldo Silva were creators of many Brazilian compositions that found their way onto the Brazilian airways with the help of white patrons. Likewise, mulattos such as Assis Valente and Dorival Caymi, provided compositions and melodies which received wide attention thanks to performers such as Carmen Miranda. As a result of his collaboration with Miranda in Rio de Janeiro, the Bahian Caymi would be one of the first popular singers to provide vivid images of the northeastern state for national and international consumption.

The class and race bias implicit in the founding of national media for the dissemination of popular culture forged a national aesthetic which heralded *miscegenation* and often celebrated *mulatismo* de facto: Yet white and mulatto performers (with few exceptions) presented, interpreted or translated music from the mostly black and mulatto popular sectors for a national audience. Nonetheless, the imagery and language reinforced the idea of a harmonious relationship among the races in Brazil. But *mulatismo* essentially nullified any possibility of the authentic representation of black music within these national forums. Patriotism both explicit and implicit ensured that positive values of 'the national' would be tantamount to musical representation in an effort to dismiss historical conflict.

Celebration of the national family, moreover, remained the umbrella under which performers and radio producers presented their talents. Many radio stars such as Carmen Miranda and Franciso Alves constantly maintained that their entire profession was dedicated to the celebration of Brazilian people and culture. Miranda held to this belief even while performing her mixed-mashed rumbas in Hollywood. In his 1937 memoir, Francisco Alves, in an effort to show his nationalist pride, reaffirmed that his principal motivation as a singer was to promote Brazil, its music, and its composers.[47] Still, the state and radio producers offered many opportunities for writers and performers to lend their talents to the edification of the nation, the state, and to Getúlio Vargas (Ein volk, ein stat und ein führer). Such was the case of the 1940 state-run competition to celebrate Getúlio Vargas' birthday, which was aired on national radio.

Herivelto Martins, particularly known for his *sambas de exalatacão* or glorifying sambas, wrote the winning composition which all but sanctified the Vargas regime as ordained by a higher force:

> If he came into the world, it was God who desired it
> The steersman who stands at the helm of my country
> And in order to follow the right path, my Brazil
> I hope that God gives you many nineteenths of April.[48]

Popular music, as this stanza indicated, was instrumental to Brazilian hagiography. The celebration of nationhood is closely connected to the celebration of history, authority, and peaceful coexistence. The final reference to Vargas' birth date (April 19, 1883) indicated the extent to which the contemporary nationalism reinterpreted the Brazilian past.

Patriotism and Celebration of Popular Music

The year 1930 was also a crucial one for politics and popular music in Brazil. Two months before the military junta took provisional power after overthrowing Washington Luiz, Sinhô often called the King of Samba, died. That same year Ary Barroso won the carnival competition with 'Dá Nela' recorded by Franciso Alves, the top male recording artist of the decade. Casa Edison, a private recording company, had staged a carnival music competition in January in the Teátro Lírico which Barbosa had also won. That year Carmen Miranda had also popularized Joubert Carvalho's 'Taí', which would help to catapult her to her position of ambassador of Brazilian popular music. Miranda's ascent to national attention mirrors that of popular music, reflecting an idealization of national integration that reflected the face of the upper classes but the soul of the common folk.

Getúlio Vargas' nationalist platform made room for popular musicians who would sing Brazil's praises abroad. As Martha Gil-Montero has so aptly put it 'President Getúlio Vargas was the first president of a Latin American republic to understand the value of propaganda in creating a favorable image of his country abroad'.[49] Vargas was equally concerned with creating a positive image of Brazil within Brazilian borders. Hence patriotism and promotion of *brasilidade* were infused into every possible corner. After the battles of 1932 and 1933, patriotism was strongly encouraged, if not required as the radio program, 'A Hora do Brasil', indicated.[50] On April 14, 1936, Lourival Fontes became director of the Nacional Department of Propaganda, and one year later the Estado Novo made patriotism a requirement for musical production giving rise to a genre that is often referred to as *samba da exaltação*.

Censorship banished inappropriate comments and lyrics, and favored a positive approach to the national family, particularly in those songs that were recorded, played on the air, or viewed during public performances.[51] Although censorship may have guaranteed patriotism on the radio from 1937-1945, and in many song recordings prior to 1937, compositions of the patriotic nature were often sincere reflections of a new era of optimism which had emerged from the modernist debates of the 1920s. Recorded music and radio programming evolved into a national carnival whose music had already become a forum for patriotic celebration.[52] The *samba da exaltação* was a product of this time.[53]

Musical compositions which enforced Brazilian national celebration and glorification of *brasilidade* and Brazilian leaders were widespread. Brazilian composers, writers and musicians frequently sent the government unsolicited musical compositions offering tributes to the Brazilian nation, its heroes, and to the Vargas government, although this route, hardly gained them opportunities to represent the nation. These compositions, nonetheless, attest to a faith in nationhood within the middle and popular sectors unprecedented in Brazilian history. In many cases, these compositions were inspired by state policies and by individuals trying to ingratiate themselves with the Vargas administration, while others were simple expressions of national pride.

The paulistas Manuel and Apolicina do Carmo's, 'Himno do Estado Novo', for example, intended to be taught in secondary schools in São Paulo, best indicates the institutionalized patriotism of the period. Dedicated to the youth of Brazil in Rodeon fashion, the hymn claims the 'November Revolution' was a founding moment in the nation's history and urged youth 'as the emerging fibers of the new race' to guide Brazil towards its future:

> Young people: Stand proudly for glory!
> Among the lands of the kind Earth
> Brazilians: Look: Liberty...
> Youth, you are Brazil[54]

Others with less formal preparation submitted their praises of the new regime in a more humble fashion. Franciso Pinto's composition '3 de Octubre' described the president as a high priest celebrating mass for a nation saved from communists and fascists, which now 'vibrates, full of *brasilidade*'.[55] Amaro Corrêa's offering 'Hymno 10 de Novembro' with lyrics by Silva Lopes,[56] and Pequeno Edison's 'Eis Brasil' indicate a musical propensity among the popular classes to validate the Vargas regime, not altogether altruistically.[57] This focus on representation of the nation in musical compositions underscored music's didactic potential and the attention that Brazilians gave musical creation in the 1930s in general.

Challenges to anti-social behavior were implicit in this patriotism of the Vargas era, and were aptly reflected in songs appearing on the radio, records, and the growing film industry. In 1935, for example, João de Barro and Alberto Ribeiro released their film 'Alô Alô Brasil', ('Hello Hello Brazil') a title taken from the first words of the radio announcer, and featuring Carmen Miranda. That year, her sister, Aurora, recorded one of Rio's more celebratory songs, 'Cidade Maravilhoso' by André Filho in which Rio is praised as 'the marvelous city' of a thousand incantations, and which has became the City's unofficial anthem. Genuine celebration of the local and the national which began in the early 1930s only intensified after the creation of the Estado Novo.

Film continued to interact with radio and popular music in official and unofficial ways. In 1936 Ademar Gonzaga and Alace Douney's film, 'Alô Alô Carnival' ('Hello Hello Carnival', also starring Carmen Miranda) made its debut to enthusiastic audiences. And one year later the reknown nationalist composer Heitor Villa-Lobos teamed up with Humberto Mauaro for their epic-like saga release 'O descobrimiento do Brasil' (The Discovery of Brazil). Ary Barroso, who served as president of the Department of Composers of the Brazilian Society of Theatrical Authors,[58] closed the decade with the now classic 'Aquarela do Brasil' which proclaimed:

> Oh! open the curtains of the past
> Fetch the black mother from the mountains
> Put the Congo King in the congo dance
> Brazil!
> Brazil!
> Let the troubadour sing once more
> a song to the melancholy moonlight
> a song of my love
> I want to see the lady
> passing through the salon
> dragging her dress with lace trimming behind
> Brazil!
> Brazil!
> For me
> For me[59]

Perhaps Carmen Miranda was one of the most important cultural ambassadors of Brazilian popular culture for Vargas whom she knew personally. As Martha Gil Montero puts it, 'The singer's vitality and gaiety matched Vargas' charismatic smile perfectly, and wittingly or unwittingly she became the dictator's most engaging propaganda tool'.[60] The rise of Miranda as a representative of Brazilian popular music was in and of itself a populist occurrence. As indicated previously, she provided an agreeable image for the display of popular, mostly black and mulatto talent. That she herself was talented is indisputable--but she was a product of her time, and saw herself as providing a positive service to all Brazilians.

Miranda's early domination of the recording industry with such classics as 'Se o Samba é Moda', (If Samba is in Fashion, 1930) 'Taí o Para Você Gostar de Mim' (It's There! or So That You Like Me, 1930), and 'Moleque Indigesto' (Incredible Boy, 1933), guaranteed her a place in the early Brazilian films such as 'Voz do Carnaval' (The Voice of Carnival, 1933), 'Alô, Alô Brasil' (1935), and 'Alô, Alô Carnival' (1936). But it was the incipient patriotism her songs promoted that makes her a product of the Vargas era, while her representation of the voice of blacks and mulattos links her with the cultural populism of modernism. Miranda was so popular that composing greats such as Pixinguinha and others of the *Velha Guarda* wrote compositions especially for her, as did young and emerging artists such as the Bahian Dorival Caymi who provided her with much of the inspiration for the Bahiana image she would take with her to Broadway and then to Hollywood.

Her hymns to the Brazilian nation and Brazilian culture include such beautiful renditions as 'Minha Terra Tem Palmeiras', written by João Barro and Albert Ribeiro, which promoted the Brazilian good land, perhaps the Brazilian equivalent to the American song 'This land is your land, This land is my land'. Moreover, the song reinforced the image of a multiethnic society at ease with itself: 'What a great land to go on a spree/ My country has cute blonds, and chocolate-colored *morenas*'. Patriotism was implicit in her rendition of Amado Regis' samba 'O Samba e o Tango', which juxtaposed the rhythm of the Brazilian samba with that of the Argentine tango, and the samba emerges triumphantly.[61]

More poignant was 'Eu Gosto da Minha Terra' (I Like My Country) by R. Montenegro, recorded with the Victor Orchestra in August of 1930:

> Of this so beautiful Brazil
> I am a daughter, I live happily
> I am proud of the race

Of pure people of my country
Look at my gaze
(For) it says that I am Brazilian
And my samba reveals
That I am a child of this country.

I am Brazilian, I have a magical charm
I like samba
I was born for this.
The fox-trot does not compare
With our samba; that is a rare jewel
I know how to say better than anyone
All the beauty that the samba has.
I am Brazilian, I live happily
I like the things of my country
 I like my country and I always want to live here.
To see the very beautiful Southern Cross
From the skies of the land where I was born
Abroad, out of tune
Samba looses its value
Yes! I'll remain in my land.[62]

'I Like My Country' is so compelling because of its unequivocal faith in Brazil. In the first stanza, the singer hails the Brazilian landscape and celebrates the Brazilian 'national race' to which she belongs. Stanza two reinforces an appreciation of popular culture such as the samba, and a rejection of foreign influences much like the *antropófagos* of the 1920s. Finally, in the final stanza, the singer rejects exile or going abroad, to remain in her national home. Coming from the voice of a woman born in Portugal, who maintained her Portuguese passport all of her life, this song is a reaffirmation of Miranda's own sense of *brasilidade*--a phenomenon that Vargas would have wanted other immigrants to affirm, particularly given the nationalist propaganda.

National pride and the adaptation of the Portuguese to the tropics was also emphasized in Paulo Barbosa and Vicente Paiva's 1935 'Salada Portuguesa', accepted as a carnival song despite the criteria of patriotism because of the opportunity to make fun of the Portuguese:

My green path
once came from Portugal.
Come my people let's celebrate carnival.

Manuel joins the parade, and so does Maria.
During the three days of merriment
Pierrô and Colombina, Father John and black Mina too.

> Grandfather already told me:
> In Brazil there is happiness.
> Carnival has existed
> since the days of Cabral.[63]

The Department of Print and Propaganda preferred patriotic compositions that tended towards exaggeration, and certainly glorification of the nation, hence the genre *sambas de exaltação*. Sebastião Lima and Henrique de Almeida's 1942 recording 'Brasil Brasileiro' emphasized pride in Brazil, its heroes and the Estado Novo. The song begins: 'My heart is small, but all of my *moreno* Brazil fits inside of it', and ends with a celebration of the Estado Novo which the narrator sings happily.[64]   Others, such as 'Glorias do Brasil', linked the nation's greatness with that of the president's, coinciding with the president's published and recorded discourse in which he appears as a benevolent patriarch of a national family.[65]

Social commentary and criticism within national pride was not altogether lacking, nor was there a concerted effort to avoid discussion of slavery or Brazil's race relations, as long as they were discussed within the confines of integration and an appreciation of 'the national'. Jourbert de Carvalho's rumba 'Sahe da Toca Brasil', for example, begins with 'Get up from the trenches Brazil.   Your place is else where', implying a greater place for the *povo*.   The song's refrain affirms that:

> Brazil, which used to be a slave quarter
> danced in the macumba, striking its feet on the ground.
> It is good not to ever forget that
> the dance is now in the ballroom.
>
> Brazil, leave the favela {the past}!
> The skyscraper is what matters {modernity}.
> It's too sad that many good people
> Loving you so much do not understand you.[66]

As the song urged unity and understanding, it directed its message to Brazilians who refused to rise up and celebrate their national heritage.   While on the one hand, another stanza seems to criticize the middle class (or descent people, *gente boa*) with lines such as 'Brazil your strong bright people did not sing', the songs also reprimands *favelados*, seemingly for their own predicament. The song typifies the position of many middle class interpreters of popular Brazilian music.   The song summarizes the ascent of popular music like samba, which moved from the favela to the ballroom with 'middle-sector' musicians. Ironically, the song urges the poor to leave the favela behind, as it celebrates the gentrification of Brazilian popular culture. This was another rendition of the whitening ideal.

As Miranda moved up the social hierarchy, she left the working class to enter the white *carioca* middle class, but her rendition of the problems of the poor and working class was not altogether far from her own early experience. Her father was a barber, and she herself worked in a hat shop before being discovered. Before leaving for the United States in 1939, songs such as 'Adeus Batucada', written by Sinval Silva, who was also Miranda's chauffeur, begins with a soft nostalgic samba beat as Miranda says good-by to her *batucada*, assuring Brazilians that she will promise to make people appreciate her Brazilian music:

> Good-bye! Good-bye! My samba *pandeiro*,
> Bamba tambourine, the dawn has already arrived...
> I will leave crying, with my heart smiling.
> I will let everyone take pride in our musical rhythm.[67]

This celebration did not prevent a series of revolts and challenges to the status quo as the 1932 Paulista revolt, and the rebellions in the interior which ended in the death of the famed couple, Maria Bonita and Lampião from Angico, Sergipe.   Challenges that were quickly and efficiently undermined through military action, or in the case of Maria Bonita and Lampião, assassination. As in the political realm, where all challenges to a populist-corporatist sense of nation were either outlawed, or severely curtailed, cultural populism assured that blackness, black pride, criticism of the state, violence, and other 'un-Brazilian' activity would be limited. Popular music, moreover, reinforced the celebration of 'the national' through three major themes: Brazil as a country of the future, Brazil as a melting pot, and Brazil as a country of enormous musical creativity.

Central to the celebration were images of the common folk, particularly of the mulatto--strong, independent, and joyous, and the mulatta---beautiful, charming and sensual.   These images, although inconsistent with the view of many of the elite provided *brasilidade* with two of its more important stereotypes. Popular culture created in the city reflected the rhetoric of the modernist intellectual, and focused on the coastal epitome of Brazilian cultural-intermingling: the *mulato bamba,* the cool mulatto. References to Indians, *caboclos* or *cafusos* in Brazilian popular music were rare.   The mulatto also served as scapegoat for society's problems, criticized for his laziness, yet praised for his unbridled passion. The focus on *cultural celebration* and the mulatto, dictated the content of compositions and performances even of many black musicians, marginalizing any semblance of *negritude* or other political expressions of blackness. Thus the image of carnival in Jorge Amado's 1931 novel *The Carnival Country* became the dominant symbol of Brazil for years to come. Not coincidentally, it was also in 1931 that Vargas created the first propaganda institution, the Department Official de Propaganda.[68]

While carnival emerged as a national symbol and an integrating force, the creators and organizers of the national parade tolerated little artistic or thematic diversity among the various *escolas de samba* participating in the official parade. Moreover, the conflicting views of *brasilidade* and modern identity in the positivist tradition of 'order and progress' called for aggressive government involvement. Officials in Rio required that *escolas de samba* represent patriotic themes or events in their costumes and music in order to participate in the official carnival parade, and many eagerly complied. Brazilians of all walks of life were concerned with forging a modern identity. 'Century of Progress' by Noel Rosa, recorded by Aracy de Almeida in August of 1937, was an ideal samba that reflected this spirit.   While emphasizing the problems of violence, it nonetheless celebrated samba as an authentic national expression in a tone that suggests a desire to convince rather than to confirm.[69]

Vargas had a clear sense of the role he wanted the popular masses to play in his own political platform, he was not the first one to attempt to impose order on the creativity of the masses that had already crammed the southern *morros*. The organization of samba schools and the imposition of a national aesthetic which would promote patriotism was central to the gentrification of carnival and the creation of a popular 'middle way' between the elite carnival balls and the spontaneous celebrations of the *morros* and other public spaces such as the famed *Praça Onze*.

The *morros*, of course, were strictly for the *povo*--but the *povo* also had its public space: Praça Onze, a public square not too far from the soon to be Ministry of Education and Health, had long been one of the major centers for public demonstration and celebration, including carnival. Not a few samba recordings were dedicated to its legendary role in Rio's carnival life, and the music and dances of blacks and mulattos. The remodeling of Rio in 1942 with the creation of Avenida Presidente Vargas would have a catastrophic effect on this public space, and the samba schools would march down this avenue for decades until the creation of the stadium, *the Sambódromo*. Grande Otelo, one of few black actors to have found a career in music and in film, and Herivelto Martins eulogized the square in the 1942 composition 'Praça Onze' (1942):

They'll put an end to Praça Onze
There won't be any more Samba School, no there won't be.
The tambourine is weeping,
The entire hillside cries.
Favela, The Samba Schools Salgueiro
Mangueira, Estação Primeira
Put away your tambourines, put them away
Because the Samba School is leaving.

Good-bye my Praça Onze, good-bye.
We already know that you will disappear;
take our memory with you.
But you'll remain forever in our heart
and one day we'll have another Praça Onze
and to your past we will sing.[70]

The remodeling of the city and the relationship of Avenida Presidente Vargas to the people's Praça Onze was the perfect metaphor of the era. The people's space was being torn down in the name of progress, and in its place was put a grand avenue in the name of their president. Still, the notion of the people and their popular culture was abundant in the recordings of the 1930s, although, as we have previously indicated, the recordings were made mostly by middle class performers, almost all white. Assis Valente's 'Recenseamento', Herivelto Martins' 'Cabaret No Morro', and Palva Ribeiro and Luiz Peixoto's 'Voltei Pro Morro' all provide images of the care-free life of the poor classes for national audiences.

This process of modifying the popular space began with the creation of the samba schools. In *A Historia do Carnival Carioca*, Eneida de Morais indicates the national nature of the celebrations that took place in Rio de Janeiro. Internal migration to Rio, particularly from the northeast, had brought together a wide array of regional musical forms which would come to bear on Rio's carnival. Most researchers agree that the first samba school, created by black and mulatto *sambistas* was founded in 1928. As with many of Brazil's national celebrations, 'official carnival' was made up almost exclusively of whites who paraded in high society clubs, although some working class groups paraded in small groups called *ranchos*. Residents of the morros had little or no opportunity for inclusion in official festivities until the dawn of the samba schools.[71]

Prior to 1932, the popular samba schools chose ironical and popular names for the musical groups such as 'Vai Como Pode' (Go Any Way You Can) and 'Deixa Falar' (Let Us Speak), and paraded in local neighborhoods without any formal organization or direction. In 1932, Pedro Ernesto, the then populist governor of Rio de Janeiro attempted, with

Vargas' support, to centralize and set standards for one official carnival parade to be held in downtown Rio, a move that would integrate the neighborhood celebrations into a unified national show.[72]

Rio's mostly black and mulatto samba schools responded enthusiastically, seeing participation as a form of legitimizing their music and providing an opportunity to shine in the national limelight. In his film on the history of samba, released posthumously as a part of the video *It's All True,* Orson Welles acknowledged that by the 1940s, carnival participants were largely black, an image that neither the Brazilian government nor the United States was enthusiastic in projecting during the years of the 'Good Neighbor Policy'. Popular music performers celebrated the wonders of samba and other black-based musical rhythms, but criticized lack of order, violence and un-social behavior, all of which were associated with the black inhabitants of the *morros*. At the same time, blacks were supposed to 'know their place' in society. Recorded music such as Aracy Almeida's rendition of Noel Rosa's 'The Root of the Problem' ('O X do Problema')[73] celebrated the *escola de samba* Estacio, for example, from the perspective of a woman who had acquired fame and glory, and received invitations to perform elsewhere. Despite her fame, she is unable (because of her apparent happiness) to leave the *morro*: 'I was born in Estácio/ I cannot change the substance of my blood/You can believe in the palm trees of the marshes/ in the sand from Copacabana'[74] Furthermore, in Brazilian popular music, the *morro* became not as a place stricken by poverty, but as one where people celebrated despite their woes.

'Rencenceamento', probably recorded in 1939, makes reference to the upcoming 1940 Census; the singer who assumes the voice of a woman from the *favela* speaks of the poverty in the *morro*, but emphasizes the role of music and celebration in making life worthwhile, not altogether without national pride:

...In 1940 in the hills, they began a census count..

...I obey everything that is law
kept quiet and then I said:
-Oh my moreno is Brazilian, he's a rifleman
and he's the type who goes out with the flag from his
  battalion.

...Our house is nothing to boast about
but we live in poverty without owing a cent
We have our *pandeiro*, we have the *cuica* and the *tamborím*
a *reco reco* and *cavaquinho* and a guitar...[75]

Others, such as 'O Imperador do Samba' (The Emperor of Samba),[76] 'Gente Bamba' (Happy People),[77] and 'Deixe Esse Povo Falar' (Let Those People Speak)[78] underscore the importance both of respect for popular music, and the importance of music to the national soul.

'O Imperador do Samba', for example, begins by asking the audience for silence, respect and order because the Emperor and the Empresses will enter. The double meaning is clear: Carnival is fantasy, but an emperor is an emperor and deserves respect. At the same time, the solemn rhythm of this particular samba lends it a seriousness that demands respect for samba music. This theme is repeated in songs like the 1939 recording 'Minha Embaixada Chegou'.[79] Thus poverty notwithstanding, popular music reinforced a patriotic celebration in which national celebration remained central even within a focrum where fantasy reigned. Within this context, similar to the modernist trajectory, blacks and even mulattos continued to be marginalized or presented in static images.

Patriotism, Mestizaje, and the Mulatto

While it is impossible to provide an exhaustive appraisal of all of the popular musical pieces performed and/or recorded which center on the mulatto, an examination of recorded music, particularly by national entertainers who received widespread national attention allows us to understand the national aesthetic, or the forging thereof. Indeed the mulatta's first appearance in musical compositions came prior to the modernist generation. At the turn of the century, even before the advent of radio, Ernesto de Souza's 'Quem inventou o mulato' was the carnival success of 1903.[80] Three years later Arquimedas de Oliveira, with verse by Bastos Tigres popularized the *maxixe* 'Vem cá, mulata', a *tango-chula*.[81] Oliveira's refrain, which implored the mulatta to embrace him: 'Vem cá, mulata/ Não vou la não' (Come here mulata/I'm not going there), projected the mulatta as a symbol of the common people, who the singer encourages (if not commands) to join the Democrats, because of their love for carnival and the common people, rather than for their political commitment.

The use of mulatta instead of mulatto suggested a gendered relationship between political parties and the people, yet what is more significant is the apolitical way in which the singer appealed to her by suggesting that the reason for the embrace is love for popular culture, affirming his right as a legitimate representative of the people. A precursor to Vargas' populism perhaps? In future generations, the lyrics to this song became less important than the title itself which would inspire other compositions, and productions, including a popular magazine.[82]

By the 1930s, descriptions of mulattos and mulattas were common in popular music. Noel Rosa's 1932 samba 'Mulato Bamba',[83] secured the mulatto a place as a national icon for the next decade. The *bamba* was known as an artful musician and dancer who was usually mulatto or black. Yet the bamba's rise as a popular symbol celebrated for his 'natural musical ability' was often juxtaposed against a propensity towards drink, an inability to work, and his inability to settle down as Rosa's composition indicated:

> This strong mulatto
> Is from Salgueiro
> To take a ride in the police car
> That was his sport
> He was born with luck
> and since he was a young boy
> he supported himself playing cards
> He never saw work![84]

In this sense the mulatto was more likely to act as a scapegoat than an escape hatch. The popularity of the vagabond or the *malandro* in popular musical compositions, which came in vogue at the end of the 1920s, implied a desire for order directly preached to the popular classes, as the words to the popular 1929 Franciso Alves recording indicated:

> I put vagrancy aside.
> I don't want to hear anything about it.
> I've begun another life
> because I can't live
> that way anymore...[85]

The nationalist propaganda against chaos and a propensity towards order necessitated a strong stand against *malandragem* and a vilification of the *malandro*, almost always with racial, if not class, overtones. The thirst for work and the willingness to supplicate individuality to the national good was tantamount to state-approved popular musical lyrics.[86]

While the *malandro* became a popular villain of the era, Vargas essentially appropriated the vocabulary of the *malandro* in his discourses to the public. His own images as president often in a suit and wearing the Panama hat was a mixture of the *malandro* and the *caudillo*.[87] At the same time, criticism of the malandro was a way to encourage work and physical exercise in an age when technical manpower and health were seen as key to modernity. Popular music such as Ataulfo Alves e Felisberto Martins' 'O negocio é casar' is typical of this tendency.[88] As was 'Eu Trabalhei' by Roberto Roberti and Jorge Faraj which celebrated work through a worker's voice who exclaimed 'I worked' with pride:

> Today I am happy,
> And I can advise;
> Who does what I used to do
> Can only better himself
> And whoever says that work
> Doesn't gain anyone a shirt
> Is completely wrong! Wrong! Wrong![89]

Vargas, the leader of the nationalist 'popular' revolution was   often referred to as 'the greatest worker'.[90]

Satirical creations also highlighted the mulatto as the national prototype *par excellence* who rejected foreign influences and assumed his *brasilidade*. Such was the case of 'Mulatto Anti-Metropolitano' by Laurindo de Almeida, which described the protagonist as one who '..prefers the morro, forgoes cinema, and has nothing to do with the fox-trot. His is the samba-canção..'[91] The 1935 release of the *marcha*, 'Mulatinho Bamba' (Smart Little Mulatto),[92] emphasized the 'good mulatto' as opposed to the *malandro:*

> Mulatinho Bamba
> Oh mulatto, my little mulatto bamba
> how you distinguish yourself when you samba
>
> In the circle he's a revelation
> When he stamps his feet
> My heart begins to beat
> And he knows how to perform a step
> Dancing with elegance
> To the rhythm
>
> He doesn't walk around armed with a knife
> Nor with a kerchief on his chest
> Nor a straw hat.
> A fine mulatto, he is well-dressed
> He has gestures and attitudes
> of a congressman.
>
> Because of this dear mulatto
> I remain at the window

All day,
When he walks by on the sidewalk
He seems like a Clark Gable...[93]

Here it is important to pay attention to the singer's narrative voice (in this
case Miranda's) which assumed the position of a black or mulatta woman
from the popular classes.   Listeners assumed that the narrator is either
black or mulatta since explicitly assuming the voice of a white women
would have been problematic, and met by some criticism.   Despite racial
democracy rhetoric, Brazil enforced a hierarchy in which inter-racial
marriages still remained taboo.   Blacks with blacks, mulattos with mulattos
and whites with whites.   No recorded song of this period treats the subject
of the inter-racial relationship of a white woman with a black or mulatto
man.

The narrative voice in the 1934 'A Voltar do Samba' (Coming
Back From the Samba), and the 1938 recording of 'Meu Radio e Meu
Mulatto' (My Radio and My Mulatto), further indicate the necessity of
white performers appropriating the voice of mulattos or mulattas in order
to sing stories of the popular classes.

Returning Home From the Samba
Oh God, I feel so tired
after returning from the *batucada*
that I participated in at Praça Onze
I won a bronze harlequin

My sandal's heel broke
And I lost my mulatto there on the pavement

I'm not interested in knowing...
Someone came to tell me
That he found you grieving
With tears in your eyes, crying.
Cry mulatto, my pleasure comes from seeing you suffer
So that you know how much I loved you
And how I suffered to forget you.

You were my friend
And I don't know why
I met you in the circle dancing
with a tambourine in your hand, keeping the beat.
Now mulatto, for you I will not do anything disrespectful
I'm going for revenge and....[94]

The image of the mulatto gained more popularity in the 1930s, thanks to the sensational if not sensual images of Brazil's most successful international author, Jorge Amado, whose first novel, *O País do Carnival* was the first in a series of exotic novels in which mulattos, and sensuality would take center stage. Moreover, his work was an explicit celebration of the mulatta with undeniable traces of misogyny.   Paulo, one of the characters, presents an unpublished poem which apparently sings to the mulatta but in reality exploits a perceived sexuality:

> I sing to the quarreling mulatta
> from Saint Sebastian of Rio de Janeiro.
> The mulatta, the color of cinnamon
> who has traditions
> who has vanity
> who has goodness
> (that goodness that makes her open her
> brown-skinned legs,
> strong,
> serene,
> for the satisfaction of insatiable instincts
> of the poor poets
> and of vagabond students).[95]

The carnival success of 1932, 'Teu Cabelo Não Nega' Your Hair Gives You Away, by the Valença brothers with Larmantino Babo, intensified the scrutiny of the mulatto. 'Teu cabelo', a *marchina*, which Alencar reports 'lends itself to satire, criticism and joking',[96] became one of the most successful carnival hits of all time:

> Your Hair Gives You Away
>
> In these land of Brazil
> Here
> You don't even have to cultivate it
> This land gives
> Black beans, many learned men, and *giribita*
> A lot of beautiful mulattas
>
> The hair gives you away
> Mulatta.
> You are a mulatta through and through
> but since color doesn't stick, mulatta,
> Mulatta,
> All I want is to love you.

You gave me a short-circuit
What a mess!
All the fuses have been blown
Incredible
Mulatta in your body's frame
Intrigue passes through.[97]

This powerful, humorous, and certainly satirical song succeeded in addressing the important issues of race and national identity in Brazil by focusing on Brazil's racial image, Brazil's national aesthetic, and its unique sexuality, all the while employing puns and double entendres. Reinforcing Brazil's image as a carnival country, 'Teu cabelo não nega' urges Brazilians that there is no reason to mourn. Among its natural resources, Brazil has many beautiful mulattas. Stanza two's sardonic political commentary is also intended to be humorous:

The hair gives you away
Mulatta,
You are a mulatta in color
but since color doesn't stick, mulatta,
All I want is your love.

The singer directly urges the mulatta to accept her true identity---that she is not white. At the same time, she cannot assume a black identity because of her light skin, but she is 'a mulatta in color only'. The last line's double meaning suggests that her color did not matter since all the singer wanted was her love. On the other hand, the song implicitly denigrates blackness, and is reminiscent of another Brazilian saying, 'branca pra casar, mulata pra fornicar e preta pra trabalhar' (a white woman is for marriage, a mulatta for fornication, and a black one for work). Here, the narrator is clearly interested in sex. Indeed this song celebrated the uncontrollable sensuality of the mulatta in the closing stanza. In this manner, the mulatta served as a conduit for comment on race and sexuality, while celebrating miscegenation as a national fact.

The mulatta woman's sensuality is also the subject of Ary Barbosa and Luiz Iglesias' duet 'Boneca de Peixe', or 'Fish Doll', recorded by both Aracy Cortes and Augusto Vasseur, and Carmen Miranda and Almirante. The sung dialogue between the male and female roles revealed a tendency towards the sexual objectification of the mulatta and the negra. The male complains that his sexual partners must necessarily be black because he is black, 'I am black and nobody cares about my tastes', white men can choose among many women. The two recorded versions use the euphemistic phrase 'Mas ha muito branco com pinta na testa', literally 'there are many whites who are guilty', but Abel Cardoso reveals that the first version of the song in 1930 contained the line '... mas há muito branco que gosta da fruta', literally 'but there are many whites who love the fruit'. This espression refers to white men who like having sex with non-white women. To the male's worries, the female singer replies that 'there are many Portuguese like that around me', but she quickly adds that she is not able to do anything because she is a 'beautiful mulatta'.[98]

'Boneca de Peixe' draws attention to the unequal power relationship among white men and black and mulatta women in post-abolition Brazil, as well as the predicament of black men. But the fact that the song was recorded twice by white performers (in black face) reveals a deeper level of marginalization of blacks similarly seen in North America, where blacks were prohibited from performing black roles. Unlike in the United States, however, whites seemed comfortable both with assuming black roles, and denouncing racism and prejudice. Brazil had a long history of civil rights rhetoric which can be traced back to the independence leaders who mimicked the French liberal cries of freedom, equality, and brotherhood while maintaining an inhuman system of slavery.

Race relations, as we have seen, was hardly an explicit topic in intellectual circles, nor was it explicit in Brazilian popular music despite the obsession with skin color. One exception, however, was Augusto Vassuer Marques' and Porto Luis Peixoto's 1939 recording 'Preto e Branco',[99] Technically a duet *batuque*, 'Preto e Branco', first recorded by Carmen Miranda (C) and Almirante (A), offers a humorous look at race relations in Brazil while satirizing Brazil's aversion to blackness:

C: They say that those whites of today are angry at all the blacks

A: What is good is black: Black is the Diamond *(Brazilian soccer player)*, and coffee...

C: Black is the 'oiá' of Mary, the wife of St. Joseph...

A: Black is the ink we write with that gives value to the paper...

C: Black is carbon that makes fire and passes through the chimney...

A: To give work to men...

C: And black was St. Benedict in whom whites have so much
      faith...

A: And the mouth of the night is black, like a black man
      from Guiné

C: The snow is sometimes more black than any black woman
      you'll see.
      Black is the hair of the Virgin...

A: And the beard of St. Miguel...

C: The feathers of the goose are Black.

A: Love pains are also.

C: Only whites don't want to be black

A: The Mulattos don't want to either
      But blacks' consolation, let anyone say it,
      Is that God made him white

C: Where was that?

A: In the soles of his feet

C: Very good![100]

Unfortunately, racial humor often came at the expense of blacks. Chapter
two illustrated how intellectuals either marginalized images of blackness or
presented them in stereotypical ways. Popular music followed that lead.
While 'Preto e Branco' begins with a very valid concern, and chronicles
Brazilians aversions to blackness, it contains a list of carefully chosen
associations of blackness which undermines any criticism.

      Stereotyping of blacks and whites in popular music was
widespread. A top 1930 hit, 'O Nego No Samba', first recorded by
Carmen Miranda with the Victor Brazilian Orchestra, praised the natural
ability of blacks to dance and the white's difficulty of acquiring these
'Brazilian talents':

      Black Samba
      Sways the hip
      Black samba
      has *parati* (a type of rum)
      Black Samba, oh oh

always on the beat
Black samba, my sweetheart
makes me crazy

In samba, whites break into pieces
In samba, a good black has a swell time
In samba, whites don't have chance, my good friend
For samba, blacks are born to do it.[101]

As in many sambas pre-dating the Nueva Canção (New Song Movement), these songs were popularly received in a celebratory fashion without a full-examination of their racist implications. In the midst of Brazil's fervent nationalism, black talents were merely explained as innate abilities. How far away from this were the theories of the turn of the century which ascribed given negative qualities to people of African descent?

Carmen Miranda's ascent to the top of the Brazilian musical world by the end of the 1930s provided us with a window into Brazilian racial hegemony. Due to her numerous travels to all corners of Brazil, and the national attention and publicity that she attained, her songs and performances provided some of the first images of Brazilian popular culture which would later be exported to the United States during 'The Good Neighbor Policy'. The image of the 'Bahiana', a black woman from the streets of Salvador, figured prominently in her repertoire after 1939 thanks to compositions by the Bahian Dorival Caymi. 'Que que a Bahiana tem' took Miranda on a path through Bahian (read: black) folklore which would ultimately lead to her appropriation of the black Bahian woman, albeit in platform shoes and excessive corporal fruits in the 1940s.

Not all of the compositions of this period which make reference to blacks or mulattos are stereotypical. 'A Preta do Acarajé', first recorded as a duet with Caymmi and Miranda in 1939 presented aspects of the Bahian folklore in non-stereotypical terms, for example, scenes describing the streets of Salvador at 10 o'clock clockwise, while emphasizing the hard work that blacks often endure to produce something pleasurable for consumption: acarajé, a fried delicacy from Bahia: 'Everyone likes acarajé', but 'no one knows the work it takes to make it'.[102] Taken as a whole, however, images of blacks, even in popular music, remained relatively static during World War II.[103]

Sinval Silva, a favorite composer of Miranda at one point in her career, was acutely aware of the importance of having both a white patron, and another career. Blacks in general, and composers in particular, were not accustomed to making money from their musical compositions or performances. Many sold their compositions cheaply to singers who went on to make a fortune. For this reason Silva always insisted that he was a mechanic. When he received money for his first recording, his father did not believe him. Although Silva felt a loyalty to Miranda until his death in 1994, the truth is that despite his success with her he died almost penniless. Indeed, Silva had earlier appeared before the court requesting to retire early because he was not able to support his family.[104]

Silva's work that focused on blacks' contribution to Brazil attained almost no attention when compared to his Miranda 'hits'. His composition, 'Negro Antilheiro', written with Herivelto Martins, told the story of black Brazilian soldiers who fought for the Allies in World War II, while 'Geme Negro' explored the theme of what can best be called black pride in Brazil. Critics often explain this lack of attention because these sambas were considered *sambas de exaltação*, but glorifying sambas by other composers received unprecedented air time during the Vargas years.[105]

Vargas' dictatorship which began in November of 1937, produced hundreds of laudatory tunes. Indeed the samba de exaltação was the norm, and like the Hollywood musical, Brazilian popular music promoted stereotypical and often uncritical images of Brazilians, particularly of the popular classes, mulattos and blacks. In 1939 Lamartine Babo underscored Brazil' racial democracy in his 'Hino do Carnaval Brasileiro' (Hymn to the Brazilian Carnival):

> All hail to the morena
> -The brown color of gracious Brazil.
> All hail the tambourine
> that comes down from the hills to create a rhythm.
> There are
> There are
> There are
> Five hundred thousand *morenas*.
>
> Blonds, orange-colored one hundred thousand
> Hail them!
> Hail them!
> My Carnival Brazil!
> Hail my sweet blond!
> Of green eyes-the color of our forest
> All hail the mulatta
> The color of coffee-our great product
> There are
> There are

There are
There are
Five hundred thousand *morenas*.
Blonds- orange - colored one hundred thousand
My carnival
Brazil![106]

Despite the underlying multi-colored patriotism of this song, conspicuously absent is a celebration of blacks. Many thousands of blondes, mulattas and *morenas*, but not one black. The essentialist rhetoric that affirmed that Brazilians were of 'a *morena* color', or 'orange white', displaced blackness from the discourse on national identity. Moreover, *brasilidade* was equated with the great Brazilian productions minus the black.

One of the first black women to be featured as a protagonist of the samba was in the 1942 hit 'Nega do cabelo duro'. This *batucada* by Rubens Soares and David Nasser, recorded by the group Anjos do Inferno, satirized a black woman 'who had weedy hair' (cabelo encapinhado) and who often goes to great length to hide it:

Hard-haired black woman,
Which comb do you use to comb your hair?
Which comb do you use to comb your hair?

When you enter the circle
Your body moves like a serpent...
Your hair is now fashionable.
Which comb do you use to comb your hair?

Your permanent hair,
Something from a mermaid,
And the people ask
Which comb do you use to comb your hair?

If you use a hot iron
It doesn't go to pieces in the sand,
You go swimming in Botafogo,
Which comb do you use to come your hair?[107]

That same year Ary Barroso's 'Aquarela do Brasil' reinforced the gaiety of Brazil with stanzas such as 'Esse Brasil lindo e trigueiro/E o meu Brasil brasileiro/Terra de samba e pandeiro', (That Brazil, beautiful and wheat-colored? It is my Brazilian Brazil/ Land of the samba and of the tambourine). Popular music had become a transforming vehicle for enforcing civil sentiments and identification with 'the national'.

Conclusion

Popular Brazilian music dominated the means of communication throughout the duration of Vargas' tenure as president of Brazil, 1930-1945. It was in perfect harmony, as José Ramos Tinhorão has indicated, with the nationalist political economic program, which enhanced Brazil's internal market production, and its cultural production. Music served as propaganda long before the Vargas era, but it was Vargas, Brazil's most effective nationalist, who was able to propagate and encourage a sense of national unity and celebration but with clear social and racial heirarchies). Heitor Villa-Lobos' *A Música Nacionalista no Governo Getúlio Vargas* indicated the states' understanding of music as a means through which to cultivate civic pride.[108]

Civic pride under the rubric of nationalism provided Brazilians of all walks of life with positive reinforcement of *brasilidade* in a modern era: a Brazil strong, unified, and unique, without the racial problems of the United States and Europe.

Nationalism thus had two faces--consolidation within and projection abroad. It was no coincidence that as the Vargas administration carefully moved to nationalize popular music and establish a middle class aesthetic through programs such as 'A Hora do Brasil', it encouraged full and complete use of the radio waves, film and recording to promote popular Brazilian music abroad.[109]

This middle class aesthetic meant the slow appropriation and transformation of tunes of the morro, and this meant selecting white performers to represent Brazil in national forums and abroad. Hence the emergence and promotion of talented white performers such as Carmen Miranda and the members of the Banda da Lua,[110] all of whom received the official blessing of Getúlio Vargas before they left for the United States in 1939. It is important to understand that the Vargas administration did not initiate this whitening but merely institutionalized a process which was occurring in all sectors of Brazilian society from the turn of the century to the end of World War II. Understandably, this whitening process in the popular sphere did not mirror Brazilian Aryanist thought promoted by intellectuals at the turn of the century. This chapter has indicated that the content of much of the popular music which focused on race and nationality maintained and celebrated images of cultural unity and miscegenation. The aesthetic bias would not be addressed until the emergence of the understudied and underestimated Experimental Black Theater by Ruth de Souza and Abdias do Nascimento in the late 1940s.

In 1946, in the wake of Vargas' resignation from the presidential office, the focus on mulattos continued in popular music, as Pereira Mattos and Felisberto Martin's song 'Mulata: Rainha do Meu Carnival' indicated:

> Mulatta, Queen of my Samba,
> Queen of my carnival,
> Mulatta if you were mine
> Although a little burnt,
> It wouldn't be so bad.
>
> I've already scorned a pretty little blond girl
> I've already scorned an infernal morena
> Only because I want to choose you, oh mulatta
> Queen of my carnival.[111]

Or João de Barro's and Antônio Almeida's 1948 classic, 'A Mulata é a Tal' which has been recorded by several contemporary artists including Caetano Veloso:

> White is white
> Black is black
> But the mulatta is the special one.
> She is the special one.
> When she passes, everyone shouts
> I'm there with you in the pan
> When she moves with her perfect figure
> I clap and beg! (repeat)
>
> Oh mulatta, the color of cinnamon
> Praise, praise, praise, praise, praise her![112]

While the celebration of mulattos and mulattas continued with essentialist fervor, blackness continued to be marginalized, humored, or avoided altogether as the 1946 carnival hit 'Bom Crioulo' attests: 'O bom crioulo dança bem' (The Good Creole Dances Well),[113] or as countless others, including 'Tem nego bebo aí' (There's A Drunken Black Man There), both sung by Carmen Costa, one of the few black radio performers that emerged in the 1940s.[114] The aversion to blackness underscored in Carmen Miranda's 1930s song 'Branco and Preto', continues to be a contemporary issue as recordings such as Gilberto Gil and Caetano Veloso's 'Haiti' (1995) reveal.

Racial democracy, as Michael Hanchard reveals, has been so pervasive as a hegemonic ideology that we can no longer continue only to debunk it; we must also show the myriad of ways that it has inhibited the emergence of an authentic expression of blackness. The denial of blackness and positive non-stereotypic expression in popular music also stymied a sense of *negritude* in an area of Brazilian popular culture which was influenced, if not created, largely by blacks. The mulatto as a middle ground between black and white has only served to reinforce the racial hierarchy in which whites dominate and blacks are ruled.

On the other hand, it is important to recognize the importance of white intellectuals, politicians, and performers such as Freyre, Vargas, and Miranda respectively who were among the first to challenge notions of the inferiority of Brazilians, and to celebrate Brazil's cultural heritage openly. As cultural populists do, they sought to represent the common people and in the process appropriated popular symbols as their own. The relationship between national music and the themes and issues presented throughout the national media was determined largely through a complicated relationship among a generations' acutely patriotic world view, historic events which influenced musicians, and a state interested in promoting views shared by an elite group of politicians and intellectuals.

Throughout Vargas' tenure as state leader, the Ministry of Education received a myriad of compositions as gifts from loyal, but not entirely disinterested, followers. Augusto Ramão, for example, composed 'Hino a Getúlio Vargas' in 1939 which bore the epigraph 'Brazil deposits its faith and its hope in the Leader of the Nation'. Manuel and Apecina do Carmo's 'Hymn to the Estado Novo', created to be sung in secondary schools in São Paulo, was a beautiful piece of propaganda created without state direction. Other compositions dedicated to the president described and celebrated specific political events from 'The 10th of November' to the 'Revolution of 1930'.[115]

The cover of Jairio Severiano's bibliographic compilation *Getúlio Vargas e a Música Popular Brasileira* reproduces a caricature from *Caretas* which best depicts the relationship of the state to the nation, and the role of race within. In the drawing, Vargas stands on a dais near a microphone as he conducts the orchestra, symbolizing a nation that has come together to create music. But who comprised the orchestra? Three male musicians: A black man from the favela playing the tambourine, dressed in a typical malandro outfit with a hat which bears the legend 'Champion of the Hill'; in the middle sits a young white man whose instrument cannot be determined, but whose hat identifies him as a member of the 'progressive' bourgeois class, and to the far right playing passionately on his violin stands the 'gran fino', a white gentleman dressed in a black suit.[116]

Blacks constituted an essential but predetermined part of the orchestra. All played to the directions of the conductor, apparently producing a harmonious tune.   The one-dimensional image, however, ignored deeper divisions based on the cultural, economic, and social baggage that each performer brought to the performance.   Moreover the viewer is oblivious to the power relations among the participants.

Popular music, samba in particular, along with Brazilian soccer are often cited by scholars as examples of Brazilian racial tolerance.   Samba and soccer often represent manifestations of social intermingling in the Brazilian public sphere or what anthropologist Roberto Da Matta has called *o codigo da rua.*   While Da Matta and others have seen these popular national forums as positive expressions of citizenship, they have not always been historically so.   Before the 1950s, blacks never played crucial role in the organization, promotion or propagation of these national icons. Blackness and black contribution were included in a corporatist manner as one element of a larger Brazilian melting pot, even in instances where that contribution was undeniable.   More often than not nationalists avoided associating an ethnic identity with *brasilidade*, although in practice this meant that white values predominated.

Notes

[1] Karl Mannehiem, *Man and Society in the Age of Reconstruction* New York: Harvest Books, 1935), 5, 15, 222.

[2] Robert Levine's periodization differs slightly in 'Esporte e Sociedade: O caso do futebol brasileiro', *Futebol e Cultura Coletânea de Estudos* (São Paulo, 1982), 21-43. An English version of this article, 'Sport and Society: The Case of Brazilian Football', appeared in *The Luso-Brazilian Review* (Vol. 17, No. 2 Winter 1980), 223-252. Utilizing Charles Miller as a focal point, Levine's first era develops from 1894-1904, the second begins with the foundation of the Metropolitan Football League until the institutionalization of foot-ball as a professional sport, 1905-1933, and finally the period of national expansion from 1933 until the completion of the Maracanã Stadium in 1950.

[3] References to the practice of football in Brazil between 1870 and 1890 abound. As early as 1872, students at the College São Luís played the game under the supervision of Catholic priests who ran the school in Itu, São Paulo.   British sailors docking in various ports often played the game during their leisure time, including in Recife and Porto Alegre.   Various sources report the English playing the game on Gloria beach in Rio de Janeiro in 1874, British workers organizing impromptu games, in Sao Paulo in the early 1880, sailors playing in front of the Guanabara Palace in Rio, and capuchin monks in Nova Friburgo, Rio de Janeiro State.   Lois Baena Cunha in his *A Verdadeira História do Futebol Brasileiro* adds that English workers practiced the sport in Belém do Pará at the site which is now the Praça Batista Campos.

[4] Among the scholars who have examined the social history of Brazilian football

are Lois Baena Cunha, *A Verdadeira História do Futebol Brasileiro* (Rio de Janeiro: Edicão Rua Araúja, 1994), 1-2. Mário Filho, *O Negro no Futebol Brasileiro* (Editôra Civilização Brasileira, 1964). Tomás Mazzoni, *Historia do Futebol no Brasil* (São Paulo, 1950). Joel Rufino dos Santos, *Historia política do futebol brasileiro* (São Paulo: Brasiliense, 1981).

[5]   Joel Rufino dos Santos makes a connection between the growth of the popular classes from 1904-1917, workers' strikes and growth of football as entertainment, 21-22. In the nineteenth century, many believed capoeira to be an uncivilized activity that had to be restricted. The penal code of 1890 severely restricted *capoeira* as one of the many offenses against public order. See João Lyra Filho, *Introducão à Sociologia dos Desportos* (São Paulo, 1974), 332 and Thomas H. Halloway, *Policing Rio de Janeiro: Repression and Resistance in a 19th Century City* (Stanford, 1993).

[6]   See Luiz Edmundo, *O Rio de Janeiro de meu tempo* (Rio de Janeiro: Imprensa Nacional, 1938).

[7]   Luiz Edmundo, *O Rio de Janeiro de meu tiempo* (Rio de Janeiro: Imprensa Nacional, 1938), see Vol. I, 82. Peter C. McIntosh, *Physical Education in England Since 1800* (London: G. Bell and Son Ltd, 1968), 38-43. For information related specifically to football in Great Britain, see Percy Marshall Yong, *A History of British Football* (London, 1968). Lima Barreto, 'O Football', *Careta* (Rio de Janeiro) August 1, 1892.

[8]   Joel Rufino dos Santos, *Historia política do futebol brasileiro* (1981), 14.

[9]   Members included William Fox Rule, J.T. Sadler, Percy W. Crew, J. Robottom, W. Jeffrey, G.H. Ford, W. Holland, R. Duff, H.J. Boyes, F.H. Robinson, F.H. Hodgkiss, N. Biddell, F.M. Ewan, H.W. Wright, P. Mantandon, C. Holland, C. P. Tomkins.

[10] Ibid, 17.

[11] Mario Filho, 6. Cricket was a different story and much more of an elite sport. Not even white Brazilians could dare participate.

[12] dos Santos, 21-22.

[13] dos Santos, 18-19.

[14] Rio's Américas and Vasco da Gama were two of the first middle class teams to sign on black players. In 1923, Vasco's racially mixed squad won the city's championship causing criticism among many, but increased their popular following.

[15] Gilberto Freyre, *Novo Mundo nos Trópicos* (São Paulo: Cia Ed. Nacional/EDUSP, 1971), 97.

[16] Filho, 5 and 213. Levine reports, however, that as late as 1958, Brazilian officials hesitated in placing players like Pelé and Garrincha during the legendary world cup match which Brazil eventually won.

[17] Orlando Ferreira, *Forja de Anões*. (São Paulo: Imprensa Gráfica da Revista dos Tribunais, 1940), 70-85, 99.

[18] Michael Roberts, 'The Vicarious Heroism of the Sports Spectator', *New Republic* (23 November 1974): 17.

[19] Ministry of Education, Department of Education, Folder 188 (1939),

Presidencia da República, Brazilian National Archive, Rio.

[20] Americo Brazilio Silvado, 'Dois Discursos Contra A Educação Militar', Presidencia da Republica, Folder 30 Ministerio da Educação e Saude Pública (1932), Brazilian National Archives, Rio.

[21] Miguel Lardies, *Coletânea de leis e regulamentos dos desportes* (6th edition) (Porto Alegre: Edicão Sulina, 1971), 27. Law Decree No. 3, 199 (April 14, 1941) established the structure for building Sports centers.

[22] Rufino dos Santos, 48-51. See also FIFA, *1904-1984: Historical Publication of the Federation Internationale de Football Association* (1984).

[23] João Máximo and Marcos de Castro eds., *Gigantes do futebol brasileiro* (Rio de Janeiro: Lidador, 1965), 50. Originally printed in the Barcelona newspaper, *El Diluvio*.

[24] Máximo and Castro, 51.

[25] Levine, 'Sport and Society The Case of Brazilian Football', appeared in *The Luso-Brazilian Review* (Vol. 17, No. 2 Winter 1980), 239.

[26] Robert Levine, 'Esporte e Sociedade: O caso do futebol Brasileiro', 27.

[27] Marcos de Castro, 'Leônidas', Gigantes de futebol brasileiro', Marcos de Castro and João Máximo ed. (Rio de Janeiro: Lidador, 1965), 114-121.

[28] Joel Ruffino dos Santos, 53.

[29] quoted from 'Sociologia' Vol. II, 375 in Mario Filho, 244.

[30] Afrânio Peixoto, 'Deporto e Disciplina', *Sports* (Rio de Janeiro) Vol. I, No. 1 (6, August 1915).

[31] Peter Wade, 'Black Music and Cultural Syncretism in Columbia', *Slavery and Beyond: The African Impact on Latin America and the Caribbean* Darién J. Davis ed. (Wilmington, Delaware: Scholarly Resources, 1995): 121-127.

[32] A national competition for a republican anthem took place on January 20, 1990 in the Teatro Lírico in Rio de Janeiro, D.F. While composers such as Francisco Braga and Leopoldo Migues, among others produced beautiful scores, the public opted for Manuel da Silva's old National Hymn, which was adopted by the republic by Decree, No. 171 on January 20, 1890.

[33] 'Decreto-Lei' No. 4. 545 of July 31, 1942, reprinted in Instituto Nacional de Estudos Pedagogicos (INEP), Música para a escola elementar (Rio de Janeiro, 1955), 15-16.

[34] National Anthem reprinted, 28.   The National Flag song composed by Francisco Braga (1868-?), and based on a poem by Olavo Bilac (1865-1918) follows a similar theme of praise of Brazilian land and people.

[35] 'Himno da Proclamação da República dos Estados Unidos do Brasil' original:
'Nós nem cremos que escravos outrora
Tenha havido em tão nobre pais...
Hoje o rubro lampejo da aurora
Acha irmão, nos tiranos hostis

Somos todos iguais ao futuro
Saberemos, unidos, levar
Nosso augusto estandarte que, puro
Brilha ovante, da Patria no altar

Liberdade! Liberdade!
Abre as asas sôbre nós!
Das lutas na tempestade
Dá que ouçamos tua voz
[36]   José Ramos Tinhorão, *A história social da música popular brasileira* Lisboa: Editorial Caminho, S.A., 1990), 233-234.
[37]   See Erika Franziska Herd, 'O radio: o amigo da madrugada', Masters thesis, Escola de Comunicação da Universidade Federal do Rio de Janeiro, 1976.
[38]   Alberto Ribeiro da Silva, 74.
[39]   'As Emissoras Mais Ouvidas no Rio', *Rádio Revista* Edição Comemorativa do Museu da Imagem e do Som (October 1985), 8.
[40]   See *Revista da Semana* March 21, 1936 and Febraury 15, 1936.
[41]   For information on Rádio Nacional see Carlos Saroldi and Sonia Virginia Moreira, *Rádio Nacional: O Brasil em Sintonia* (Rio de Janeiro: Instituto Nacional da Música, 1984).
[42]   Alberto Ribeiro da Silva, 45.
[43]   Silvian Goulart, 26 Note 14.
[44]   Júlio Barata to Lourival Fontes, February 29, 1940, Departamento de Imprensa e Propaganda, Presidência da República, Lata 510, Brazilian National Archives, Rio.
[45]   Departamento de Imprensa e Propaganda, 'Relatório' 1941, Presidência da República, Lata 510, Brazilian National Archives, Rio.   The Vargas administration made a strong effort to establish liaisons with internationals enterprises, but so did enterprises in the United States, particularly during the Good Neighbor Policy, 1933-1947.   In 1944, for example, Secretary of the National and Inter-American Music week Committee wrote a letter to Verges asking for support for a week of festivities in celebration of hemispheric music.
[46]   Claus Schreiner, 92-94.
[47]   Franciso Alves, *Minha Vida* (Rio de Janeiro: Brasil Contemporaneo, 1937), 86.
[48]   Heloisa Paulo, *Estado Novo e Propaganda em Portugal e no Brasil*.   The Portuguese original reads 'Se veio ao mundo, foi Deus quem quis./O timoneiro que está no leme do meu país/E para que siga o rumo certo, meu Brasil./Deus que lhe dê muitos dezenove de Abril'.
[49]   Gil Montero, 121.
[50]   Created in 1931, 'A Hora do Brasil' ('Brazil's Hour') served as one of the many official forums for the promotion of brasilidade.   After 1939, Brazil's came under the jurisdiction of the newly created Department of Printing and Propaganda.
[51]   See Sérgio Cabral, *Ensaios de opinião* in which there is an essay entitled 'Getúlio Vargas e a musica popular brasileira'(Editora Inúbia, RJ, 1st edition, 1975).
[52]   Citing the 'Relatorio do DIP-1941', Alberto Ribeiro da Silva reported the number of radio programs submitted to be modified and the number of musical compositions.   In 1941, for example, the DIP censured 2,971 programs and 9,363 musical compositions (mostly the lyrics).

[53] The *samba de exaltação* encouraged a glorification of Brazil and included such classics as 'Aquarela do Brasil', 'Canta Brasil', 'Terra de Ouro', 'Desperta Brasil', and 'Viva o Meu Brasil'. See HMB027, 'Samba de Exaltação', Museu da Imagem e do Som, Rio de Janeiro.

[54] Manuel and Aplecina do Carmo, 'Himno do Estado Novo' Aplecina do Carmo to Getulio Vargas, September 24, 1938, 'Agência Nacional', Folder 123, Ministry of Education and Public Health (1938), Arquivo Nacional, Rio de Janeiro.

[55] Gustavo Capanema to Getulio Vargas, November 11, 1938, 'Agência Nacional', Folder 123, Ministry of Education and Public Health (1938), Arquivo Nacional, Rio de Janeiro.

[56] Amaro Corrêa to Getúlio Vargas, January 18, 1938, 'Agência Nacional', Folder 109, Ministry of Education and Public Health (1938), Arquivo Nacional, Rio de Janeiro.

[57] Pequeno Edison to Getúlio Vargas, September 22, 1938, 'Agência Nacional', Folder 109, Ministry of Education and Public Health (1939), Arquivo Nacional, Rio de Janeiro. Compositions such as these were often accompanied by requests for monetary aid, a job, or funds to buy musical instruments.

[58] This Sociedade known as SBAT was another official intellectual organization which supported, if only tacitly Vargas' nationalist trajectory.

[59] Ary Barbosa, 'Aquarela do Brazil', (1939), HMBO27 Museu da Imagem e Do Som, Rio. English translation from Claus Schreiner, 113-114.

[60] Gil Montero, 70.

[61] 'Carmen Miranda: The Brazilian Fireball', (SH114) Sussex, England: World Record Club, 1982, Side 1, No. 5.

[62] Carmen Miranda (New York University Library), 'Eu Gosto da Minha Terra' (3/30), Band 8. Original Portuguese:
Deste Brasil tão formoso
eu filha sou, vivo feliz
tenho orgulho da raça
da gente pura de meu país
Sou brasileira, reparem
no meu olhar, que ele diz
E o meu sambar denuncia
que eu filha sou deste país

Sou brasileira, tenho feitiço
Gosto do samba, nasci para isso
O fox-trot não se compara
com o nosso samba, que é coisa rara
Eu sei dizer como ninguém
toda a beleza que o samba tem
Sou brasileira, vivo feliz
Gosto das coisas do meu país

Eu gosto da minha terra
e quero sempre viver aqui

Ver o Cruzeiro tão lindo
do céu da terra onde eu nasci
Lá fora descompassado
o samba perde o valor
Que eu fique na minha terra

[63]   Paulo Brabosa e Vicente Paiva.
        A minha caminha verde
        Já chegou de Portugal
        Vamos todos minha gente
        Festejar o caranaval

        Sai Manuel mais a Maria
        Nos três dias de folia
        Pierrô e Colombina
        Pai João e Negra Mina
        O vovô já me dizia
        No Brasil há alegria
        Desde o tempo de Cabral
        Que existe o carnaval.

[64]   Reprinted in Jairo Severiano *Getúlio Vargas e a Música Popular Brasileira*
        (Rio de Janeiro: Fundação Getúlio Vargas/ CPDOC, 1982), 34.

[65]   Ibid, 29.

[66]   Original Portuguese:
        Brazil que foi senzala
        Dançou na macumba batendo o pé no chão
        E bom que não te esqueças nunca
        que a dança agora é no salão

        Brazil deixa a favela
        O arranha-céu é o que recomenda
        E é pena que muita gente boa
        te querendo tanto e tanto não te compreenda

[67]   'Adeus! Adeus! Meu pandeiro do samba
        tamborím de bamba, já é de madrugada...
        Vou-me embora chorando, com o meu coração sorrindo
        E vou deixar todo mundo valorizando a batucada'

[68]   A Lei da Segurança approved on April 4, 1935 was first used to censure the
        leftist newspaper *A Pátria*.

[69]   Recorded September 9, 1936.

[70]   Written in 1943, 'Praça Onze': 'Vão acabar com Praça Onze/Não vai haver
        mais/Escola de Samba, não vai/Chora o tamborim/Chora o morro
        inteiro/Favela, Salgueiro/Mangueira, Estação Primeira/Guardai os vossos
        pandeiros, guardai/ Porque a Escola de Samba sai/Adeus minha Praça Onze,
        adeus/Já sabemos que vais desaparecer/Leva contigo a nossa Recordação/ Mas
        ficarás eternamente em nosso coração/E algum dia nova Praça nós teremos/E o
        teu passado cantaremos'. Heriveto Martins's samba 'Laurindo' tells the tale of

a man who wakes up the morro with tales that 'Praça Onze still existed'. The people travel to the *morro* in the hopes of creating samba, only they find all along that he has duped then, needless to say, they return. Another samba (written in 1944) by Haroldo Lobo and Cristovam de Alencar, 'Bom Dia Avenida' welcomes 'Avenida Rio Branco, but nonetheless declared 'Só quem viu a Praça Onze/Acabar tem direito à Avenida/ Em primeiro lugar'.

[71] Alsion Raphael, 'From Popular Culture to Micro enterprise: The History of the Brazilian Samba Schools', *Latin American Music Review*, Vol. 11, no. 1 (June 1990): 73-83.

[72] Ibid. For a more complete history of the *escolas de samba* see Sergio Cabral, *As Escolas de Samba-Quê, Quem, Como e Porquê* Rio de Janeiro: Fontana, 1974.

[73] September 9, 1936.

[74] For a reproduction of this original tune see the CD *Revivendo Noel Rosa* with Mário Reis and Aracy Almeida, 'X do Problema', Revivendo Músicas Comércio de Discos, Ltd, (Track 6). Orginal Portuguese verses quoted: 'Nasci no Esteacio/Não posso mudar minha massa de sangue/Você pode crêr que palmeira do Mangue/na areia de Copacabana'.

[75] Assis Valente, 'Recenseamento' originally recorded in 1940 by Odeon can also be found on the CD *Carmen Miranda: The Brazilian Recordings* (West Sussex: Harlequim, 1993, song number 12.

[76] Waldem M. Da Silva, 1937. This song refers to the carnival practice of crowning Emperrors and Empresses of the Hoy Spirit.

[77] Written by Synval Silva.

[78] Arlindo Marques Jr. and Roberto Roberts.

[79] 'Carmen Miranda: The Brazilian Recordings' (West Sussex: Harlequim, 1993, song number 12. by Assis Valente (probably recorded in 1939).

[80] Edigar de Alencar, *O carnaval carioca através da música* 5 ed. (São Paulo, Franciso Alves, 1985), 92.

[81] Ibid, 98.

[82] Words to 'Vem cá mulata' cited in Edigar de Alencar, 98. The respected actress Maria Lino would cause a scandal in her debút of this *maxixe* since the dance was considered obscene and inappropriate for public performance.

[83] popularized by Mário Reis (recorded on July 7, 1932).

[84] Letter to music of Noel Rosa from CD *Revivendo Noel Rosa* by Mário Reis and Aracy de Almeida (Comércio de Discos).

Esse mulato forte
é do Salguiero
Passear no tintureiro
era o seu sporte
ja nasceu com sorte!
e desde pirralho
vive a custa do baralho
Nunca viu trabalho!

E quando tira o samba

e novidade
Quer no morro ou na cidade
Ele sempre foi o bamba
As morenas do lugar
Vivem a se lamentar
por saber ele não quer
se apaixonar por mulher

O mulato e do fato
e sabe fazer frente
a qualquer valente
Mas não quer saber de fita
nem com mulher bonita

Sei que ele anda agora
aborrecido
porque vive perseguido
sempre, a toda hora
Ele vai se embora
para se livrar
do feitiço e do azar
das morenas de lá
Eu sei que o morro inteiro vai sentir
Quando o mulato partir
Dando adeus para o Salgueiro
As morenas vão chorar
Vão pedir pra ele voltar
E ele então diz com desdém
Quem tudo quer nada tem!

[85] Franciso Alves, 'A vadiagem' 1929: A vadiagem eu dexei/Não quero mais saber/ arranjei outra vida/Porque deste modo/Não se pode mais viver.....

[86] Cláudia Neiva de Matos, *Acertei no milhar: malandragem e samba no tempo de Getúlio* (Rio de Janeiro: Paz e Terra, 1982), 158-159. On this topic see Sérgio Cabral, *Getúlio Vargas e a música popular brasilera: ensaios e opinião* (1975), 40. Wislon Batista and Ataulpho Alves' samba 'O Bonde São Januário' is often cited to indicate the extent to which the regime often changed lyrics and meaning. The original which apparently focused on unsocial behavior was changed to promote work when it was finally recorded in 1940.

[87] Heloisa Paulo, *Estado Novo e Propaganda em Portugal e no Brasil*, 65.

[88] Originally recorded in 1941, the lyrics are partially reproduced in Silvana Goulart, *Sob A Verdade Oficial. Ideologia, Propaganda e Censura no Estado Novo* (São Paulo: Editora Marco Zero, 1990), 21.

[89] Recorded in 1941, reprinted in Alencar, 286. 'Eu hoje sou feliz,/E posso aconselhar;/Quem faz o que eu já fiz/Só pode melhorar../E quem diz que o trabalho/Não dá camisa a ninguém/Não tem Razão. Não tem. Não tem'.

[90] Martins Castelo, 'O samba e o conceito de trabalho', *Cultura e Política* 2 (22) 1942: 174. Silvano Goulart, *Sob a verdade oficial*, 23.

[91] Laurindo de Almeida, 'Mulato Anti-Metropolitano' recorded in April 1939. Lyrics reproduced in Abel Cardoso Junior, *Carmen Miranda: a cantora do Brasil* (1978), 457.

[92] Written and composed by Ary Barboso-Kid Pepe with the Victor Band 'Diabo do Céu'.

[93] Ibid.

Mulatinho Bamba
ô mulato mulatinho bamba
como desacata quando samba

Na roda é uma revelação
Quando ele bate o pé
bate o meu coração
E sabe decidir um passo
sambando com elegância
dentro do compasso

Não anda armado de navalha
nem lenço no pescoço
nem chapéu de palha
Mulato fino é alinhado
tem gestos e atitudes
de um deputado

Por causa deste mulatinho
eu fico na janela
o dia inteirinho
Quando ele passsa na calçada
parece o Clark Gable
em 'Acorrentada'

[94] O Deus, eu me acho tão cansada
ao voltar da batucada
que tomei parte lá na Praça Onze
Ganhei no samba um alerquim de bronze

Minha sandália quebrou o salto
e eu perdi o meu mulato lá no asfalto

Eu não me interessei saber
Alguem veio me dizer
que encontou você se lastimando
com lágrimas nos olhos, chorando
Chora, mulato, meu prazer é de te ver sofrer
para saber quanto eu te amei
e quanto eu sofri para te esquecer
Eu tive amizade a você
Eu mesmo não sei por quê...
Eu conheci você na roda sambando

com o tamborím na mão, marcando
Agora, mulato, por você não faço desacato
Eu vou a forra e comigo tem (ora se tem)
ou este ano ou pro ano que vem....

[95] Jorge Amado, *O Pais do Carnaval* (São Paulo: Martins, 1931), 28-29. Original poem:
'Eu canto a mulata dos freges
de São Sebastião do Rio de Janeiro...
A mulata cor de canela
que tem tradições,
que tem vaidade,
que tem bondade,
(essa bondade que faz que ela abra
as suas Coxas morenas,
fortes,
serenas,
para a satisfacão dos instintos insatisfeitos
dos poetas pobres
e estudantes vagabundos'

[96] Alencar, 210.

[97] 'Carnaval de 1932', HMC011, Museu da Imagen e do Som, Rio de Janeiro, Brasil. Portuguese original:
Nestas terras do Brasil
Aquí
Não precisa mais prantá (Mourn)
Qui dá
Feijão muito doutô e giribita
Muito mulata bonita

O teu cabelo não nega (The hair gives you away)
Mulata
Que tu és mulata na cor (that you are a mulata through and through)
Mas como a cor não pega (but since color doesn't stick mulata)
Mulata
Mulata eu quero o teu amor (All I want is to love you)
Me deste um curto-curcuito
Que bruito
Que inté queimou-se os fusíveis
Incríveis
Mulata nos teus dois quadros de fama
Passa a corrente da 'Trama'

[98] Abel Cardoso, 438-440 *Carmen Miranda* (1996), CD #4, track 15.

[99] The original recording of May 2, 1939 can be found on the remasterized disc 'Carmen Miranda: The Brazilian Recordings' (West Sussex: Harlequim, 1993), song number 10. 'Preto e Branco' was recorded by Aracy Côrtes in 1930.

[100] The duet included Carmen Miranda (C) and Almirante (A).
C: 'Diz que esses branco de agora tem raiva dos pretos inté

A: Pois ôio que é bom é preto, preto é o diamante e o café

C: Preto é o oiá de Maria, esposa de São José

A: Preto é a tinta que escreve e dá valô ao papé

C: Preto é o carvão que faz fogo e sai pela chaminé

A: P'ra dá trabaio p'ros hôme assustentá as muié

C: E preto foi São Benidito a quem os brancos faz tanto fé

A: A boca da noite é preta, como preto da Guiné

C: A neve às veis é mais preta que uma preta quarqué
    Preto é os cabelo da Virge

A: E as barba de São Migué

C: As pena do ganso é Preta

A: Pena de amô tambem é

C: E só branco não qué sê preto

A: Mulato tambem não quer
    Mas o consolo dos pretos, deixa falá quem quisé
    E que Deus faz ele branco

C: Onde que foi?

A: Mas foi na sola do pé

C: Muito bem!'
[101] Ibid.
Samba de nêgo
quebra os quadri
Samba de nêgo
tem parati
Samba de nêgo, oi, oi
sempre na ponta
Samba de nêgo, meu bem
me deixa tonta

Num samba, branco se escangaia
Num samba, nego bom se espaia
Num samba, branco não tem jeito, meu bem
Num samba, nêgo nasce feito
[102] Almir Chediak, *Songbook: Doryval Caymmi* (Rio de Janeiro: Lumiar Editora, 1994), 48. The original recording can be found on the remasterized disc 'Carmen Miranda: The Brazilian Recordings' (West Sussex: Harlequim, 1993).

[103] 'Carmen Trata a Seu Público Como Uma Imensa Família', *Diário da Noite* (Rio) August 9, 1955 File 'Carmen Miranda', Museu da Imagen e Som, Rio.

[104] Folder 'Synval Silva', Museu da Imagem e Do Som, Rio. Interview with family Silva, February 13, 1997, Rio de Janeiro.

[105] Folder 'Synval Silva', Museu da Imagem e Do Som, Rio. Interview with family Silva, February 13, 1997, Rio de Janeiro.

[106] Lamartine Babo, 'O Himno do Carnaval Brasiliero', 1939 (lyrics reprinted in Alencar, 269).

Salve a morena
-A cor morena do Brasil fagueiro
Salve a pandeiro
Que desce o morro pra fazer a marcação...
São
São
São
Quinhentas mil morenas!

Louras cor de laranja cem mil...
Salve!
Salve!
Meu carnaval Brasil!
Salve a lourinha!
Dos olhos verdes-cor da nossa mata...
Salve a mulata!
Cor do café- a nossa grande produção!
São
São
São
São
Quinhentas mil morenas
Louras-cor de laranja cem mil...
Salve!
Salve!
Meu carnaval
Brasil!

[107] Alencar, p. 295.
'Negra do Cabelo Duro' original Portuguese:

'Nega de cabelo duro
Qual é o pente que te penteia?
Qual é o pente que te penteia?

Quando tu entras na roda
o teu corpo serpenteia...
Teu cabelo está na moda:
Qual é o pente que te penteia?

Teu cabelo permanante,
Qualquer coisa de sereia

E a pergunta sai da gente:
Qual é o pente que te penteia?
Misampli a ferro fogo
Não desmacha nem na areia
Tomas banho em Botafogo,
Qual é o pente que te penteia?

[108] Heitor Vila-Lobos, *A Música Nacionalista no Governo Getúlio Vargas* (Rio de Janeiro: Departamento de Imprensa e Propganda (DIP), n/a. (Reprint copy, Ministry of Culture, Rio de Janeiro).

[109] Tinhorão reports that Vargas even authorized the transmission of a Brazilian music program via short waves to the Germans, not to tout racial democracy but as a way of asserting Brazilian independence form United States' demands.

[110] One of the members of the band was black.

[111] Lyrics reprinted in Loris Rocha Pererira, *Velhos Carnavais* (São Paulo: Câmara Brasileira do Livro, 1994), 36.

Mulata, Deusa do meu samba
Rainha do meu carnaval
Mulata, se tu fosses minha,
Mesmo queimadinha
Não fazia mal

Já desprezei uma lourinha bonita
Já desprezei uma morena infernal
Só porque eu quero te eleger, oh mulata
Rainha do meu Carnaval

[112] Loris Rocha Pererira, 53.

[113] Ibid, 53.

[114] For information on Carmen Costa see João Carlos Viegas, Carmen Costa: Uma Cantora do Rádio (Rio de Janeiro: Editora Revan, 1991).

[115] Ministro da Educação e Saude Pública, Departamento de Educação, Folder 188 (1939), Brazilian National Archive, Rio.

[116] Jairo Severiano, *Getúlio Vargas e a Música Popular Brasileira* (Rio de Janeiro: Fundação Getúlio Vargas/CPDOC, 1982), cover.

5. Afro-Brazilians and Civil Rights: Ethnic consciousness versus cultural nationalism

> Never speak disrespectfully of society...
> Only people who can't get into it do that.
>
> Oscar Wilde, *The Importance of Being Earnest*

> Long live our Revolution.   Brazil will ascend like a balloon.With Getúlio, Brazil moves ahead
> With Getúlio, Brazil won't fall. Let's have more bread on the table. Getúlio is a friend of the poor.
>
> Carolina Maria de Jesus, quoted in Robert M. Levine and José
> Carlos Sebe Bom Meihy,
> *The Life and Death of Carolina Maria de Jesus*

One year after the triumph of the Vargas Revolution, Jorge Amado published his acclaimed *O Pais do Carnival* (*The Carnival Country*) and blacks like Carolina Maria de Jesus were celebrating. Carnival, the national forum for celebration and merriment, was an apt metaphor for a country which wished to project an image of diversity and tolerance. It is telling that Vargas, nonetheless strictly controlled or attempted to control Brazil's images abroad through D.I.P. and others mediums of censorship. Vargas promoted the 'national family' comprised of *gente boa*, or descent people, which excluded blacks for the most part. Ironically, historians are indebted to visiting American artists in the late 1930s and early 1940s such as Genevieve Naylor and Orson Welles for preserving images of ordinary Brazilians from distinct walks of life since they were often able to work outside of the purview of D.I.P.[1]

Even in the 1940s, Orson Welles was able to demonstrate the fallacies of Brazilian nationalist rhetoric. The 'carnival image' obscured the social reality and the entrenched social order which relegated blacks to second class citizens. Even carnival itself was quickly being gentrified. Like their white counterparts, Brazilian blacks and mulattos participated in the forging of Brazilian nationalism, but from different social contexts. Nationalism could not stymie completely black and mulatto challenges to

178

the status quo, or the call for greater civil rights, but it did shape the discourse that blacks would use within the political reality of the Vargas regime. The relationship between Brazilian blacks and the state would change, engendering a new dialogue predicated on the emerging definition of citizenship. Clifford Geertz's 1960s description of the dialectic clash between civil sentiments and primordial sentiments partly accounts for the character of the black protest from the proclamation of abolition to the end of World War II. Primordial sentiments which may provide the basis of groupings and divisions according to the shared experience of race, in the nationalist fervor of the Vargas years, became secondary to civil sentiments which required an allegiance to unity, nationhood, and *brasilidade*. On the one hand, primordial associations became subordinate to nationalist goals officially through law and censorship, and unofficially as a result of the euphoria associated with nationalist change, since blacks willingly supported the Vargas regime. The state cultivated limited ethnic identification within a static conceptualization of nationhood in so far as ethnic identification contributed to nation-formation.[2]   Brazilians perceived political and cultural unity as essential to the achievement of its nationalist goals, thus black mobilization began within a discourse of patriotism.

This chapter examines the nature of black civil rights discourse and its relationship to the black conceptualization of the nation in the 1930s and 1940s. It will be particularly important to understand how Vargas' nationalist practices helped to shape the limits of black political and cultural expression and how blacks' organized and voiced their protests.   An examination of black Brazilian voices and their understanding of their civil rights helps us to deepen our understanding of the relationship between black ethnic expression within the dominant Brazilian national identity.

Mandating civil rights implies a 'civil society', governed by a set of written or unwritten laws which define the relationship of the state to citizens.[3] Raymond Williams has emphasized the relationship between civil, social organization, and ordered society, pointing out that citizens, members of a society, have rights based on theories of individualism that date back to the sixteenth century.[4] John Locke, for example, believed in the inherent right to life, liberty, and property against arbitrary government. Based on fundamental human rights derived from natural law, civil rights encompass a wide range of guarantees presumably agreed upon by members of society.[5] Thomas Paine clarified the relationship between human and civil rights:

> Natural Rights are those which appertain to man in right of his existence. Of this kind, there are also intellectual rights, or rights of the mind; and also all those rights of acting as an individual for his own comfort and happiness, which is not inurious to the natural rights of others. Civil Rights are those which appertain to man in right of his being a member of society. Every Civil Right has for its foundation some natural right pre-existing in the individual, but to which his individual power is not in all cases sufficiently competent...[6]

According to Ian Shapiro, the purpose of rights in society is to afford a pluralistic account of good.[7] Civil rights entail the rights of persons as members of a given community and must be defined by that community, depending on the state and the rules which bind government. Though civil rights may change during unusual circumstances such as war or other disruptive crises, a written document such as a constitution, lays down the national framework which relies on laws of enforcement involving the principal branches of government: legislative, administrative (executive branch) and judicial. Locke argued that one of the presuppositions on which law is based is recognition of the law's authority.[8]

As Elisa Larkin Nascimento, wife of Abdias do Nascimento, one of Brazil's militant civil rights activists, points out the law is the only peaceful solution to problems of civil rights for many black Brazilians. It is also the solution which is less costly socially.[9] But Brazil's laws have never been quite clear on how to enforce violations of civil rights of blacks. In the 1930s and 1940s, Brazil was still a country marginalized by underdevelopment, and where widespread disenfranchisement occured. Its democratic institutions have been historically weak, and its authoritarian leaders have shown little interest in guaranteeing civil rights in general, much less those of blacks in particular. Moreover, the historically precarious economic conditions prohibited more than three quarters of the population access to the law. A series of factors including ignorance of civil rights, lack of education, misinformation about the law after abolition, and general disenfranchisement inherited from the patriarchal and racist tradition render politics and activities in the public domain off limits. Even though 'all are equal before the law', in Brazil civil rights movements necessarily entail a third dimension: that of consciousness raising and education within the Afro-Brazilian community.[10]

In the 1920s, black political voices were drowned out by the *tenentes* revolution of 1922 which sought reform in the name of the popular masses. Meanwhile, the modernists, as we have already seen, orchestrated their nationalism in the world of letters, calling for the inclusion of the popular masses in its vision of Brazilian-ness. Few blacks, however, had access to the national media of the time. Indeed, Black representation and importance to the Brazilian national culture was through assimilation and thus the mulatto represented them. Blacks were throwbacks to the past. Despite the overwhelming influence of the corporatist philosophy during the 1930s, blacks continued to resist and speak out, but post-abolition forms of resistance adapted to the new era.[11]

What role did blacks play in forging the modernist aesthetic? The answer to that question provides another interpretation to the so-called mulatto escape hatch. Few blacks participated in modernism, although revered mulattos such as Mario de Andrade brought an appreciation of blacks to the national aesthetic (see Chapter Two). Modernism's aversion to an explicit treatment of blackness in favor of a search for an integrative nationalist model contribuited to a spirit of investigation and search for national roots.

The Afro-Brazilian current within modernism tended to focus on *mestizaje*, and demonstrated a preference towards the mulatto. Guilhermino César, João Dornas Filho and Aquiles Viváqua edited the newspaper *Leite Crioulo*, (Creole or Black Milk) a supplement to the *Estado de Minas* (first issue published on May 13, 1929) the anniversary of the abolition of slavery. According to Fernando Correa Días, the movement was provincial and had little impact on national dialogue,[12] while Gutemberg Mota e Silva considered it racist, particularly in its blatant and unanalytical use of black stereotypes.[13] Nonetheless, as Antonio Sergio Bueno remarks, *Leite Crioulo* represented one of the sole forums which attempted to give expression to the black presence within the modernist current.

How would blacks begin to voice their own concerns under such a paradoxical framework? How would they frame their preoccupations? No visible black organization defied unwritten laws which downplayed racial conflict from the national territory until the rise of the Frente Negra Brasileira, the Brazilian Black Front, in the 1930s, precisely during a political watershed which opened up opportunities for the middle and popular classes. During the first two decades of the twentieth century, the black press flourished. Following in the footsteps of national trends, blacks took advantage of the improvements in technology to publish a series of newspapers in the first phase of black journalism that Roger Bastide affirmed grew from 1915 to 1930.[14] Not coincidentally most of the newspapers were based in São Paulo or Rio de Janeiro.[15] One of the precursors of the Black Front was a concrete group centered around the newspaper publication the *Clarim da Alvorada*. They were well informed on social legislation and laws that affected blacks in the United States.[16] Another black group was the Sociedade Benificiente 13 de Maio, which was active before the dawn of the Brazilian Black Front.[17]

Black Discourse, *Brasilidade*, and the Vargas Regime: From the Frente to TEN

In the summer of 1933, after Hitler had assumed power in Germany, the International Work Conference was held in Geneva. The Minister of Work of the German government began a speech which would illustrate the perception of the world about Brazil: 'It is unbelievable that I, a representative of Germany, only has the same vote that competes with those semi-savage countries of blacks from America like Brazil'.[18] The Germans attacked Brazil because, in their view, Brazil represented the antitheses of Hitler's racist ideology: a country claiming internationally that it had achieved racial harmony. That Brazil's inhabitants were, to a large degree, mestiços and mulattos was seen as proof, and a model for the world to follow.[19]

During the fervent 1930s, few challenged the Brazilian national mythology. Even the Brazilian Black Front, (*Frente Negra Brasileira*) the major black civil right's organization during the Vargas era, was assimilationist in focus. To the question, 'who are we?' the leadership of the Black Front, assumed the framework of nationhood to model their response. Issues of integration, national and racial pride confirmed Brazilian blacks' faith in *brasilidade and* the black race. Most scholars agree that the Black Front represented the first major movement to gain national attention, but few are clear as to how many other groups were formed in other states throughout Brazil. The Black Front emerged within a highly euphoric and optimistic milieu of the 1930s and cannot be understand only as a manifestation of black civil rights but also as another response to the nationalist matrix of the 1930s. The Black Front (or the Front) became the first national organization to attempt to consolidate all black demands under one umbrella group.[20]

Founded on September 16, 1931 in São Paulo, the Front's members came from the poor sectors of Brazilian society, although the Front received support from many intellectuals, and the small black professional class. The creation of the Black Front marked an important step in the consciousness movement from a national perspective, since it was the first national movement that brought together blacks and mulattos in São Paulo but with affiliations all over the country. Two years later, *A Voz da Raça*, its journalistic forum began publication.[21]

The Front's initial impact was unprecedented for a national black organization. On October 12, 1931, the Front drew up its statutes. The organization had three separate, but related units: an armed sector, the Milicía Frentenegrina, under the direction of Raul Joviano do Amaral, included paid agitators who went out into the community to stir support; a newspaper, *A Voz da Raça*; and a political directorate, comprised mostly of black intellectuals and professionals. Aiming to promote race consciousness and respect among blacks and mulattos, the Black Front's popularity was so great (at one point the Black Front boasted a membership of over 200,000 blacks and mulattos), that by 1936, it was able to register as a political party.[22]

Arlindo Viega dos Santos, the Black Front's first general president called for the union of blacks in order 'to help Brazilian powers be Brazilian'. This was a euphemistic way of combating Brazilian nationalistic racist practices which ignored the African element, while at the same time promoting order and a sense of community among blacks. The Front called for the 'definite, total integration of the Negro in all of Brazilian life'. Florestan Fernandes correctly contended that the most important change that this black organization brought to the community was psychological. Blacks began to change their self-concept regarding status and social roles. The Front's bylaws stressed the political and social unity of all blacks on a national scale.[23]

The influence of Brazilian nationalism and the authoritarian style of governance prevalent at the time had an indelible mark on the Front. In addition, Santos provided a controversial leadership style similar to Vargas's populist-like authoritarian style with a marked paternalistic attitude towards the masses. The comparison to Vargas is not without warrant. The Front's directorate came mostly from the black professional class. The late independent black activist, José Correia Leite, went as far as to say that the Front borrowed many organizational tactics from Italian fascism, and Kim Butler has elaborated upon that influence. The directing council was comprised of forty members, including a president whose powers were 'absolute'.[24]

The members of the Front considered themselves 'real nationalists', as opposed to those that only spoke of equality rhetorically. In one of its official pamphlets sent to the federal government in Rio, the Front declared itself ready to fight for and to defend the nation's interest. The Front's organizational structure mirrored Vargas' corporatist structure; attempting to include all blacks from maids to intellectuals to those few involved in business. The leadership was subdivided into three levels: a grand council of twenty that included a chief and a general secretary; an auxiliary council formed by district sub-chiefs; and a military unit under the direction of Raul Joviano do Amaral who formalized a rigid disciplinary training program and appointed honorary majors and colonels, usually chosen from among the council's members.[25]

The Front never espoused rebellion, however, only integration through reform. Like the dominant nationalist writers who promoted national heroes, the Front pursued four major aims: Undermining the traditional racial domination by openly attacking color prejudice through demonstrations and publications; encouraging racial pride and competition with whites on all levels, to extract the Negro from his or her exploited position; fighting against apathy and indifference in the black community; and re-educating whites in order that they see the importance of the Negro to *brasilidade*. The Directorate, as George Reid Andrews has pointed out, seemed limited to blacks from white-collar professions despite its overwhelming support from the working classes.[26]   The leadership, nonetheless, encouraged their members to take an unwavering line against racism and discrimination while raising consciousness within the community from a grassroots perspective.[27]

According to Francisco Lucrecio, secretary of the Front from 1934-1937, the movement directed itself to blacks in particular, but also to the nation in general. It was a call for action within the black community rather than a protest of the white. The *Frentenegrinos,* as Front members were called, carried identification cards, and had a reputation as honest, hard-working blacks who would not tolerate prejudice or discrimination. Clearly influenced by the new political opening which afforded them the possibility to organize, they waged a war against racism and social prejudice to defend a nationalist-racial unity program. In the spirit of reconciliation, the Front vowed to work closely with all races in Brazil in a patriotic manner, stressing that they were not in any way racist or separatist, a wise course of rhetoric to pursue given the nationalist spirit of the time.[28]

Indeed, the Front had much in common with other contemporary nationalist groups. The Front's leader, Viega dos Santos, an ardent monarchist desired order and stability in the black community as well as in the nation at large. Like many men of his generation, he saw nations falling into chaos and disorder. To combat this anarchy, he espoused a national discipline which called for 'the restoration of the family, the church, and the school'. Most remarkably, however, he called for a strong head of state, reasoning that 'without a king, there is no peace, there is no prosperity, there is no respect, there is no order, there is no discipline in society'.[29]

The Front's newspaper *A Voz da Raça* had two mottos (which appeared at the top of every publication), reflecting the dual agendas of the Front. The first connected the group with other generation units: 'God, Race, Family'. The Front promoted traditional values that had been lost during the republic, sharing much in common with both the integrationists and the Catholic writers. In addition, Santos' ideas about monrachy were anachronistic. He considered himself a monarchist, and maintained a paternalistic view of the masses. Indeed, his passionate distaste for communism stemmed from his views that communism subverted the natural intellectual order.[30] Within this traditional world view, Santos and his co-leaders promoted a sense of community based on racial experience as the newspaper's other motto clearly indicated: 'Only Blacks Feel Color Prejudice In Brazil'. At the same time, the Front placed the burden of black change fully within the black community when he remarked that blacks had been resistant to progress, and that their lack of education and family values had contributed to their marginalization. Thus the leaders defined their goals within the community to promote family values and education.[31] Along this vein, the Front opened a small primary school on Libertade Street in São Paulo to prepare students in civics, music, languages, and history. They were motivated by a final goal to encourage the integration of blacks and mulattos into schools of higher education and eventually the society at large. The Front's leaders advocated education and self-help programs in order to facilitate further integration, calling on black youth to become educated in order to lead the nation into the future.[32]

Influenced by the national euphoria of the time and, in particular, the nationalist slogan of order and progress, the Front never espoused violence nor civil disobedience of the law. Leaders promoted discipline and order within its ranks so that *frentenegrinos* could be distinguished from other blacks in the community. To a certain extent, this raised the level of pride among this unit, but it also created a 'clique mentality'.[33] Discipline and dependability were important attributes that the Front promoted among blacks in order for them to take their rightful place as nationally minded Brazilian citizens. The Black Front saw itself as the vanguard of the community in the tradition of the many blacks who had historically acted as soldiers on behalf of the *patria*. Encouraging its members to respect the flag as it symbolized the union of the Brazilian nation, the Front admonished a national sense of identity: 'Blacks united for a strong Brazil'.[34]

According to the Front, unity was necessary to conquer disorder, in part, caused by the increasing foreign influences in Brazil. They protested that after China, Brazil had more illiterates than any country in the world, yet foreigners could come to Brazil and fare quite well. Denouncing the growing foreign influences, the Front called for the intellectual and cultural emancipation of the nation from foreign hands, echoing the call of the *antropófagos*.[35] Anti-immigration rhetoric had long become a part of the state's nationalistic discourse, which the Black Front readily adopted. Rapid immigration to São Paulo from the turn of the century had, in many instances, displaced black workers, thus the Front had a legitimate claim.[36] Reid Andrews has indicated that the Front was able to capitalize on the anti-immigration sentiments by pressuring President Vargas to appoint more blacks to São Paulo's Civil Guard which they believed was dominated by foreigners.[37]

During the São Paulo 'Constitutionalist Revolution of 1932', the Black Front's directorate supported Vargas' federal government against the paulista revolutionaries. The conflict came to an end in October 1932 when constitutionalist forces surrendered to the federal government after hundreds of paulistas had lost their lives.[38] In the aftermath, the secretary general of the Black Front traveled to Rio to meet with President Vargas, expecting political or moral compensation for the Front's support. According to Jaime Correia Leite, Arlindo Viega dos Santos' inability to procure any benefits from the federal government resulted in his eventual expulsion from the group, and the election of a new president, Justiniano Costa.[39]

Although the Black Front established its headquarters in São Paulo, it maintained connections with groups throughout the nation under Costa. While some scholars have argued that the establishment of the Black Front signaled the emergence of the incipient black middle class or even a black elite in São Paulo, it is important to emphasize that the ranks of the Front were filled by a myriad of blacks and mulattos from the lower and middle classes. The appearance of the Front marked a desire on the part of many black leaders to politicize their constituents and to pursue mechanisms deemed as important for the pursuit of their agenda: education, economic and political participation. All this despite Reid Andrews' report that specific political commentary and goals were consistently absent from the Black Front's newspaper, *A Voz da Raça*.[40]

One of the challenges of the Black Front was not how it could balance the director's elitist or middle-class views with its popular support, but one of rhetoric. Indeed, it is hardly possible to speak of a strong black middle class or elite in São Paulo in the 1930s given the occupations (journalists, accountants, clerics, secretaries, etc.) and backgrounds of the leaders of the Front. The Front's aspirations of becoming a middle-class institution were supported by some precisely because they put the burden of economic and political participation upon blacks. The Front urged more blacks and mulattos to pursue careers in commerce and business in an effort to promote black capitalism and self-reliance.[41]

Women were also important constituents of the Front as evidenced by the creation of the 'Departamento Feminino da FNB' (Women's Department of the Black Front).[42] This department served as a forum for the promotion of the ideas of black women in Brazil who opposed sexual discrimination, harassment, and exploitation,[43] many of whom came from the working class. Even though the Women's Movement had procured the right to vote in 1932, Afro-Brazilian women and popular-class women felt alienated from the women's movement. At the Second National Feminist Convention held in Bahia in July 1934, the delegates had resolved to support women in their quest for political office, but only endorsed upper or middle class women from prestigious family backgrounds.[44]

Many Afro-Brazilian women saw the Front as more in line with their goals. Together they forged a sense of pride and dignity, promoting a forum for mutual support. Many of the women worked as domestics, as clerks in stores, and in the growing manufacturing and transport industry. Already by 1933, women who joined the movement were known as *frentenegrinas* and had a reputation for being strong, assertive, and dependable women who would not tolerate harassment. This reputation had both its advantages and disadvantages. Many employers specifically asked for *frentenegrinas*. Others would not hire them because of their involvement in a movement which many conservatives considered racist and anti-Brazilian.

The Black Front also worked with other black organizations from time to time in the promotion and celebration of black culture and heroes.[45] In November 1936, Front president Justiniano Costa and secretary Francisco Lucrecio invited the local government of São Paulo to participate in the inauguration of a special *salão* at the headquarters of the Front dedicated to José do Patrocínio. In part this was an important public relations move, but it also indicated the Front's interest in cultivating a good relationship with the state government and the state press.[46] Indeed the mainstream press had commented favorably on 'a new attitude among Brazilian blacks'.[47] Support for the Front ran high in many circles, as long as its goals did not conflict with the broader nationalist agenda.

The organization was not by any means without its internal problems. It was difficult to come to a consensus among all the different factions that comprised the group. Dos Santos' monarchist views also proved problematic, leading to his departure from the Front's directorate. Santos aside, the Black Front still had its internal problems. A call for racial unity even within the context of the national order seemed redundant to many black and mulattos who did not see a need for an organization based exclusively on race or color. Part of this was the desire to avoid issues of race while the nationalist rhetoric of the Vargas regime exasperated the chances that the directorate could consolidate the aims of the majority of the blacks. Thus, the very regime that the Front supported would lead the group to its eventual demise. The Vargas regime's institutionalized paternalism, through decrees and rhetoric, was too powerful a force, and seemed aimed to 'keep blacks in their place'.

At the same time, the Front's nationalism and promotion of *brasilidade* cannot be overemphasized. Brazil had to be built for the benefit of all Brazilians including poor blacks and mulattos. Arlindo Viega dos Santos realized that self-consciousness had to come from within. He believed that it was incumbent upon blacks themselves to prepare for their entrance into the new emerging capitalist society and to earn respect through their own actions. He was painfully aware of the negative stereotypes not only of the blacks' docility, but of their laziness, and it was against these stereotypes that the Front fought.

Vargas was a shrewd politician who understood the importance of balancing mass support and assuring the elite that Brazil was good for enterprise. The many decrees that his provisional government issued assured the masses that he was indeed 'on their side'. Despite Vargas' ban on all political parties in 1936 with the creation of the Estado Novo, the Black Front generally supported his actions. They continued support of *brasilidade*, and their faith in the government attests to Vargas' success at appeasing the popular classes in general.[48]

Similar to other social and political groupings of the 1930s, the Black Front was influenced by the national euphoria and hope of the new nationalist government. They were a part of a cultural matrix which demanded integration and national allegiance, and like their predecessors of the nineteenth century, contributed to the tradition of nation building. This fact is underscored by the Front's own characterization as a counterforce to the integralists, who they believed were destined to divide and destroy Brazil with their racist assumptions. Moreover, in its appeal to the Ministry of Education and Public Heath for support, Front leaders utilized a nationalist rhetoric imbued with essentialist anti-immigrant attitudes. They believed, for example, that the integralists could never form part of the nationalists platform because they came from 'Italian fascists from São Paulo, and sons of Germans from the south'. Blacks, in the Front's view, had for three centuries lived and worked in this land, and had developed a sincere love for the *patria*.[49]

In the tradition of other black Brazilians who fought for their country in the independence wars and the War of the Tripple Alliance, and other nationalist battles, the Front offered its military wing complete with 'disciplined blacks' conscious of their duty as patriots. Indeed, they believed that blacks were better equipped than any other social or political group in defending the interests of the nation. The Front's ultra-patriotic commitment was hardly altruistic, however. In exchange for its support, blacks sought to establish a relationship with the government that would earn them support in acquiring land, and establishing a host of other institutions such as primary and professional schools, and economic cooperatives for blacks.[50]

While many in the government and in the press criticized the Front as an extremist movement, the Front also had influential friends without whom they would have been doomed. In 1937, for example, *A Noite*, the Paulista newspaper, defended Front delegate Francisco Napoleão, against unjust incidences of prejudice and misunderstanding. Earlier Napoleão had voiced praise for Minister of Works, Agamemnon Magalhães, which led to repeated criticism of nepotism and extremism by both the Front and the Minister of Works. In a bold move, *A Noite* defended the Front who was 'weary of extremist ideas or actions', while praising Minister Agamemnon for dialoguing with the group.[51]

Despite the Front's candor, its support of the nationalist program and its supporters in São Paulo, by late 1937 its existence as a national entity was put in serious doubt. The headquarters in Rio had not been open yet, since the police had denied them a license under the pretext that the regime was in a *estado da guerra*, a fact that the Front would subsequently lament owing to the fact that it had already been recognized by the Electoral Tribunal, and had begun to receive overwhelming support from the working classes in Rio.[52]

The Front's participation in the dissemination and promotion of black culture on a national level was likewise limited, and the Front never received support from the Ministry of Education and Public Health for its stated goals. Conferences held by the Front received little national attention compared to official state functions, and those organized by councils and recognized with intellectuals such as Gilberto Freyre. In a presumptuous article in *O Jornal* in November entitled 'Os problems do negro e do mulato no Brasil', the author warned that blacks might not be able to organize a conference about black culture in an objective manner.[53] While the article praised the organizers from moving away from 'black problems as a pathology', since it represented 'an advance from the days of Nina Rodriques who was convinced of the black and mulatto inferiority', the author warned that the congress should not be led astray by black interests.   Gilberto Freyre was also critical of the congress because he believed that its organization was hasty and that the involvement of the State of Bahia might compromise its integrity.[54]

Carlos de Andrade, then director of the Ministry of Education and Public Health's cabinet, underscored the state's concern with the black group which he believed was adapting certain social concepts contrary to the civil and constitutional order of Brazil, in particular a 'social politics of races'. Despite the Front's unequivocal support of the Vargas regime, its pronounced agenda centered around the edification of the black community which contradicted a centrist policy designed to eliminate not only actual racial conflict but any rhetoric which would lead to social instability.[55]

Drummond's distance from the Black Front reflected a general ambivalence towards racial mobilization on the one hand, and an aversion towards any ideology which it regarded as extremist, i.e., contrary to the nationalist agenda of the presiding regime. Yet it is clear that the Vargas administration did not fully understand the depth of support that the Front harbored for the federal government's nationalist agenda, despite its Paulista base. In its memorandum to the Ministry of Education and Public Health, the Front emphasized its goal to assist in 'the salvation of Brazil', seeing itself as 'the only living nationalist force capable of avoiding, in the hour of struggle the desecration of Brazil'.[56]

After 1937, the Front attempted to regroup as a cultural association, but the damage to group morality was too severe. Individual members feared being victimized or being branded non-Brazilian.   In addition, Vargas' authoritarianism exasperated their chances for survival. Most important, however, were the labor codes which indicated to many workers of all ethnicities that Vargas was indeed 'Father of the Poor'. Despite spiraling inflation, government pay increases meant that Front workers were less inclined to adamantly oppose the regime. The political elite's rhetoric wooed them. The state promoted traditional values and identified with them through the magic of *brasilidade*.

Growing political pressure under the Estado Novo clearly indicated the continued supremacy of the upper class whites. Vargas' measures were in keeping with the general policy to limit internal opposition as much as possible. The reforms that began from the top-down created problems and antagonisms within the system. Organizations such as the Front which did not feel its position being positively redefined were more likely to resist change. Unfortunately, it was precisely groups without economic or political power that had put their faith in the new regime that suffered the consequences of the changes. Because of their disadvantaged position, they were unable to resist the powerful dictatorial mechanism which encouraged national unity.   Many Brazilians encouraged nationalism and pride, but instituted a policy which relied on deep-rooted prejudices against those former descendants of African slaves as well as others who had been historically displaced by the traditional system.

The celebrations surrounding the 50th anniversary of the abolition of slavery on May 13, 1938 served as an indicator of the progress of race relations under the Estado Novo.   The only national black organization was in ruin.   Black cultural organizations such as the São Paulo-based Clube Negro de Cultura Social (Black Club for Social Culture) joined in for the celebration of the event with a nationally created 'Black Commission for the 50th Anniversary of the Abolition of Slavery'. The public fanfare seemed another official overture intended to galvanize popular support, but without any broader political or social goals that would impact on the black community. According to Correia Leite, one of the leaders of the Black Club for Social Culture:

> After the festivities for the 50th Anniversary of abolition ended, the group was encouraged to dissolve. But Borba [José Assis Barbosa], one of the directors of the newspapers *O Clarim d'Alvorada*] was able to dialogue with the police department and the club was allowed to continue, only as a non-black cultural entity so much so that we had to remove the word 'black' from our name.[57]

Other black organizations, including a group that tried to reorganize from the remnants of the Black Front, were likewise barred. What resulted was a return to the 1920s where *clubes de baile*, or dance clubs, provided the only forums for black social engagement, but within an explicitly non-political climate. Political discourse by blacks was forced underground in clandestine groups such as Jabaquara until the end of the Estado Novo in 1944. Blacks congregated in informal settings, particularly in the private homes of men such as Correa Leite or around so-called 'cultural activities'.[58]

One year before the end of the Estado Novo, blacks in Rio who had been in close contact with the black movement in São Paulo would emerge with the second black national movement since abolition, the Teatro Experimental do Negro (Black Experimental Theater or TEN). Given this historical experience of explicitly black organizations, TEN emerged as a cultural entity at a time when the political discourse was moving slowly towards democracy.

In 1943, President Vargas had met with President Roosevelt in Natal, Rio Grande do Norte discussing issues of collaboration against fascism in Europe. The following year Brazilian troops would be sent to Naples, Italy to combat the powers of the Axis. The idea of troops combating fascism abroad would be grossly out of step with dictatorship at home. The move towards a democratic *abertura*, or opening, had started taking shape. On October 24, 1943, a group of *mineiros* (from the state of Minas Gerais) signed the 'Manifesto of the Mineiros', calling for the return of democratic rights to Brazil. Afro-Brazilians slighted by the effects of nationalism emerged tentatively with the creation of TEN which was first conceived as a cultural forum for black cultural expression on the stage.[59]

Democracy among the races continued to provide students of Brazilian social reality with a powerful mythology which served as the basis for the eventual absorption of blacks into the dominant white culture. Thus TEN was received as anti-Brazilian or influenced by North American thinking as well. To reach and affect the Brazilian population, and reinterpret Brazilian reality, blacks were compelled to reassess the nation's myths--taking the dominant cultural myths as a point of departure. Only after the fall of the Estado Novo would TEN attempt to exorcise the modernists' myths from Brazilian consciousness.

The Teatro Experimental do Negro and the Legacy of the Vargas Regime

The Estado Novo had been detrimental to grassroots and civil rights movements, although it had fostered an important appreciation for national culture. Despite the official rejection of blacks and blackness as representative of Brazilian culture in favor of 'a cosmic race' theory, blacks continued to be not merely contributors to Brazilian music, food, and national folklore, but participants in nation building. Black Brazilian soldiers fighting fascism in Italy returned home as heroes. By the end of the war, the Estado Novo had already given way to a new period of democratization. Not coincidentally this new opening allowed for the emergence of the second mass organization of black Brazilians in the post-abolition era.

In the dawn of Getúlio Vargas' nationalist regime, 1930-1945, and two decades after the modernist movement in Brazil, the new revolutionary black theater became the instrument for liberation for many Afro-Brazilians. Following in the Negritude movement of the Caribbean, Brazilian artists and intellectuals in the *Teatro Experimental do Negro* (TEN) set out to destroy the dominant myths used for exploitation of the black masses and to create new myths of liberation, at times romanticizing the African contribution. TEN transformed blacks into national heroes, removing them from the bottom of the corporatist mythology. In this way, they would combat racism and the dominant national myths that continued to allow prejudice to exist without calling into question the value and ethnic background of Brazilian heroes. During this period, the Teatro published the journal *Quilombo* which allowed many Brazilian thinkers, both black and white, to contribute their ideas with the goal of wiping out discrimination in Brazilian society.

In order to promote their ideas of Brazilian culture, they first had to address the ideas of the modernists. TEN revisited the symbols, but not the framework of analysis which centered on the nation. Yet TEN and its founders were no less patriotic than the modernists a decade earlier, nor did they promote black nationalism. The counter-myths that they created were central to the ideas of the national Brazilian family. TEN addressed the issues of the mulatto as hero of Brazil, racial democracy, and Brazilian modernization.

Black theater in Brazil was in itself a revolutionary concept for the 1940s, as black artists and intellectuals came together to forge a new vision, which recognized sectors of society notably missing from Brazilian history.[60] TEN attempted reinterpreting national Brazilian myths with the enlightened black hero at its center.[61] TEN constructed a new national myth by relying on the black experience with two primary goals: to destroy the myths that dehumanized and treated blacks as anachronistic, but favored the mulatto; and to create the myth which adequately reflected the way that blacks experienced the world. Afro-Brazilian religion would be of paramount importance to this process. According to cofounder Abdias do Nascimento, TEN recalled the African past, and showed the resiliency of that heritage through the *candomblé* religion and other cultural aspects. The theater served as the secular and intellectual forum for showcasing the black experience, and in this way served as a surrogate platform for the nation which lacked a black perspective.[62]

As the writers of the 1920s and 1930s forged a united, syncretic nation, the members of TEN saw syncretism as an element of black resistance and not as accommodation. That the African influence survived despite slavery and oppression evidenced that resistance. The *quilombo*, a necessary web of the resistance and survival of the slaves during the colonial period, had existed because slaves were badly treated. In this same way, TEN saw their existence as a necessary protest against white domination in an industrialized era. The Portuguese had quickly destroyed the *quilombos* in order to deter other slaves from fleeing and to punish those that did. Thus since the colonization of Brazil, the Portuguese system had become adept at instituting measures that stymied popular mobilization.[63] TEN recognized many similarities between the Portuguese desire to stamp out the quilombos and the Brazilian government's constant quests for destruction of the sacred houses of *candomblé*, its prohibition of samba celebrations in certain neighborhoods in Rio, and its harassment of Afro-Brazilian organizations.[64]

In addition to dramatic plays, TEN became the major black forum for the discussion and dissemination of its ideas. Subtitled 'Life, Problems and Aspirations of Blacks', the organ acknowledged that black Brazilians, had not received their rightful place in Brazil, socially or culturally. At the same time, TEN assured Brazilians that they were neither separatist nor interested in creating a ghetto for black intellectuals, but rather that they were obliged to fight against discrimination as an undemocratic practice which undermined the nation.[65] Since blacks were a subculture that lacked access to the dominant means of communication, TEN encouraged Afro-Brazilian and all those who believed in Brazil to speak out, listing its objective as:

(1) To collaborate in the formation of a consciousness that there was no superior race nor was there natural servility;
(2) To eradicate color prejudice;
(3) To pursue policies so that blacks be admitted with scholarships to private, state, and military schools;
(4) To combat racism, following the code of conduct of the Brazilian Constitution; and
(5) To define precisely the crime of racial discrimination in Brazilian legal codes as in the United States and the Cuban Constitution of 1940.[66]

The reference to the other national constitutions deserves special mention. In opposing the racist attitudes of many Brazilians, TEN called for the institutionalization of laws that clarified discrimination, but within the Brazilian legal and constitutional framework. Although laws did not eradicate discrimination in either the United States or Cuba, their existence in writing would legitimize TEN's struggle and provide a legal framework for redress. The state never followed TEN's education recommendations, some of which looked oddly similar to affirmative action programs in the United States. Many politicians could avoid addressing race since more than fifty percent of the population did not have access to education for class reasons.

On February 20, 1945, the *Correio da Manhã* defied the Estado Novo's censorship of the press by publishing former presidential candidate José America de Almeidas' candid criticism of the Estado Novo. Almost two months later, the government declared a general amnesty of all political prisoners, the second watershed that paved the way for presidential elections at the end of the year. In that election, General Eurico Gaspar Dutra, a Vargas ally was overwhelmingly elected to the presidency. Moreover, due to Brazilian election policy that allowed a candidate to run for congress in more than one state, Vargas was elected congressman by nine states, and senator for two.

Despite Vargas' undeniable mark on the new generation, the dictatorship had ended. A rise in anti-fascist rhetoric, urged on by French activists such as Jean Paul Sartre and Albert Camus, swept over Brazil. Brazilians had helped the Allies win the war in Europe, and Brazil too would change. Under these conditions, TEN expanded its cultural focus becoming more and more political well into the 1950s. TEN began to directly attack the modernist myths, looking closely at the issues of the national family, miscegenation, and so-called racial democracy. But TEN cautiously continued to promote its own sense of *brasilidade*. In an unofficial manifesto 'Nós e a Sucessão' (We and the Succession), the group declared, 'We are not creating cysts, we are not pleading for minority rights, we do not intend to create a problem in the country'. The organization assured Brazilians that its interests were in the best interests of the nation.[67] Theater, as a mirror and reflection of society, afforded blacks a symbolic space from which to launch their civil rights campaign. On the stage, blacks sought out the opportunity to materialize their struggles.[68]

Although TEN never received as much popular support as the Black Front had received in the early 1930s, it had influence all over Brazil. In São Paulo, Porto Alegre, and Santa Catarina, organizations with direct links to TEN arose.[69] By the end of the 1940s, TEN, along with several other Brazilian interest groups, organized the First National Negro

Congress in an attempt to foster scientific research on black issues. In an address to the Congress, Abdias do Nascimento lamented blacks' lack of access to the major means of national communication. TEN did, however, operate on two assumptions. First, that many blacks were organized around religious or entertainment circles because there was no strong black middle class nor a national black intelligentsia;[70] and second, that the masses did not have the preparation to define their own problems, and therefore had been co-opted by the nationalist rhetoric of the dominant culture.[71]

TEN's emergence at the end of the Estado Novo reflected a change in the way blacks organized. Benefiting from the work of the Black Front, TEN balanced the challenges of political and social denunciation, and cultural and community edification. Similar to the leaders of the Black Front, TEN assumed a didactic role within the black community which some writers have confused with elitism. Unlike the Black Front, TEN was vigorously pan-African, although in the tradition of black Brazilian organizations unequivocally affirmed its *brasilidade*.[72] At the same time, the group kept close watch over the emerging pan-African forums. To promote further interest in 'black issues', each year TEN recognized scholars and artists who dedicated their energies to the promotion of black culture by awarding four annual awards: Luiz Gama, Mãe Preta, Cruz e Souza, and Zumbi dos Palmares. The Luiz Gama Award was of particular import as it was given to the one person who had contributed to harmony in racial relations in the international arena.[73]

TEN entered into a direct dialogue on the issue of national identity. *Quilombo* editors included a column entitled 'Racial Democracy', which promised to point out events and issues that attacked the racial democracy myth in order to forge a new concept of racial democracy based on social equality. To this end, *Quilombo* invited prominent intellectuals and artists to contribute to the newspaper. Not surprisingly, almost two decades after the publication of *Casa Grande e Senzala*, Gilberto Freyre reiterated his belief in Brazilian racial democracy, in *Quilombo*. Although recognizing a color prejudice, Freyre acknowledged that Brazil had never been polarized along racial lines. There was never a concerted effort of black against white, Aryan against Jew or European against Indian. At the same time, Freyre affirmed that blacks in Brazil were Brazilian 'of the Latin Race', and not African. Freyre implored Brazilians to be aware of separatist ideologues who wanted to separate Brazilians. It may seem ironic that he might appear in *Quilombo* given TEN's agenda. His anti-separatist message was even more ironic since this was a criticism that TEN often received.[74]

The appearance of Freyre, one of the architects of the myth of racial democracy in *Quilombo* was curiously important to the life of the black movement. Freyre's appearance in *Quilombo* legitimized TEN's existence in the public's eye, since he was well-respected by the Brazilian public. It also illustrated the willingness, if not obligation, that members of TEN felt in order to avoid projecting themselves as black separatists. The power of Freyre's presence in the initial phase of the publication of the journal was a direct result of the power of modernist thought even after the Estado Novo. Only in the 1950s would TEN become increasingly militant.[75]

Clearly many blacks and whites saw that Brazil had to resolve serious questions of race relations in the post World War II era, prompting Estanislau Fischlowitz to call this period the 'Age of the Racial Question'. As World War I and the stock crash had led the modernist to reevaluate the elitist way of examining Brazilian culture, Fischlowitz saw the end of World War II and the division of Europe as an end of the supremacy of the white race, and a re-examining of race relations around the world.[76]

In 'Contatos Raciais no Brazil', Guerreiro Ramos attempted to demystify the myth of racial democracy, by pointing to the different types of contacts in different regions of Brazil. Ramos declared that regional phenotypes may have existed but, there was no definite pattern of racial or cultural contact in Brazil. Racial democracy notwithstanding, white culture was always the dominant culture, despite the existence of the mulatto population, many of whom considered themselves white. Moreover, Ramos affirmed that the mulatto was not a hybrid cultural category but a separate class which adopted the dominant class values. Ramos' arguments mirror those of the Cuban Elías Entralgo who made the distinction between mulattos *blancoides* (white-like mulattos) and mulattos *negroides* (black-like mulattos).[77]

For black women slighted by the dominant aesthetic values, TEN organized beauty pageants which promoted a 'black aesthetic'. There were two annual events: 'The Fish Doll' and the 'Queen of the Mulattas'. TEN, with the generous collaboration of sponsors, offered an annual monetary prize for the prettiest black woman in Rio de Janeiro. The directors of these competitions would choose the darkest women in the black community in an effort to counteract the brainwashing of Brazil's white aesthetic.[78] Although these beauty pageants have since been denounced as sexist enterprises, TEN's intention was to promote a new Afrocentric aesthetic vision, or at least question Brazil's avoidance of blackness, and its abuse of black women.

In the same vein, a regular column entitled 'Fala Mulher', appeared in *Quilombo*. Edited by María Nascimento, the column explored the woman's voice in Brazil. Articles ranged from the role of domestics in teaching white children to articles on etiquette and health.[79] TEN also established the Congresso Nacional das Mulheres Negras which served as a center mainly for professional women, domestic workers, and female artists. The female sector of TEN called for the integration of women of color into social life. In the spirit of self-help, they carried out several major activities: a literacy campaign, a Children's Theater for the recreation and education, and several educational seminars for mothers.[80]

TEN also forged racial pride and awareness by immortalizing Brazil's black and mulatto heroes, but also lauded white activists who fought for Civil Rights.[81] Thus, *Quilombo* ran a series of articles on the forgotten blacks such as Francisco José do Nascimento from Ceará, Cosme das Balaidas,[82] Chico Rei,[83] O Negro Pio,[84] João Cândido, and others.[85] In anticipation of the one hundred years of the abolition of the slave trade (1850), Orestes Barbosa called attention to historians who 'forgot' to include people of color who contributed to the Brazilian democracy: João Cruz e Souza,[86] Andre Rebouças,[87] Patrocínio,[88] Luis Gama,[89] Henrique Días,[90] and Zumbí.[91] In an effort to frame this celebration of Brazilian heroes in nonracial terms, TEN also honored many whites, including Artur Ramos, who they called a 'true scientist'. Contrasting him to Freyre, *Quilombo* evoked his work which was 'motivated by the spirit of science and not by Christian piety, lyricism, or *saudade*'.[92] Likewise they accepted some mulattos as important to their struggle, while rejecting others. Men such as Machado de Assis and Lima Barreto were claimed as heroes of color.[93] In its celebration of white Brazilians, TEN attempted to indicate that it was not a racist organization.

TEN aimed to show that the modernists and the generations before them used select mulattos to construct the idea that Brazilians had no prejudice. The heroes lauded as being mulatto were in fact considered white due to the process of *branqueamento*.[94] Under Nascimento's leadership, TEN endeavored to promote the African culture as the base of Brazilian culture. Their heroes, more often than not, were blacks and mulattos who had fought in the struggle of freedom of people of color throughout Brazil. In many instances, TEN relied on myth-making just as the dominant intellectual units had, concentrating on the symbol rather than the substance of individual personalities-- but this was a counter-attack against the dominant mythology.[95]

In spite of their opposition to the symbol of the mulatto, Nascimento once remarked that the problem with the mulatto is that he must understand that he is black. He must become, in the terminology of Elías Entralgo, a *mulato negroide*. Such mulattos became important to TEN's agenda and were perceived as possessing a black consciousness. TEN made it clear that the first lesson that the mulatto had to accomplish was to learn to be black. Cruz e Souza and Marío de Andrade were two such mulattos who had learned. Yet, the distinction between the biological and the social distinctions of race and consciousness were still evident. Blacks of this generation looked at Mario de Andrade as one of their own. He was venerated as a man of color, and as a 'letrado', who was interested in literary emancipation. Whenever he appeared in the journal *Quilombo*, his name was preceded by 'O mulatto'. TEN selected mulattos whom they thought represented black consciousness.[96]

While TEN clearly celebrated *brasilidade* and assured Brazilians of their loyalty to Brazilian development, the group also defied the narrow focus of nationhood which limited pan-African associations. Isolation had led to further marginlization, and TEN saw the advantages in connecting their cause with the cause of others in the hemisphere. In so doing, TEN illustrated the importance of blacks to different American communities throughout the hemisphere. The purpose was two fold. First, in pointing out the contribution of blacks throughout the hemisphere, TEN was calling attention to Brazil's exclusion of blacks in national life. Second, and more importantly, these type of strategies served to edify the Brazilian black population from their oppressed location. In this way pan-Africanism provided another opportunity for Brazilians to learn about the contributions of black people abroad, which would ultimately edify the national community. One example was TEN's focus on Cuba's Antonio Maceo, (1848-1948) the 'Titan de Bronce' to show how other Latin American countries with strong African influences celebrated their diversity.[97] Their overt contact with Afro-Americans was unprecedented.

The modernists had been anti-foreign, and anti-American to the extent that they promoted the unity and uniqueness of the Brazilian nation because of its history, the combination of different cultures, and the richness of natural resources. One senator in Parliament was more explicit when he reported that any racism present in Brazil was a direct result of North American style democracy filtering into Brazil. The idea that racism and race relations were worse in the United States was a common perception among many Brazilians and North American scholars. Existence of organizations like the K.K.K., segregation, and Jim Crow laws were vivid manifestations of the unjust U.S. system. But TEN adopted a different stand.[98]

In addition to providing information about the black experience in North America, TEN revealed the implications of looking at Brazil as a better society than the United States. Although there was no official segregation in Brazil, TEN showed that barriers to integration made Brazilian blacks feel segregated. Rather than being xenophobic, TEN called for collaboration with North American blacks who had achieved many successes despite their position in society.[99] Brazilians also pointed to other international events that had an impact on black people. TEN often referenced the Constitution of Cuba of 1940 as well as the American Constitution as worthy models for the Brazilian parliament to imitate.[100]

One TEN publication, 'Os Arianos de Criciuma', stated emphatically that prejudice in Brazil was just as devastating as in the North, except in Brazil, the mulatto made it more complicated. Miscegenation in Brazil meant, according to TEN, the disappearance of the black. In the United States, on the other hand, black consciousness survived since laws mandated that the racial orientation of all mulattos would be towards the black.[101] At the same time, blacks revealed that the so-called northern imperialist threat discussed by Brazilian nationalists did not mean that the U.S. had more social and racial problems than Brazil. As a consequence, many writers and newspapers in Brazil accused TEN of being financed by the United States. Without explicitly requesting them to be outlawed, the dominant newspaper *O Globo* stated: 'One must fight it at once without undermining the rights the Negroes are invoking that which have never been refused them'.[102]

Black entertainers who were known worldwide were also applauded as favorable manifestations of North American benefits. Marian Anderson was one such example. Born in Philadelphia, she studied both in the United States and in Europe, and was afforded opportunities which no black Brazilian could imagine. *Quilombo* focused on other North American artists, from Josephine Baker to Katherine Dunham, who received special mention on her trip to perform in São Paulo, when she was quoted by a French journalist as saying that blacks in Brazil should not voluntarily segregate themselves. Yet, while visiting São Paulo, she herself was a victim of discrimination and later told TEN that she was quoted out of context.[103]

Brazilian intellectuals associated with TEN also took a great interest in the French-Caribbean black pride movement. Roger Bastide, who traced the importance of blacks to the French Antilles as well as to France, also contributed to TEN's journal.[104] The movement criticized and opposed all racist acts around the globe. 'Racismo, A Herença de Hitler' by Daniel Rops explained that the United Nations Declaration on Human

Rights looked pretty on paper but called for its implementation in all societies. They criticized the fact that it was signed by South Africa, indicating that the United Nations was not serious in implementing its ideals.[105]

The Role of the United States

Members of TEN were intent on showing their white counterparts in Brazil that the information fed to them about the United States was largely false. Blacks in Brazil were no better off than their U.S. counterparts. The brutality and exploitation were the same, but many black activists recognized a different historical process in Brazil which allowed for certain advantages for blacks in both regions. TEN understood that in the U.S., for example, the black family was historically more stable since under slavery they lived together in huts as a unit. Under slavery in Brazil, most slaves lived together in the *senzalas*.[106] In Brazil there was never a desire to preserve the family unit as a work force since, according to Nascimento, it was much cheaper to acquire more slaves. A large plantation in Brazil could consist of a thousand slaves, whereas in the United States there were from sixty to one hundred slaves. Nascimento thus refuted arguments of the benign nature of Brazilian slavery. As far as blacks were concerned, their status in Brazil in the 1940s seemed far behind that of blacks in the United States in economic and sociological terms.[107]

Culturally and religiously however, blacks in Brazil were afforded various opportunities not afforded to blacks in the United States, who were stripped of their African cultural identity in the majority of cases. But TEN and it leaders were sure to demonstrate that this was not due to any innate quality of the Brazilian nation, or the benevolent nature of the Portuguese or the Catholic Church. The cultural resistance found in Brazil was a direct consequence of historical circumstances. The large concentration of slaves allowed them to preserve certain customs and religious values. The nature of slavery in the cities allowed blacks to gather together more frequently. To a certain degree the imposition of the Catholic religion allowed African cults to survive since many of the practices were analogous, but Catholicism was not a dominant force in the United States.[108]

Despite TEN's comparison of their situation with that of blacks in the United States, its focus remained national. Its main purpose was to increase awareness among blacks of their own contribution to Brazilian society, and to clarify how the ideology of *racial democracy* had harmed black consciousness. To acknowledge that blacks' contribution to Brazil was through miscegenation was to sanction the validity of the genocide of blacks in Brazil. Blacks were being encouraged to absorb Portuguese values, to react and think like the Portuguese. This was a part of a plan of genocide which Nascimento defined not only in terms of killing physically, but culturally, politically, and economically. Against this backdrop, TEN organized an umbrella of activities aimed at attacking the roots of Brazilian racism and white supremacy.[109]

Although they began in an artistic forum their plans for integration were deeply political. The members of TEN demanded proper treatment of all its citizens in politics, economics, but especially in education. In 'Queremos estudar', one of the students of TEN, the ex-vice-president of the Associação Metropolitana de Estudantes Secundarios, documented the discrimination against blacks in the Brazilian school system. Blacks had failed, for example, the military medical examinations only because they are black. One of members, Haroldo Costa also named several private schools including Notre Dame de Sion which refused to accept blacks. Indeed, the mere existence of TEN was a miracle as the Ministry of Education had failed to give the organization funding to help in their educational and literacy campaigns.[110]

With TEN's backing, José Correa Leite, founder of the Associação dos Negros Brasileiros and the director of the newspaper *Alvorada* announced his candidacy for Congressman. Geraldo Campos de Oliveira, director of TEN in São Paulo, also announced his candidacy for Congressman soon after.[111]   TEN moved to a new level of political consciousnesss in the late 1950s, seeing the secret ballot as a weapon in the struggle for their rights. Leaders encouraged blacks to vote for those candidates who had the peoples' interest at heart. In Porto Alegre, there was a call to participate in the political life in order to modify their lack of status during the Vargas dictatorship.[112]

The new black politicians declared that racial democracy should not be a luxury of the Brazilian Constitution or a slogan without content or without reflecting the daily existence of the Brazilian people. Abdias do Nascimento, for one, saw the 1950's election as a test of this equality, and called for more black and mulatto candidates. Nascimento himself announced his own candidacy for Congressman in Rio de Janeiro, D.F. The political wing of TEN, the Comité Democrático Afro-Brasileiro, established in 1945, had now come to maturity.[113]   In addition to launcing their own candidates, in the interests of blacks, TEN sent a letter to all political parties in the D.F., asking them to develop programs which would stimulate the interests of the people of color. The letter asked explicitly for them to list all their black and mulatto candidates.[114] Despite this daring gesture, political parties were never strong institutions in Brazil and did not see blacks as a valid interest group with whom they had to contend.

Conclusion: The Impact and Legacy of Black Challenges

After the military coup of 1964, the activities of TEN ceased. Abdias do Nascimento went into 'voluntary' exile in the United States. In the late 1970s, during the period of *abertura* the literature from the black voice began to emerge once more. *O genocidio do negro brasileiro* which was subsequently translated into English in 1979 is one example. Nascimento, all too aware that his words might have fallen on deaf ears inside of Brazil, reiterated that the failure of black consciousness was due to *branqueamento*. He turned to the international arena participating enthusiastically in many of the pan-African movements while continuing his writings and political activities.[115]

In her book, *The Brazilian Empire*, Emilia Viotti da Costa raised several important points about this new generation of revisionists and their challenges to Brazil's social mythology. This is not to suggest that the writers of the 1920s and 1930s were unaware of racial prejudice, but rather that later writers influenced by the ideas of World War II were more sensitized to racial prejudice and discrimination. The modernist generation responded to the nationalist impulse of the 1930s. Interest in race relations was highlighted after World War II. The UNESCO special project which studied race relations in Brazil was evidence of this.[116] Charles Wagley, for example, and other scholars concluded that there were less racial tensions in Brazil, but that one could not deny that Brazil was founded on a society of distinct castes, and that the legacy of that prejudice was found in many regions in Brazil.[117]

Although Viotti da Costa overlooked the struggle of blacks against the dominant mythology, she is correct in asserting that the 'attack on the myth came out of a political struggle against the traditional oligarchies which reached its climax in the sixties'. Yet this too must be qualified. Viotti referred primarily to a new generation of social scientists who were emerging as a new generation of dominant intellectuals. Guided by the spirit of social science, they focused on the realities of distinct regions, from which they could draw data and analyze it in a scientific fashion. These new intellectuals came from São Paulo, and many of them were from the middle sectors who did not depend on the traditional system of clientele and patronage.[118]

The 'New School', (U.S.P.) supported by the state, was in a favorable location to disseminate its ideas locally and internationally. Unfortunately, the events of 1963-1964 dispelled the challenges, only in the post-military era are Brazilians beginning to reassess the importance of the University of São Paulo (U.S.P.). On the other hand, other nonacademic groups in other parts of the county also emerged. The União dos Homens de Côr (Union Of Men of Color) founded in Rio de Janeiro in 1949, like TEN, attempted to lobby in political circles to affect policy changes that would benefit blacks and mulattos, especially in the areas of education and employment.

In São Paulo, it was not until the 1950s that another group emerged approximating the size and character of the Black Front. In December 1954, several blacks from mostly lower middle-class backgrounds formed the Associação Cultural do Negro (A.C.N.). Like the Teatro Experimental, the name of the organization was a misnomer of a sort. Activities ranged from cultural, intellectual to economic and political, but concern for racial consciousness ranked high on the list. To this end, they later initiated a literacy program and established courses in black culture. As Clóvis Moura has already shown, many of these organizations lay dormant or disintegrated after the coup, only to re-emerge in the late 1970s.[119] Regardless of the strength of the group, it received little attention from the national press and was in a most disadvantageous position to promote its ideas. U.S.P., on the other hand, made huge strides in the international arena, providing them a national forum for questioning of the traditional myths.[120]

In any society, the psychological importance of the hero cannot be overestimated. The hero enunciated the values of its society and culture. For the modernists in the context of nationalism the hero was the mulatto or the *mestiço*. Certain historical facts apparently pointed in this direction: widespread miscegenation, the color spectrum, and the Portuguese adaptation to the tropics, for example. However, identification with this hero was fueled by the emotions of nationalism and patriotism, embodied in *brasilidade*.

While the Black Front treated blacks and mulattos as part of the same constituency, it was TEN that revealed that identification with the mulatto meant for most Brazilians, identification with his whiteness. It was not a true depiction of a complete social mixture. Blacks found that they were ignored to a large extent after abolition. For this subculture, new myths were necessary to raise consciousness within the 'little circle' of consciousness in order to effect changes within the 'big circle'. The new Brazilian hero would be the black man, who through no fault of his own, occupied the lowest level of the Brazilian social hierarchy.[121]

The numerous black movements that arose, regardless of their success, indicated that racial democracy was at best a myth.[122] Nonetheless, Maria Isabel Abreu has rightly concluded that color was just one of the criteria of the social hierarchy which encoded levels of education, personality, and connections.[123] The examination of color or race alone outside of the political and cultural developments engendered by nationalism does not adequately explain Brazilian black reaction to their economic and political disenfranchisement.

Even though both the Front and TEN attempted to represent the black voice on a national level, individual supporters, both black and white had very different ideas of how to promote black interests. Many of the original members who first joined TEN were primarily artists interested in promoting the art form. Ruth de Souza was one such participant who saw the political activities as secondary to art. Haroldo da Costa and Wanderly Batista broke away from TEN to form the Teatro Foclorico Brasileiro.[124] The directors and planners of the first National Congress of the Black Brazilian recognized its intellectual biases and vowed to concentrate on the popular masses and their contribution to Brazilian culture.[125]

Blacks in Brazil remained incessantly divided over the way in which to pursue civil rights, through individual means or through the forging of a black community within a Brazilian nation. To be sure, in the 1930s and 1940s, black Brazilians often encouraged community to action and dialogue through newspapers and discussions, but mass support of black movements prior to the 1980s had always been weak. On the one hand, the deplorable conditions of the rural black families who tended to migrate to the cities in larger numbers compared to their white counterparts made political, economic, or cultural mobilization difficult. Political uncertainty and repression also discouraged mass protest. On the other hand, the pervading cultural populist nationalist program provided a framework and a rhetoric which promoted the inclusion and integration of blacks as essential members of the national family, thus making mobilization based on race unnecessary. Those persons who identified with the struggles of the Front or TEN would have their loyalty to Brazil questioned.

Mulatto-black relations within this framework further diminished the impact of black demands. Many mulattos who could 'pass for white' did.   On the other hand mulattos such as José Correia Leite were unwavering in their insistence of a black identity, although his relationship with official black organizations proved problematic. Education, money, and fame could also enhance one's chances of assimilation into the dominant white culture. Thus, the words from Oscar Wilde rang true in Brazil: only those people who cannot get into society criticize it. The fluid system that allowed for movement along a social race, tended to look at black movements as segregationist, racist, and influenced by the United States, allowing nationalism to avoid the issue of discrimination against blacks.

It is important to reiterate that even the 'so-called' national focus of the black movement emerged largely out of Rio de Janeiro and São Paulo, and became 'national' because of the centralization of industries, media, and peoples in those two southern cities. In different areas of Brazil, racial and ethnic interaction varied drastically and affected the dynamics of mobilization on the part of blacks. Even so, black militancy remained a subset of Brazilian nationalism not a competing ideology. Indeed, as we have seen, *brasilidade* had become so powerful a force that black criticism of Brazilian racism went hand in hand with a strident patriotism.

Notes

[1]   Robert Levine, *The Brazilian Photographs of Genevieve Naylor, 1940-1942* (Durham: Duke University Press, 1998) and Orson Welles' recently restored films in *Its All True* (Paramount, 1994).

[2]   Clifford Geertz, 'The Integrative Revolution: Primordial Sentiments and Civil Politics in New States', *Old Societies and New States: The Quest For Modernisty in Asia and Africa* Clifford Geertz ed. (Glencoe, Illinois: Free Press, 1963), 105-157.

[3]   One of the principle documents which lays down the rights of citizen was influenced by the American Revolution. See *The Declaration of Rights of Man and the Citizen* (August 27, 1789).

[4]   Raymond Williams, *Key Words* (New York: Oxford University Press, 1976), 48.

[5]   John Locke , *Essays on the Law of Nature* W. von Leyden ed. (New York: Oxford University Press, 1965), 99 and 147-159.

[6]   Thomas Paine, *The Rights of Man* (London, 1791), 43-52.

[7]   Ian Shapiro, *The Evolution of Rights in Liberal Theory* (Cambridge University Press, 1986), 274-276.

[8]   Locke, 147.

[9]   Elisa Larkin Nascimento, *Dois Negros Libertários: Luis Gama e Abdias Nascimento* (Rio de Janeiro: IDEAFRO, 1985), 18. In addition to the Constitution, the United States has a Bill of Rights, but many countries do not.

The 1791 Bill of Rights advocated by George Mason was enthusiastically supported by James Madison, the Father of the Constitution.
[10] José Alvaro Moises, 'Constituinte e Direitos Humanos', *Constituição e Constituinte* Maria Rosa Abreu ed. (Brasília: Editora Universidade de Brasília, 1987), 42.
[11] This decree which attempted to destroy all records, from ownership papers, ship logs, religious documents, etc. would not allow many 'whites' in society to be traced back to African origins. In short it was a part of the whitening campaign of the time. Contrary to popular belief, all documents were not destroyed.
[12] Fernando Correa Días, 'Gênese e Expressão Grupal do Modernismo em Minas' in *O Modernismo* Affonso Avila (org.) (São Paulo: Perspectiva, 1975): 165-177.
[13] Gutemberg Mota e Silva, 'Criolismo: 50 Anos Depois. A Resposta de Minas ao Antropofagismo', *Jornal do Brasil*, April 7, 1979, 6.
[14] Roger Bastide, *A imprensa negra em São Paulo* (São Paulo: Perspectiva), 1973, 131. Some of the more important newspapers include *O Menelick* (1916), *A Rua* (1919) *O Xauter* (1918), *O Alfinite* (1919), *O Bandeirante* (1919), *A Liberdade* (1920), *A Sentinela* (1922), *O Kosmos* (1923), *O Getulino* (1924) *O Clarim d'Alvorada* (1928), *Elite* (1928).
[15] For an analysis of the black press in São Paulo see Míriam Ferrara, 'A imprensa negra em São Paulo', Ph.d. dissertation, 1983. See also C. Moura and Ferrara, *Imprensa negra* (São Paulo: Imprensa Oficial, 1984).
[16] 'A Lei do Lynch', *O Clarim D'Alvorada*, 28, September 1930, n.p. See also 'Destroe o Paternal Imperialismo Norteamericano', *O Clarim D'Alvorada*, 28 September 1930, n.p.
[17] Given the size of Brazil it is not surprising that many groups formed in the period 1922-1937. Many had strictly recreational agendas, while others were interested in the promotion of culture, education, art and the well-being of blacks and mulattoes in general. None of these groups had the impact and organization of the Frente Negra Brasileira Some of the better known groups were the Grêmio Recreativo Kosmos, Associação José Patrocinio, Associação dos Negros Brasileiros, Centro Cívico Beneficiente Mães Pretas, Centro Cívico Palmares, Clube Negro de Cultura Social, Federação dos Homens de Côr, Frente Negra Socialista, Legião Negra Brasileira, Movimento Afro-Brasileiro de Educação e Cultura, Organização de Cultura e Beneficência Jabaquara. Florestan Fernandes provides a more complete list in *The Negro in Brazilian Society*, 453. See Appendix for the newspapers and journals published by these black units.
[18] Dr Estanislau Fischlowitz, 'Século de Questão Racial', *Quilombo* II, No. VI (February 1950): 3 and 8.
[19] Ibid, 8.
[20] 'Nós E A Frente Negra Brasileira', *O Clarim D'Alvorada*, September 23, 1931, 2.

[21]   Clóvis Moura lists some of the irmandades in *Brasil: As Raizes do Protesta Negro* (São Paulo: Editora Global, 1983), 49.   They include Senhor do Bomfim, São Bendito, Santa Ifigênia, São Jorge, São Elesbão, Santo Antônio de Catagerona, São Gonçalo, Nossa Senhora do Rosario.

[22]   'Estatuos da Frente Negra Brasileira', *A Voz da Raça*, May 1937, n.p. Valdecir Mello, *1978-1988 10 Anos De Luta Contra O Racismo* (Salvador: Movimento Negro Unificado, 1988) 64-79.   See also Clóvis Moura, *Brasil: As Raízes do Protesto Negro* (São Paulo: Editora Global, 1983).   Moura provides a good descriptions of black movement in the state of São Paulo using some primary sources and interviews.

[23]   Florestan Fernandes, *The Negro in Brazilian Society* Jacqueline D.Skiles et al trans. (Atheneum and New York: Columbia University Press, 1969), 210-222.

[24]   Jose Correia Leite and Cuti, *E disse o velho militante José Correia Leite* (São Paulo: Secretaria Municipal de Cultura, 1992).   See Kim Butler, p. 116.   Butler provides a chart of the organization's hierarchy.

[25]   Ibid.

[26]   George Reid Andrews, *Blacks and Whites in São Paulo, Brazil 1888-1988* (Madison: University of Wisconsin Press, 1991), 9. 150 and note 67 page 305.

[27]   'O que pretendem os negros frentenegrinos brasileiros com o nome Frente Negra Brasileira' *A Voz da Raça*, fevereiro 1937, n.p. It was important for the black community to stress action.   Blacks were socially and culturally conditioned, as were white Brazilians to venerate the black Mother, but not to establish conditions so that the black and brown offspring could compete fairly with their white counterparts. The Frente actually did not call for any 'going back to African ways movement', like their Garveyite counterparts in the Caribbean.   They essentially acknowledged Brazil as a Western society in which the European political and economic system dominated.   Blacks were encouraged to adopt and learn the 'white' way of doing things and to be their best at whatever they did. Many of the women who joined the Frente were clerks and maids known as 'Frente Negra Girls', and were admired for their honesty, bravery and industrious qualities.   On the other hand, many were avoided by employers who considered them 'trouble'.   The idea of the importance of consciousness raising is taken from V.P. Naipaul, *India: Wounded Civilization* (New York: Alfred A. Knopf, 1977), Ch.8.

[28]   Francisco Lucrecio, 'Memoria Histórica A Frente Negra Brasileira', no publisher, 332-342.   See also Francisco Lucrecio, 'A Constante Fundação de Núcleos Frentenegrinos', *A Voz da Raça*, September 1936, n.p.

[29]   Arlindo Veiga dos Santos, *Idéias que marcham no silêncio* (São Paulo: Patria-Nova, 1968), 109-111.   Although published in 1962, the author espoused these views as early as the 1920s.   He was extremely anti-Republican and it is believed that he supported the 1930 revolution that challenged the politics of the republic.   Kim Butler's recent book *Freedom Given Freedoms Won: Afro-Brazilians in Post-Abolition São Paulo and Salvador* (1998) likewise places the Frente's ideology in historical context p. 120-123.   Butler stresses the dual

influences of Catholicism and Integralism in the philosophy of the Front's leader Arlindo Viega dos Santos.

[30] Arlindo Veiga do Santos, 'Limpando O Campo', *A Voz da Raça*, September 2, 1933, 1. 'Limpando o Campo' was a regular column which dealt with religious rejuvenation of moral values in Brazil. See also Benidito Vaz Costa, 'Profissão de fé', *A Voz da Raça*, November 1937, n.p. In *Blacks and Whites in São Paulo, Brazil, 1888-1988*, George Reid Andrews reports that the motto was a borrowing from the integralist party. Other mottos from black newspapers followed similar practices.

[31] 'Inimigo do negro', *A Voz da Raça*, August 31, 1935, 2.

[32] 'Atenção Frentenegrinos' *A Voz da Raça*, February 1937, n.p.

[33] This 'clique attitude' among the Frente is seen in 'Preso como extremista o presidente da Frente Negra Mineira', *A Voz da Raça* April 1936, 1. The Frente was responding to an article that claimed that the President of the FNM was arrested. However, the man arrested was Claudio José da Silva. The Frente claimed that this man was never a member of the Frente much less president, since the organization held to such high values.

[34] 'Frente Negra Brasileira', *A Voz da Raça*, November 1937, 1. See also 'Cultura e Nacionalismo', *A Voz da Raça*, February 1937, n.p.

[35] Paraiso dos extrangeiros', *A Voz da Raça*, January 1937, n.p.

[36] George Reed Andrews, 151.

[37] Ibid.

[38] Herculana de Cavalha e Silva, *A revolucão constutionalista* (Rio de Janeiro: Civilização Brasileira, 1932), 421.

[39] José Correia Leite and Cuti, 103-105. All black organizations in São Paulo did not support Vargas. Men and women from Legião Negra, for example, fought with the constitutionalists.

[40] Abraham Monk, *Black and White Race Relations in Brazil* (Special Studies Council on International Studies, State University of New York, 1971), 36.

[41] 'Os negros e o comércio', *A Voz da Raça*, August 1936, n.p.

[42] 'Associação Cívica Feminina', *A Voz da Raça*, December 1936, n.p.

[43] 'Associação Cívica Feminina', *A Voz da Raça*, dezembro 1936, n.p.

[44] Morris J. Blachman, 'Selective Omission and Theoretical Distortion in Studying the Political Activity of Women', in *Sex and Class in Latin America*. June Nash and Helen Icken Safa eds. (South Hadley, Massachussetts: J.F. Bergin Publishers, 1980): 245-257.

[45] Several articles in *A Voz da Raça*, August 19, 1933 are dedicated to this topic.

[46] 'A Frente Negra de São Paulo Vae Homenagear o Sr. Armando de Salles', *O Jornal* November 18, 1996, Miscellaneos Newspaper Clippings, General Sector, Folder 1, DOPS, Archive of the Political Police, Rio de Janeiro.

[47] 'Movimento de arregimento de raça negra no Brasil', *Diario de São Paulo* September 17, 1931, 5.

[48] 'O negro em face da situação atual', *A Voz da Raça* (November 1937), n.p.

[49] Frente Negra Brasileira, 'Memorial', October 25, 1935, Folder 31, Ministry of

[50]   Education and Public Health, (1931), National Archives, Rio de Janeiro.
Frente Negra Brasileira, 'Memorial', October 25, 1935, Folder 31, Ministry of Education and Public Health, (1931), National Archives, Rio de Janeiro.

[51]   See 'A Frente Negra Brasileiira solidária com o ministro do trabalho' *A Noite* (Nov 1937), 9 and 20, found in Miscellaneos Newspaper Clippings, General Sector, Folder 1, DOPS, Archive of the Political Police, Rio de Janeiro.

[52]   Ibid.

[53]   Miscellaneous Newspaper Clippings, General Sector, Folder 1, DOPS, Archive of the Political Police, Rio de Janeiro.

[54]   Miscellaneous Newspaper Clippings, General Sector, Folder 1, DOPS, Archive of the Political Police, Rio de Janeiro.

[55]   Carlos Drummond de Andrade to Secretary of the Presidency, April 2, 1936, Folder 31, Ministry of Education and Public Health, (1931), National Archives, Rio de Janeiro.

[56]   Frente Negra Brasileira, 'Memorial', October 25, 1935, Folder 31, Ministry of Education and Public Health, (1931), National Archives, Rio de Janeiro.

[57]   José Correia Leite and Cuti, *E disse o velho militante José Correia Leite* (São Paulo: Secretaria Municipal de Cultura, 1992), 137.

[58]   Ibid, 139.

[59]   J. Oliveira de Meira Penna, *Em berço esplêndido* (Rio de Janeiro: Liv. Gráfica, 1974).

[60]   It is important to remember that Alejo Carpentier laid out his theory of magical realism in the preface of his book *El reino de este mundo*. Gabriel García Márquez would then carry these concepts to its most popular literary expression in *Cien años de soledad*. The Rastafarians began in the 1930s, with the crowning of Ethiopian Emperor Ras Tafari. They are more religiously based than other members of the Negritude movement. Influenced to a great extent by Marcus Garvey, the Rastafarians considered themselves displaced Africans, calling for a return to Africa, at the expense of the Western capitalist.

[61]   For a good background source on the Rastafarians, see Leonard E. Barret Sr., *The Rastafarians* (Boston: Beacon Press, 1977). Also see Samuel E. Brown, 'Treatise on the Rastafarian Movement', *Journal of Caribbean Studies* 6, No. 1 (1966).

[62]   Flora Edwards Mancuso, 'The Theater of Black Diaspora: A comparative Study of Drama in Brazil, Cuba and the United States' Ph.D. Diss. (New York University, 1975), 116. Candomblé is a complicated, yet very well organized Brazilian religion, with priests and priestesses, orixás and a supreme creator Olorum. The study of the mythology involved here and their syncretism is another interesting study which lies outside the scope of this work.

[63]   Seymour Drescher, 'Brazilian Abolition in Corporate Perspective', *The Abolition of Slavery and the Aftermath of Emancipation in Brazil* (Durham: Duke University, 1988), 429-460. A poem by Joaquim José Lisboa poignantly explains the motivation behind the creation of quilombos: 'Os escravos pretos

lá/ Quando dão com maus senhores/Fogem', from 'Descrição Curiosa', *Negros e Quilombos Em Minas Gerais* (Belo Horizonte, 1972), 23.

[64] Abdias do Nascimento, interview by author, 16 May 1991 Rio de Janeiro, tape recording, Abdias do Nascimento's residence, Rio de Janeiro. For information on the evolution of samba see Alison Raphael, 'From Popular Culture to Mico-Enterprise', *Latin American Music Review,* II, No. 1 Spring/Summer 1990.

[65] Abdias do Nascimento, 'Nós',*Quilombo* I, No. I (dec. 1948): 1 and 6. Abdias assured his Brazilian readers that he would react unfavorably to segregationist tendencies even on the part of blacks that his organization was 'not a 'black politic' but rather a black desire to be Brazilian'.

[66] 'Nosso Programa', *Quilombo*, I, No. I (December 1948), 3.

[67] Ibid.

[68] Pericles Leal, 'Teatro Negro do Brasil', *Quilombo* II, No.VI (February 1950): 11. See also 'Teoria e Práctica da Psychodrama', *Quilombo* II, No. VII-VIII (March-April 1950): 6-7.

[69] 'Noticias de TEN', *Quilombo* I, No. II (December 1948): 7.

[70] Abdias do Nascimento, 'Epiríto e Fisionomia do TEN' (discourse on opening of the National Negro Congress 9, (May 1949) reprinted in *Quilombo* I, No. IV (May 1949): 11. Ricardo Mueller's accused TEN of elitism in his book published to commemorate 100 years of abolition in Brazil. See 'Identidade e cidadania: O Teatro Experimental do Negro', T*eatro Experimental do Negro.* (Rio de Janeiro: Centro de Estudos da Fundacen, 1989): 11-53.

[71] Ibid. This paternalism stemmed from a desire to order the demands and agenda of the black community: to eradicate illiteracy, to educate, to exert political power, etc. Intellectual paternalism is seen in one instance when a young writer is praised for his aristocratic sensibilities ('O jovem Ironides Rodrigues, escritor de sensibilidade aristocrática'). The young Ironides Rodrigues, writer with an aristocratic sensibility), which is seen as positive. This was common to Latin American intellectuals in general and Brazilian writers in particular. In order to legitimize their ideas, they elevated their subjects (in this case the position of blacks) to the level of aristocracy.

[72] Social history was best defined by James Lockart in his article 'The Social History of Colonial Latin America: Evolution and Potential', *Latin American Research Review,* (Spring 1972).   He defined Social History as the investigations of the informal, the un-articulated and the daily and ordinary activities of human existence. An article on the Congresso do Negro Brasileiro stated that Blacks in Brazil will no longer be content being relegated as a 'peça de museu'. See *Quilombo* II, No. V (January 1950): 1.

[73] *Quilombo* I, No. IV (May 1949): 7. For prize announcements for 1948 see 'Laureas 1948', *Quilombo* II, No. V (January 1950): 12. In 1948, this honor was given to Dr. Ralph Bunche for his role in the Jewish-Palestine conflict. The Mãe Preta was awarded to Mary MacCleod Bethune, while the Zumbi dos Palmares went to Senator Hamilton Nogueira in the national orbit. Cruz e Souza was given to the most prominent writer; Artur Ramos. The recipient of

another occasional award, the Dragão de Mar, which went to the black who had made strides in theater. This was Ruth de Souza, one of the co-founders of TEN

[74] Gilberto Freyre, 'Democracia Racial: A Atitude Brasileira', *Quilombo* I, No. I (December 1948): 7.

[75] Ibid.

[76] Estainsilau Fischlowitz, 'Século da Questão Racial', *Quilombo* II, No.VI (February 1950): 3.

[77] Guerreiro Ramos, 'Contatos racias no Brasil', *Quilombo*, I, No. I(December 1948): 8.

[78] 'Concursos', *Quilombo* I, No. I (December 1948): 7. The winner of the first Rainha das Mulatas was María Aparecida Marques, a public school professor and radio announcer. The second year winner was Mercedes Batista. Maria Tereza was elected Boneca de Peixe in 1948.

[79] María Nascimento, 'Crianças Racistas', 'Fala Mulher', *Quilombo* I, no I (December 1948): last page.

[80] 'Instalado o Conselho Nacional das Mulheres Negras' *Quilombo* II No. VII-VIII (March-April 1950) 4. A teatro infantil is essentially a kid's theater.

[81] Reference to the 19th century indigenista book *Iracema* by José de Alencar. That is to say as Alencar described the Tupí-guaraní from his ivory tower perspective, so many writers wanted to describe the black influence in a fockloristic form.

[82] Leader of anti-slavery rebellion in Maranhão in the middle of the nineteenth century.

[83] Chico Rei was a legend/hero of Minas Gerais who was brought to Brazil from Africa, despite being of royal ancestry. He was able to buy his freedom from the rich minerals he discovered and was known to help other slaves to obtain their freedom.

[84] O negro Pio was a conductor of masses in the coffe plantations of São Paulo.

[85] Edmar Morél, 'Dragão do Mar', *Quilombo* I, No. IV (July 1949): 5. João Cândido was the leader of a Marine revolt in Rio de Janeiro in 1910.

[86] João Cruz e Souza was a Brazilian poet of African descent (1861-1897).

[87] André Rebouças (1838-1892) was a black abolitionist and an advocate of the monarchy who left Brazil for Africa when Don Pedro II was dethroned.

[88] José Patrocinio was also an abolitionist.

[89] Luis Gama (1830-1882) was a mulatto abolitionist.

[90] Henrique Días was the Brazilian son of a freed blacks who fought in the campaign against the Dutch in the seventeenth century.

[91] Zumbí was the leader of the 'Republic' of Palmares.

[92] Senador Hamilton Nabuco, 'Presença de Joaquim Nabuco', *Quilombo* II, No. V (January 1950): 3.

[93] 'Rui e os escravocratas', and 'A Morte de um grande amigo', *Quilombo* II, No. V (January 1950): 3.

[94] This is an interesting social phenomenon typical of many Brazilians even

today. Stereotypes exist where a black person living in Copacabana is perceived as being less black or more white (moreno) than a person of the same color living in one of the favelas around Rio. In Brazil, whites from Bahia are often referred to as 'white from Bahia' (branco da Bahia), denoting the fact that they are probably not pure white.

[95] J.S. Guimarães, 'A força do Preto na Economia Nacional', *Quilombo* I, No. I (December 1948): 6. The author of this article traces the importance of blacks to the Colony, the Empire and the Republic. It is important to point out the not so subtle distinction between preto, negro and moreno. Negro denotes the general concept of Black as a Race. *Moreno*, depending on the region of Brazil refers to people of dark complexion (Brown skinned). Preto on the other hand refers to people of very dark complexion.

[96] 'Grandeza de Mario de Andrade' II, No. VI *Quilombo* (Febraury 1950): 2. Intellectuals are faced with a pool of resources with which to forge their myths. The invention does not occurs in the choice process. It is in this way that historians and writers share a commonality. The choice of their subjects and their events, despite their desires of objectivity, illustrate some latent agenda.

[97] 'Antonio Maceo o Titan de Bronze', *Quilombo* I, No. II (December 1948): 8.

[98] 'O Racismo Ante O Parlamento' *Quilombo* I, No. II (May 1949): 6. See also the article 'K.K K., organização terrorista dos Estados Unidos', by W. Hardin Hughes translated for TEN by João Conceicão from *Negro Yearbook* (1947).

[99] 'Imprensa Negra Americana', *Quilombo* I, No. III (May 1949): 5. Facts about the black community in the U.S. were plentiful. Brazilians discovered, for example, that the black community in the United States had its own flourishing press which had begun in 1827 with the publication of the *Freedom Journal*.

[100] Abdias do Nascimento, 'Nós e a Sucessão', *Quilombo* I, No. III (June 1949): 1.

[101] 'Os Arianos de Criciúma', *Quilombo* I, No. III (June 1949): 4.

[102] The article originally appeared in *O Globo* April 13, 1950. It was translated and reprinted for an editorial commentary in *The Pittsburgh Courier* April 29, 1950. Both articles were cited by *Quilombo* II, No. VII-VIII (March-April): 5.

[103] 'Marian Anderson, símbolo da unidade americana' *Quilombo* I, No. III (1949): 4. See 'Nos E Katherine Dunham', *Quilombo* II, No. VII-VIII (March-April): 11. Also see interview with Katherine Dunham by Yvonne Jean published in *Correio da Manhã* June 1950 (supplementary) 9. The incident of discrimination against Ms. Dunham apparently had to do with the mix up of her hotel reservation. It was never determined whether the error by the hotel was intentional or not. An article on Josephine Baker appeared in *Quilombo* II No. VI (February 1950): 2. In an article on the famous North American boxer Joe Louis, the author begins 'In spite of discrimination, the U.S. has many famous Black personalities in all aspects of life'. See 'Joe Louis no Brasil', *Quilombo* II No. VII-VIII (March-April 1950): 4.

[104] Roger Bastide, 'O movimento negro francês', *Quilombo* II, No. VII-VIII (March-April 1950): 3.

[105] Daniel Rops, 'Racismo, A Herança de Hitler', *Quilombo* I, No. II (May 1949): 2.

[106] Abdias do Nascimento, interview by author, 16 May 1991 Rio de Janeiro, tape recording, Abdias do Nascimento's residence, Rio de Janeiro.

[107] Ibid.

[108] Ibid.

[109] Ibid.

[110] *Quilombo* I, no I (December 1948): 4. Apparently the Ministry of Education did provide funding to other theatrical and education related groups. Various politicians such as the Mendes de Morais, from the Prefeitura had promised funding but never came through. TEN also waited to see if the promise made by Café Filho, Rio de Janeiro Congressman, would materialize.

[111] *Quilombo* II No. V (January 1950): 2. See also 'Candidato a Deputado por São Paulo', *Quilombo* II, No. VII-VIII (March-April 1950): 5.

[112] 'O Negro e as Eleições', *Quilombo* II, No. V (January 1950): 3 and 'Ministro, Senadores E Diplomáticos Negros', *Quilombo* II, No. V (January 1950): 8.

[113] 'Candidatos Negros E Mulatos', *Quilombo* II, No. VI (January 1950): 1. The announcement of Nascimento's candidacy to the legislative assembly of the D.F. appeared in *Quilombo* II No. VII-VIII (March-April 1950): 1. Formed in 1945, the Comitê published its declaration with twenty five demands, among them the democratization of the nation, abolishment of discrimination in specific sectors of the government such as diplomacy and the erection of a monument dedicated to José do Patrocínio. The document was signed by twenty members of the central committee including Abdias do Nascimento, Solano Trinidade, Ironides Rodrigues and Martins Texeira. This document is reprinted in its entirety in Clóvis Moura, *Brasil: As Raízes do Protesto Negro* (São Paulo: Editora Global, 1983), 150-152.

[114] 'O TEN se dirige aos Partidos Politicos', *Quilombo* II, No. VII-VIII (March-April 1950): 5.

[115] Abdias do Nascimento, *O genocídio do negro brasileiro: processo de um racismo mascarado* (Rio de Janeiro: Editora Paz e Terra, 1978). Translated into English: *Mixture or Massacr ? Essays on the Genocide of a Black People* trans. Elisa Larkin Nascimento (New York: Afrodiaspora, 1979). In *Mixture or Massacre?*, the author re-interpreted miscegenation as a genocide of the Brazilian black. According to Nascimento, in Brazil a very special Luso-Brazilian type of racism had emerged that was subtle, diffuse but powerful which has led to social lynching of black people. Some of these mechanisms included miscegenation, color prejudice and racial discrimination along with a biased immigration policy. Like Florestan Fernandes, Nascimento documented cases of discrimination, but in the cultural as well as in the economic realm. The persecution of the Afro-Brazilian religion, the disdain for African influences even in Art and Music continued to create an atmosphere which has encouraged the Brazilians, who are in the majority of African descent, to turn away from anything that is black. Another ex-member of TEN, Haroldo Costa,

became a prominent television producer and has written on various related topics. His book, *Fala Crioulo* used oral history to document different views on being black in Brazil from various Brazilian citizens. It was a new type of Brazilian testimony in which different blacks from different backgrounds are given an opportunity to express themselves. Such was the case of Vera Lúcia Couto de Santos, the first black Ms. Brazil. She recalled vividly the racism she experienced from comments such as 'This black (creole) is involved in white affairs, she buys everything good and even what is better'. Costa also interviewed famous Brazilians, like Pelé, as well as maids, porters and practitioners of *Candomblé*. See Haroldo Costa, *Fala Crioulo* (Rio de Janeiro: Editora Record, 1987).

[116] A good source which outlines this study is Roger Bastide, 'Race Relations in Brazil', *International Social Science Bulletin* IX, No.4 (1957), 6-15.

[117] Emilia Viotta da Costa, *The Brazilian Empire Myths and Histories* (University of Chico Press, 1985), 236-137. Charles Wagley ed. *Race and Class in Rural Brazil* (Paris: United Nations Educational, Scientific and Cultural Organization, 1952). Harry W. Hutchinson who wrote the essay on 'Race Relations in a rural community of the Bahian Recôncavo' in *Race and Class in Rural Brazil*, 16-46 maps out the different racial attitudes in the rural Northeast. Attitudes in general show a prejudice towards both the indigenous groups and blacks, but there was a complex relationship that depended on individual contact, family background and class. The series of questions and surveys taken show no conclusive results. For example many people preferred *pretos* as workers, whites considered *caboclos* the most attractive people, while many caboclos preferred to be called mulattos.

[118] Emilia Viotta da Costa, *The Brazilian Empire Myths and Histories* (University of Chico Press, 1985), 244-246.

[119] Clóvis Moura, *Brasil: As Raízes do Protesto Negro* (São Paulo: Editora Global, 1983), 58-59.

[120] Florestan Fernandes, *The Negro in Brazilian Society* Jacqueline D.Skiles et al trans. Atheneum and New York: Columbia University Press, 1969), 221.

[121] In the traditional theater of Aristotle, the *anagnorisis* is the point at which the hero becomes enlightened. He realizes what he is doing and either modifies his behavior or fails to change.

[122] Gilberto Freyre, 'Tipos socioantropológicos no romance brasileiro', *Ciência e Trópico*, 2 (1974): 7-26.

[123] Abreu, Maria Isabel. 'Cultures in Contact with the Making of Brazilian Society', *Revista Interamericana de Bibliografía* 30 (1980): 164-172.

[124] Interview Summer 1990.

[125] 'Interesse Nacional', *Quilombo* II No. VII-VIII (March-April, 1950): 3.

6. Conclusion:
Race and national culture, the legacy of the 1930s

> Hoje en dia eu constato que a situação do crioulo no Brasil já melhorou muito, deu uma subida há mais consciencia. Infelizmente a infra-estrutura do sistema não dá muito condição. O analfabetismo, por exemplo, continua sendo a maior epidemia para o negro brasileiro. De qualquer maneira vamos galando pouco a pouco os escalões socias. Eu pessoalmente sempre defendi a tese de que é evidente que existe alguns requícios de racismo en certas pessoas, o cara e racista e pronto. Tem gente que não gosta de português, tem gente que não gosta de judeu e tem gente que não gosta de negro. Mas mesmo estes têm que agüentar evidências contra as quais nada podem. No dia 15 de abril de 1981 eu recibi em Paris o prêmio 'O Esportista do Século', quem recebeu foi Pelé, um negro. Um negro brasileiro. São essas coisas...

Pelé, Haroldo Costa, *Fala Crioulo*

Nem tudo mundo pode ser Pelé

Emanuel Batista de Endrade, Haroldo Costa, *Fala Crioulo*

As self-appointed national leaders to order what they perceived as chaotic, and to consolidate the Brazilian nation, the populist and nationalist intellectuals were paternalist and essentialist in their approach to national culture. Brazilian nationalism in the 1930s was corporatist and aimed to homogenize diversity through the forging of a single national identity. Given the isolation of the Indian, and the historical struggle between the African and the European in Brazil, the mulatto--an American identity-became an important symbol of the fraternity of both groups. Promoting a 'mulatto nation' implied a lack of racial prejudice, where eminent mulattos represented the genius of blacks. By and large, the creation of Latin American heroes took place with the intention of praising those who had forged a fraternity among citizens, but revealed a white European bias.

This work has illustrated the importance of approaching national myths which attempt to convey a particular group of people in a stereotypical fashion with a critical mind. Hayden White has indicated that '[h]istorical situations are not inherently tragic, comic or romantic.

All the historian needs to do to transform a tragic event into a comic situation is to shift his point of view or change the scope of his perceptions'.[1] The perceptions of the dominant classes in the 1930s created the national myths that would be the focus of attention throughout the remaining century. These myths, were propagated through the most popular medium of mass communication in Brazil in the 1930s and 1940s: popular music.

After the end of World War I, there was a marked change in the way intellectuals and political leaders regarded Western culture. Different cultural manifestations indicate this dimension: fauvism, cubism, futurism, surrealism, Negrism, primitivism, indigenism, as intellectuals challenged the traditional values and constructed new conceptualizations of their nations.[2] Latin American writers utilized the emerging technology, particularly advances in printing, publishing, and radio, to propagate nationhood. National identity emerged as a consequence of the definite institutionalization of the idea of the nation-state and their political and economic power in the international capitalist world market. As Cornelia Navari asserted, the nation-state became 'a polity of homogeneous people who share the same culture and the same language, and who are governed by some of their number, who serve their interests'.[3]

In 1918, President Woodrow Wilson, in his discussion of the settlement at the end of World War I, declared that the basic requirement for a government's legitimacy should be its sovereignty as a nation-state. That the United States had a growing influence in Latin America determined to a large extent the political ideologies of nation-states in the rest of the Americas. In Brazil, the 1930 Vargas Revolution provided the political forum through which the nation-state was able to institutionalize a unique cultural identity. This generation's cultural elite replaced the country's traditional economic elite who would begin sculpting a new sense of nationhood.[4] Despite the appearance of numerous intellectual groups, which espoused different ideas of the nation, there were more similarities among the groups than differences.   The common denominators bonding the myth makers of this generation were class and education. The dominant intellectuals shared similar social experiences which placed them in a favorable situation as caretakers of Brazilian national culture.

Paramount in the minds of the forgers of the union was a desire to homogenize 'national culture'. Given Latin America's social history with its racial, class, and regional stratification, national homogeneity was dubious. Indeed the nature of culture dictates otherwise. Human cultures are not standardized ways of life.   In the Americas, owing to the heterogeneity of immigrant backgrounds, national cultures are even more difficult to homogenize ethnically. It is almost impossible to arrive at a generalized 'total culture' in reference to social organization, technology, and ideological systems, since culture is a constant dynamic of action and interaction. Thus, 'national culture', or what is perceived as 'national culture', is necessarily a sociopolitical construct propagated by the dominant media, and formal national institutions responsible for the dissemination of culture. At the same time, like nationhood itself, 'national culture' assumes an unquantifiable organic quality which members of the nation recognize (or perceive) as uniquely theirs.[5]

Given the historical position and perception of blacks in society, national culture--that promoted officially by the nation-state and recognized by Brazilians as constituting *brasilidade*--was anti-black. Until the late 1970s, whites and blacks avoided confronting discourse about race, and the legacy of slavery in public forums. For whites, Brazilian blacks were better treated than blacks anywhere in the diaspora. For blacks, any manifestation of black pride or civil rights had to be framed within a larger construct of national unity, a togetherness that overlooked the political and economic inequalities between the two races. In multicultural nations, subcultures mutually influence one another, but each one's representation in the national images is determined by their social rank and how they entered the society. In Brazil, this meant that blackness would play a determined, static, and marginal role in the image of the modern Brazilian nation.[6]

In forging a common identity in a populist era, the political and intellectual elite employed the rhetoric of populism which attempted to create a wide coalition across classes. The 1930s and 1940s saw the emergence of a myriad of populist movements in Latin America, reflecting the growing concern to somehow account for the popular sectors in general rather than the organized working class and its leftist or anarchist affiliations. In creating bridges across racial divides, nationalists evoked the sense of Brazilian patriotism, calling upon its citizens to celebrate *brasilidade*. This was particularly apparent in public forums of popular culture, such as samba, Brazilian popular music, soccer, and other cultural manifestations.

For Brazilians, the primary concern was to infuse a sense of pride and to downplay any vestiges of conflict. Historically, Africans had played a major role in the economic, social, and cultural formation of Brazil, but to claim that their contribution to their respective societies was on par with whites denied the historical exploitation and their present status as cultural minorities. Focusing on the mulatto became expedient, an 'escape hatch' from political and economic discourse aimed at ameliorating the condition of the majority of blacks, since miscegenation had indeed occurred. Never mind that mulattos intermarried, constituting a separate class with a distinct way of thinking from both the black and the white, although upwardly mobile mulattos identified with the white dominant class. Racial democracy overlooked social stratification and *color* prejudice!

Brazilian nationalism maintained an apparent non-racial agenda, while reinforcing static images of both blacks and mulattos in important cultural expressions, particularly popular Brazilian music. Popular media programs such as the radio program, *A Hora do Brazil*, instilled nationalism and pride in union. Limited black participation in soccer also indicated a certain discomfort with blacks as national representatives, despite the overwhelming popular support for black athletes such as Leônides. That prejudice and racism still existed in Brazil in the 1930s was evidenced by this apparent oversight. The supporters of political and cultural centralism supported integration as long as it was kept on a theoretical level. When concrete steps were taken for real integration, they were vehemently opposed. Black groups that attempted to challenge the dominant myths were branded as racist or unpatriotic.[7]

At the same time the nationalists' rhetoric constantly compared the situation of Brazilian blacks to blacks and the underclass in other countries, particularly the United States. Anti-North American rhetoric became an essential part of the quest for new national status and independence. Due to the historical role that the United States played in the region, Brazilians defined themselves in reference to the dominant nation in the hemisphere. The United States was often portrayed in mythological language as a predominantly Anglo-Saxon political system with undesirable cultural characteristics. That these feelings were a part of a wider nationalist movement is evidenced by the fact that they arose despite (or perhaps because of) the strong economic dependence and political cooperation between the Vargas regime and the United States especially during World War II.

Nationalization, the economic arm of nationalism, bolstered more support from its citizens. The state seizure of industries, however, did not benefit the masses, but rather the ruling elite who could justify these moves in the interest of the nation.[8] Nationalization under Vargas was devoid of long term beneficial change for the masses. In a cultural sense, it allowed the elite to further the belief of the cultural flaws of the United States. From this vantage point, white Brazilians proposed a North-South rhetoric in which the South had to protect itself from the

United States and other foreign powers. That the United States social system was racist and relegated blacks to an inferior civil status allowed Brazilians to claim a cultural and social superiority, and a level of racial equality unseen in the north. In addition, white Brazilians often blamed the existence of racism in Brazil on U. S. influences.

Brasilidade embodied three crucial processes: racial mixing, Brazilian cultural uniqueness, and love of independence. The generation writing from the 1920s to the 1950s took refuge in the past. While other Latin American countries such as Perú and México reinterpreted the 'glorious' indigenous past,[9] Brazilians relied on the positive aspects of Africans combined with the tolerance of the Iberian.

Nationalists who promoted these populist images and heroes in the attempt to centralize Brazilian culture from the end of World War I to the end of World War II were highly successful. Brazil had stymieing black social mobilization even though the actual social conditions of blacks and other minorities including women may have been worse.[10] Brazil's national writers received worldwide attention and corroboration from European and North American scholars, who investigated the accomplishments of the racial paradise with United Nations' sponsorship in the 1950s. Even in the black American press before the 1950s, the image of Brazil as a racial democracy was unchallenged and used as an example that enslavement did not necessarily lead to discrimination.[11]

The relationship of nationalism to civil rights and race consciousness in Brazil was not dissimilar to that in other Latin American nations. Nationalism and the forging of a unified national identification have played significant roles in mitigating racial and class tensions in a number of Latin American countries. In many respects, nationalism compensated for the guilt of oppression of the bourgeoisie. The new enlightened intellectuals lent a sympathetic ear to the popular masses who they now saw themselves as distinctly American and *mestizo/mulatto*. Curiously, the majority of these intellectuals saw the African cultural presence as important, but the pure African as *fortunately* disappearing.

The Cuban Angel Pinto's summation of the position of blacks in Cuban history applies equally to Brazil:

> As time goes by, the conviction that the 'black capital mistake' consists and has consisted in not realizing that he is a prisoner of the philosophical doctrines of the slave owners when slavery as a social regime of production emerged and was created simultaneously with the state, as the instrument of domination destined to subject those that had been enslaved. At the same time, it was a philosophy or a perception of the world and of

life that served to explain and justify their right to exploit those that had been enslaved. For the black, unfortunately, the philosophy continues today to be nothing more than the systematic expression of a method for the acquisition of the truth, a useless entertainment for idle and lazy people.[12]

The Black Response

Employing internal categorizations of race in Brazil, the number of persons classifying themselves as blacks (Negro) had diminished significantly. By the 1930s, immigration policies in Brazil after abolition had succeeded in attracting white immigration and whitened the population in absolute terms.   Nevertheless, the degree to which miscegenation contributed to this is doubtful. In the case of Brazil, the white population, in the majority migrated to the under-populated southern parts of Brazil and the São Paulo regions. The relatively rapid upward social mobility of immigrants led to further marginalization of blacks. The historic creation of a large 'colored' sector with certain but limited privileges allowed them to acquire a separate cultural identity. With the dawn of nationalism, the sectors were unable to identify themselves through a racial consciousness, and thus were the first recipients of the national consciousness movement.

Black groups, nonetheless, rebelled against their stereotypical representation and their social oppression. By and large, during the period 1930-1950, black movements remained patriotic and unwavering in their support of *brasilidade*. Blacks challenged Brazilian racism within the cultural and political system, rather than question the legitimacy of the national system. The unit of analysis remained the nation and national edification ranked high on blacks' agendas. Rather than discard the tenets of the nationhood *brasilidade*, anti-imperialism, independence, the 'Fear of the Negro' and the mulatto hero, black intellectuals reinterpreted their meaning and called for true integration.

The black civil rights activists of the 1930s espoused traditional values of family, *patria*, religion, and order as well as social and economic progress. Interested in economic well-being and social advancement, they believed themselves to be no less nationalistic than their white counterparts, but perhaps better than any other movement of this century they understood the relationship between economic and political power. The Black Front cannot be called revolutionary in a political sense. Its leaders stressed the importance of acquiring capital and responsibility in the business world. With the Estado Novo, however, the organization disappeared.

In a moment of political *abertura*, TEN emerged. Though the overall political impact of the movement on blacks was probably negligible, it marked the most comprehensive movement of blacks prior to the 1980s. TEN's framework for the dissemination of their ideas were predetermined by the classic myths institutionalized by the writers of the 1930s; racial democracy, the mulatto nation, independence, and anti-North Americanism. Abdias do Nascimento, TEN's director, called for the creation of a true racial democracy. In regards to their stance on imperialism, they rejected any type of dominance of one nation over another, yet they did not see their status as better than blacks in the United States. While T.E.N pointed out the possible validity of a mulatto nation, they believed that the mulatto had to learn to be black.

Yet TEN's own manner of organization indicated the influence of national constructs. TEN's leaders heralded the importance of culture in alleviating the problems of blacks, and often saw its role as didactic, if not paternalistic. Moreover, TEN acted as a vanguard of the blacks, essentially to wake up blacks to their own cultural contribution. They believed that blacks had been 'duped' by whites who had robbed them of their identity. As Abdias do Nascimento stated: 'the mentality of our population of color is still pre-literate, pre-logical. The written or logic techniques, the concepts, the ideas haven't reached them successfully'.[13] Despite the modernist-like rhetoric, TEN's commitment to grassroots activities through literacy campaigns, popular journalism, and other community activities sets the group apart from the nationalist intellectuals.

Paternalism had played a major role in the forging of the nation. Learned men saw themselves in a position to provide protection for the nation. Only they, as owners and forgers of national culture could, in their didactic way, right the ills of the nation, so constructed and defined by them. They attempted to cast a dominant view of culture in a static way to explain to Brazilians their civic duty to promote unity and pursue the preservation of culture. In their attempt to include popular culture, they ignored the changing nature of culture and the existence of various subcultures interacting in the constant process of formation and adjustment.

Beyond Vargas

The 1964 military coup, which put an end to Vargas' political legacy, stifled any meaningful contribution to any national debate on race, culture, and social issues and other issues which lay outside of the military's new modernization scheme. Like Vargas, however, the military regime was macroeconomic oriented and continued the rhetoric of the nation as a family. Censorship and repression prevented any meaningful challenge to the new regime, motivated by a desire to see Brazil rise to dominance rather than to address the social inequalities still endemic to Brazil. Moreover, military leaders believed that with economic growth these problems would disappear. Still, many intellectuals and artists were forced into exile. In economic terms, nationalism broadened to include national cooperation, although Brazilian superiority still played a major role.[14]

As Anani Dizidziendo has pointed out in his study of the position of blacks in the 1970s:

> There has been a consistent if perhaps not intentional alliance of politicians, administrators, the aristocracy, academics, workers, artists and others- politically and ideologically at variance though they might be- vis-à-vis the plight of the black Brazilian: for their own reasons they refuse to recognize that the special problems that a black person encounters as a result of his color and his heritage require special solutions.[15]

It was highly desirable for the political and intellectual elite to establish a status quo position in which the Brazilian military regime would overlook the ethnic implications on national identity and concentrate on the economic growth which would in theory benefit the nation at large. It is not surprising that the middle sectors supported the 1964 military coup since they too desired a return to order after the chaotic period under President Goulart, 1960-1964.[16]

In other words, the anti-democratic coup was at least initially popular. This may have been due to the growth of the middle class under the industrialization and growth from 1930-1960. The compositions of both the working classes and the middle classes were changing drastically. The notion of order, progress, and cultural unity were ideals held by a majority of Brazilians. The military regime would promise to bring this in the 1960s. But was there a revision of the cultural images? the mulatto nation? or racial democracy? As late as 1963, the American Charles Wagley reiterated that Brazil was a racial democracy in the political and economic sense, but not in the social sense.[17] Brazilian politicians further embellished the myth of racial democracy to the benefit of Brazil's international image. The ascendance of black athletes, especially in soccer on the world arena was another venue through which the government illustrated and promoted their pride in racial harmony.[18] But perhaps more importantly, the generation of writers influenced by modernism continued to promote images of *mestizaje* and miscegenation in literature, print journalism, and popular music.

Bahian author Jorge Amado, for example, was particularly adept at exploiting the *mulata* or the *morena* as the symbol of Brazil. His packaging and marketing of Brazilian folklore continued in the tradition of racial democracy. Amado's writings are based almost exclusively on Bahia, yet he himself made his novelized reality represent Brazil. Works like *Dona Flor and Seus Dois Maridos* (1966), *Tereza Batista Cansada de Guerra* (1972) are indicative of Amado's style. Amado attempted to create a magical atmosphere with which he blessed Brazil. Yet he considers himself more of a journalist-historian than a novelist. He described Brazilian culture as sensual, mulatto, and vibrant. Despite his earlier incarceration for being a member of the Communist party, Amado did not challenge the social relations of Brazil, but continued a patriotic rhetoric.[19] Well into the military dictatorship, Amado continued to support the idea of Brazil as a racial democracy. In 1977, he remarked that 'our outlook on life is fundamentally anti-racist, based on intermingling'. Amado failed to mention the government's total avoidance of the issue of race.[20]

At the same time, black groups in Brazil that attempted to form cultural celebrations to celebrate their African heritage were still being called segregationist and racist. This was a case of the victim being ostracized for crying for help. A prominent newspaper, *A Tarde*, reported that 'we do not have a racial problem. This is a great happiness of the Brazilian people'.[21]

The national government did not turn its back on 'culture', however. Rather, the new Ministry of Culture adamantly promoted 'national culture' through the development in the communication industries, particularly in film and television, although records and radio remained powerful mediums for the dissemination of 'national culture'. The *cinema novo* movement which gained momentum during the 1960s attempted to discover Brazilian reality as the modernists before them had attempted to do in literature. Individual filmmakers celebrated their ability to bring social relevance to their artistic work.[22]

These filmmakers were directly influenced by the modernist heritage and cultural populism. In search of their cultural roots, they too turned to the Indian and African cultural traits of Brazil. Whether they took 'a hard look at racism', as Aufderheide reports, may be doubtful. Nonetheless, they looked for popular heroes in the colonial and independence eras. Slave revolts, the *quilombos*, and other forms of protests were brought to the screen. Carlos Diegues' *Ganga Zumba* made in 1963 focused on the heroism of the leader of Palmares. The coup of 1964 (particularly after 1968) had a chilling affect on film as it did over the entire country. Yet movies with popular class themes such as the Joaquim Pedro dos Santos' 1964 film *Macunaíma,* based on Andrade's classic, appeared to make use of both humor and symbolism.[23]

Much of *cinema novo* in Brazil depicted national subcultures in a romantic light. Historical films allowed black actors to become main characters, but few Brazilian dramas had blacks as protagonists (One of the few films was *Orfeu Negro*, a French musical production, of a sort). For the most part, Brazilian films which dealt with the subcultures and particularly the African elements, were presented as docudrama, historical films, or comedy. Even the film *Xica da Silva,* (1976) which spoke about the decadence of the colonial lifestyle and sexual exploitation of slave women at the same time reinforced stereotypes about black women in the 1970s. Contemporary black political issues were not addressed within mainstream culture largely because new national institutions such as the Special Assessor for Public Relations (AERP), the military's propaganda machine, reinforced the idea of a nation of content citizens without internal conflicts.

While African-Americans where shouting slogans such as 'Black is Beautiful', and 'Power to the People' in the United States, Brazilians were encouraged to live the new national motto 'Brazil: Love it or Leave it!' Authoritarianism played a significant role in propagating national identity and in marginalizing challenges to this presumed unity. By 1970 the dictatorship was celebrating an 'economic miracle', Brazil had captured football's coveted World Cup, and Miguel Gustavo's *marchina* 'Pra Frente Brasil' (Onward Brazil) had become somewhat of an unofficial national anthem. The military dictatorship had embarked upon an insidious nationalist campaign in which censorship and tight state management stifled criticism and sent thousands of dissenters into exile. Popular music, given its enormous communicative power, was closely monitored, and a host of performers including Caetano Veloso, Gilberto Gil, and Chico Buarque were invited to leave. Geraldo Vandré's 1968 'Pra Não Dizer que Não Falei de Flores' (So That They Do Not Say That I

Did Not Speak About Flowers), considered subversive, illustrated the tension between national solidarity and silence. These tactics had precedence in the Vargas administration from 1930-1945. The national ideology which defined the nation in the 1930s, once institutionalized and propagated, became a part of the national consciousness, continually being forged. Even those individuals who attempted to revise those myths were bound by the parameters. The notion of racial democracy and Brazilian cultural uniqueness are far from irrelevant today. Consciousness, after all, is built on archetypes, which according to Jung cannot be totally discarded.

The new Constitution of 1967, in part, reflected the spirit of the Constitution of 1937 in its authoritarian style.[24] The Constitution declared that 'racial prejudice will be punished by law', although prejudice was ill-defined and ambiguous. Moreover, military rule was a setback for grassroots and civil rights advocates who could be branded 'subversive' according to a host of arbitrary laws. Even prominent social scientists from the University of São Paulo, who spearheaded a renaissance in Brazilian academics, would later fall out of favor with the military regime because of their focus on social issues including race.[25]

These scholars such as Florestan Fernandes focused their attention on blacks in the urban areas since Brazil's military emphasized industrialization as a key component of their modernization scheme. Fernandes showed that modernization and the emergence of a competitive social order developed slowly and did not eradicate to any significant extent the social class system. In fact, capacity for social revolution was stymied. At the same time, participation in modernization required material and psychological skills as well as technology which Afro-Brazilians lacked. Fernandes argued that Afro-Brazilians were extremely handicapped, owing to the debasement of slavery, pauperism, and isolation over history.[26] According to Fernandes, '[it] is the Negro who represented the paradox of Brazil's capacity to erect a modern society'. Social conditions would have to improve for them and they would have to be systematically integrated into the growing urban cultures.[27]

The fact that the post-1964 military regime was a technocracy cannot be over-emphasized. It accounted for the drive to rid Brazil of dependency and to lead the nation into greatness. The new technocrats attempted to capitalize on workers' patriotism, but not to allow them to participate in the political process. Strikes were declared illegal and a new Constitution was created and passed by the legislature in 1967.[28] According to Viotto da Costa, the military's desire to further silence dissent and to entrench a tradition of order was felt in the academic institutions as well.   Two important academics, Octavio Ianni and Florestan Fernandes, critical of Brazilian social and racial paradigms in Brazil, were forced to retire early from the University of São Paulo in 1969.[29]

The worldwide oil crisis at the end of the 1970s coupled with rising interst rates shocked the Brazilian military into reality.   Much of the 'economic boom' had been financed by borrowed money, and as hard currency was siphoned off to pay for oil, Brazil's balance of payments suffered.   The military slowly began to relinquish its power.   In 1979 General João Figueiredo began presiding over the period that would begin the political opening, *(abertura)*, or return to democracy, which culminated in the elections of 1985.[30] After considerable debate, Brazil received a new Constitution in 1988.

The Civil Rights Movement did not wait for a new Constitution however.   The political climate, which allowed for the election of President Figuieredo who pledged to restore democracy, motivated Afro-Brazilians.   The Movimento Negro Unificado or MNU founded in 1978 emerged in São Paulo as an umbrella organization, embracing ideas of both the Frente as well as TEN.   The M.N.U. emerged at a time when there was growing protest against the policies of the military dictatorship and focused on many of the same issues as its predecessors: discrimination, prejudice, and lack of jobs.   The 1980s also brought new issues: police brutality, health care, battered women, the rights of children, and the rights to religious expression.[31]

The political shift in the 1980s was an opening that the MNU seized to promote equal rights.   The newly-felt presence of the Afro-Brazilian-led Civil Rights Movement was seen with the celebration of 'The International Day for the Elimination of Racial Discrimination' on March 21, 1983 in Rio.[32] The revision of the Brazilian Constitution that began in 1986 presented a national forum for civil rights' advocates to influence national law and attitudes concomitantly.   Abdias do Nascimento, founder of TEN and a close ally of the M.N.U., called for the Constitution to define racism as a crime against humanity; institute mandatory literacy campaigns; guarantee *'insonomia racial'* in all Brazilian life, including compensations for collective indemnity for more than four centuries of racism which would include a guarantee of property for black communities and black peasants; to prohibit *vadiagem* to be defined as a 'penal infraction', and to abolish the death penalty.[33] While all of these demands were not met, the 1988 Constitution was nonetheless a victory for civil rights activists and heralded a new period of dialogue between blacks and the national government.   Only in this period was discrimination specifically clarified as a national crime '...subject to imprisonment'.[34]

Today, black political organizations, cultural associations, grassroots organizations are experiencing a renaissance. Black political and cultural consciousness is and the rise. Black Brazilians have reached out to its Latin American and North American neighbors through various pan-African forums such as the Congress of Black Culture in the Americas. Black non-governmental organizations in major cities such as Salvador, Rio, Belo Horizonte and São Paulo are beginning to make an impact on the lives of Brazilians often without state support.[35]

Still, the tensions between black culture and national culture remain today, although many changes have benefited blacks. Blacks and mulattos constitute a vital and significant number among Brazil's cultural and popular ambassadors. There are a handful of black Brazilian congressional representatives including Benedita da Silva, Brazil's first black woman in congress, and Brazil has its first black cabinet minister, albeit in the realm of sports, an arena now closely associated with the popular classes. The appointment of the new Minister of Sports, Edson Arantes do Nascimento, popularly known as Pelé, still represents the exception rather than the rule. Nascimento's position is unique for two major reasons. First, he emerged as one of Brazil's most popular national heroes as a result of his performance in the 1958 World Cup, which Brazil won. Pelé managed to maintain that position for the next two decades, throughout the Brazilian dictatorship. Second, and paradoxically, Pelé has publicly claimed that he has never experienced discrimination in Brazil because of his race.[36]

According to many black activists, Pelé's position is a poignant example of the power of whitening today. Indeed for many Brazilians, Pelé is not black, Pelé is simply 'Pelé', a Brazilian hero. Others explain that Pelé adheres to a patriotic rhetoric because of his important position in society, lending credence to the belief that ethnic identity remains secondary to national identity. The rhetoric of complaint does not become a true patriot. Still, Pelé's political appointment in the 1990s is indicative of a type of change that has come with the democratic transformation since the late 1980s. And Brazil has become more comfortable with its diversity. At the 1998 World Expo in Lisbon, Portugal, Brazil chose to cover its entrance with portaits of Brazilians from all walks of life and from all ethnicities, races and mixtures, for example. Similarly, Brazil's 1998 World Cup national squad reflected a diversity on the national scale unimaginable in the 1930s.

In other arenas such as Brazilian popular music similar developments are underway. While the production of Brazilian popular music now lies in the hands of few Brazilian or multinational companies, black writers, composers, and interpreters are not uncommon. Moreover, black heroes, and themes continue to flourish, now from a myriad of perspectives within the growing musical industry.

Despite these changes, and although Brazilians today readily admit the cultural impact of Africans on Brazilian culture, many Brazilians would still prefer to avoid associating 'blackness' with their Brazilian identity. Blackness continues to represent poverty, marginalization, and backwardness associated with countries in Africa or nations in the Caribbean such as Haiti. In 1992, musicians Caetano Veloso and Gilberto Gil poignantly criticized and dramatized Brazilian's relationship to 'blackness' in a song entitled 'Haiti':

> When you are invited to climb up the *adro*
> of the Jorge Amado Foundation [in Salvador]
> To see from up high the line of soldiers, almost everyone black
> Beating the heads of black *malandros*, and mulatto thieves
> And others almost white, treated as if they were black
> Only to show the other 'almost blacks'
> (and they're all almost black)
> And to show the 'almost whites' [who are] poor like blacks
> How blacks, poor people, and mulattos, and 'almost whites
> almost blacks' [who are] poor like blacks are treated.
> It doesn't matter if, at that very moment, the entire world could
> be focusing its eyes upon the very place where slaves were
> punished
> And today a beat, a beat...
>
> ...Nothing is important...No one is a citizen
> If you go to see the celebration in the Pelo, and if youdon't go
> Think of Haiti. Pray for Haiti
> Haiti is here. Haiti is not here![37]

'Haiti' is an important symbol for the racial tensions that Brazil has historically experienced, but have become particularly acute in the modern era. It is not so much that prejudice exists in Brazil, prejudice against peoples of African descent lingers throughout the Americas. For so long Brazilians have claimed that it did not exist. Brazilians have rightly criticized outsiders, particularly North Americans, for their insistence on separate racial identities, while they ignored their own deep-rooted prejudices. Popular expressions and language passed down from generation to generation continue to provide examples: 'branco por procuracão' (white by proxy), 'melhorar a raça', (improve the race), 'a coisa está preta' (what a black situation, referring to a terrible situation) and 'no Brasil não tem discriminacão, o negro sabe seu lugar' (in Brazil there is no discrimination, the black knows his place) are indicative of the same phenomenon. Other examples exist in music, songs, and a myriad of other popular expressions.[38]

Latin American culture may be a product of cultural intermingling and miscegenation, but the position of blacks must be re-examined.[39] Brazilian nationalist ideologies of the 1930s coincided with the emerging nationalist ideology of many other Latin American nations. Black intellectuals (in the Gramscian sense) within Brazil pursued a consciousness raising of their own. It is important to reiterate the words of V. S. Naipaul when he stated that [national] consciousness-raising is a process without which a persecuted sector can be wiped out.[40] As statistics have indicated, blacks were being assimilated into the Brazilian mainstream throughout history, physically though miscegenation, but psychologically through myths of racial democracy, and patterns of behavior that encouraged upwardly mobile blacks to consider themselves if not mulattos, *morenos*, but certainly not *pretos*.

At times, many Afro-Latin stereotypes enforced positive stereotypes of blacks as gifted emotional beings, while whites were rational. This was also typical of many black and mulatto writers of the period, who turned to 'primitive cultures' during the general disenchantment between World War I and World War II. The dominant intellectuals were not completely successful, in that protests arose, signaling that the level of inculcation was certainly not fully complete. Black militancy arose precisely becaue of blacks' inability to become a part of the middle class.

Since the nineteenth century, the state had become the instrument of rationalization of the nation. Nationalist intellectuals assisted in the process of rationalizing and ordering the nation, and therefore became the broker between the state and the popular masses. Their cultural-political power allowed them to organize the thoughts of (for) the nation, according to the following hierarchy:[41]

Figure 6.1 The Organization and Propagation of National Culture

Nation-State
Marshals of the state
Dominant Intellectual Authority
(Concentrated in Rio and São Paulo)
*
*
*
*

institutionalizes
Ideas
through
Means of Communications
*
*
*
*
*

(Publications)
From upper-middle class
Validates ideas
*
*
*
*
*

Ideas
Access to the (Popular) Media
Radio********************Music
Propagated
*
*
*
*

Masses

Intellectuals, no matter how radical they may attempt to become, are influenced by current philosophical trends. They, as Antonio Gramsci has so eloquently put it, are that stratum that exercises organizational functions in the field of production as well as in the field of culture and politics. Influenced by their own agendas and backgrounds, their ideas reflect the influence of a generational *weltanschauung*. This world view is dependent upon, but not limited to the sociopolitical environment of the time.[42]

Each society has its basic institutions. The idea of the 'nation' provides the base on which those institutions are built. History cannot be discarded, but how it is interpreted depends on social relations, time, space, and politics. As Juan Rial rightly points out, real acts are not symbols, nonetheless, they are conceived on a symbolic level and within a national forum become representative of national emotion. Nationalist-minded intellectuals together with the political elite maintained the status quo as long as that vision continued to enrich their concept of self, and enhanced the idea of community to which they belong.[43]

The change that began in 1930 was populist-corporatist in nature. Its ideas were institutionalized and matured into the Estado Novo which disallowed any challenges to the status quo. It is important to reiterate that both the Black Front and TEN emerged during periods of democratic *abertura*. Still, given their location in the Brazilian superstructure, their effect on Brazilian consciousness was minimal. The modernist interpretation of Brazilian reality remained classic.

As Frank Kermode has affirmed, there are two ways of maintaining a classic: establishing its access to the contemporary mind and its ability to be accommodated to the new reality. The process of accommodation is an intimate relationship between citizen and text. Texts (written or musical) can come to mean something that they do not specifically state by the propagation of symbols which register or make connections to the present situation through some metaphor or symbol. TEN's challenge, as valid as it may have been, was not seen by the population at large as a reflection of the Brazilian experience. Of course, this perception was directly related to the level of inculcation towards a utopian version of Brazilian culture.[44]

Even in the post 1960 era, Brazil promoted institutionalized myths. Racial democracy and miscegenation will continue to play an important role in the identity of Latin America, a region dominated by North American political and economic influences. It is common that one generation reevaluate the ideas and myths of the one before. Intellectuals, politicians, artists, and even the layman will continue to reinterpret and redefine their national cultures. New mechanisms will arise in a world that has become increasingly more volatile and where communication has become more rapid. Nonetheless, future generations will not have the luxury of a *tabula rasa*. The base has already been constructed in the national psyche. The generation of 1930 attempted to create a given vision of their rcountry. They responded to the ideas of the prior generation based on political accidents and ideas that made their chosen approach expedient at the time. Nonetheless, their interests were still tied to the existing political and economic powers. It may be that challenges will only be heard and taken seriously when there are changes in the social structures which reflect more closely the national mythology. Yet with these changes there may be no need for a forging of a national consciousness.

Notes

[1]   Hayden White, 'The Historical Text as Literary Artifact', *Tropics of Discourse* (Baltimore: John Hopkins University Press, 1978): 81-98.

[2]   Guillermo de Torre, *Historia de la literatura de la vanguardia* (Madrid: 1965), 23-24.

[3]   Cornelia Navari, 'The Origins of the Nation-State', *The Nation-State* (New York: St. Martin's, 1981), 13.

[4]   Ibid, 20.

[5]   Brain K. Taylor, 'Culture: Whence, Wither and Why?' *The Future of Cultural Minorities* (New York: The Macmillan Press Ltd, 1979), 9-29.

[6]   Ibid, 20-25.

[7]   Claudio Velez, 'Centralism, Nationalism and Integration' published report. (Budapest: Center for Afro-Asian Research, 1969).

[8]   Fulgencio Batista, *Cuba Betrayed* (New York: Vintage Press, 1962), appendix-economic references and 202-207.

[9]   See such indigenista writers as the Peruvians Haya de la Torre and José María Arguedas.

[10]   June E. Nash 'Feminism, Women's Suffrage and the Suffrage Movement in Brazil 1850-1932', *Latin American Research Review* 15, no 1 (1980): 65-111. The author argues that few women gained social mobility and that they are still considered second class citizens. Similar arguments are found in Morris J. Balchman, *Eve in a Democracy* (New York: New York University, IberoAmerican Language and Area Centers, 1973). Little work is done on the struggles and challenges of the Japanese in Brazil, although much is known about their deplorable conditions as indentured servants in the Saõ Paulo area.

[11]   David J. Hellwig, 'Racial Paradise or Run-Around? Afro-North American Views on Race relations in Brazil', *American Studies* 31 (Fall 1990): 43-60.

[12]   Angel Pinto, 'El Negro, La Constituyente y la Constitución', *Democracia* La Habana, 1939 (A conference given to the Sociedad Adelante reprinted in Tomás Fernández Robaina, 162-163). This article is partially cited in Tomás

Fernández, *El Negro en Cuba 1902-1958* (Havana: Editorial de Ciencias Sociales, 1990), 162.

[13] Abdias do Nascimento, 'Espiritú e Fisonomia do Teatro Experimental do Negro', (discurso pronunciado na A.B.I. no ato da instalacão da Conferencia Nacional do Negro, May 1949), *Teatro Experimental do Negro*, 79-80.

[14] Octavio Ianni, *Crisis in Brazil* Phyllis B. Eveleth trans. (New York and London: Columbia University Press, 1970), 170. To a certain extent to which the nationalist model of development was abandoned in favor of international association during the presidency of Juscelino Kubitscheck (1956-1960).

[15] Anani Dzidzienyo, 'The Position of Blacks in Brazilian Society', *The Position of Blacks in Brazilian and Cuban Society* (London: Minority Rights Group, 1979), 9.

[16] Octavio Ianni, 212. Ianni states that the middle class was docile. I prefer the use of the word middle sectors, which include some working class people, artesans and those of both that belong to the literate population. In addition, docility implies apathy. Brazilians chose among their options given their limitations.

[17] Charles Wagley, *Introduction to Brazil* (New York: Columbia University Press, 1971).

[18] Pelé is quoted as saying that there was no prejudice in Brazil, see Anani, *The Position of Blacks in Cuba and Brazil*, 7.

[19] 'Publisher's Weekly Interviews: Jorge Amado', *Publisher's Weekly*, (23 June 1975), 20. Gilberto Freyre had also written an article for the *Courier* entitled 'The Afro-Brazilian Experiment', *Courier* (May-June 1986): 24. In his typical nationalist pride, Freyre indicated that Brazil can be looked at as a model for the new African nations since she (Brazil) created a new civilization based on the African element, but without discarding the importance of the European which was essential to the consolidation of the nation.

[20] Jorge Amado, 'Gods and Men Have Mingled', *Courier* (May-June 1986): 25.

[21] 'Bloco Racista, Nota Disonante', *A Tarde*, 12 fev, 1917 reprinted in *10 Anos de Luta Contra O Racismo*. Salvador, Bahia: M.N.U., 1988), 10. This article was a criticism of the Bahian musical group Ilê Ayê who used prominent signs such as 'Mundo Negro' (Black World), 'Black Power', 'Negro para Você' (Black For You). In an interview, Margareth Menezes, a Brazilian singer from Bahia, relates the so- called reverse discrimination that she as a black artist experienced when she attempted to join the group under question. She was denied because she was too light skinned. See *Beat* 10, no. 2, (1991); 46-17.

[22] Patricia Aufderheide, 'Brazil', *World Cinema Since 1945* William Luhr ed. (New York: Ungar, 1987): 70-85.

[23] Carlos Diegues, *Ganga Zumba* (Rio de Janeiro: Copacabana Films, 1964). The film Macunaíma was a loyal representation of the Andrade text.

[24] Constitutional Amendment No. 7 May 22, 1964 suspended provisionally and in part Article 141 which enumerates Individual Rights and Guaranties.

[25] Florestan Fernandes, *The Negro in Brazilian Society*. Jacqueline D. Skiles et al

Trans. (Atheneum and New York: Columbia University Press, 1969). Original book entitled *A integracão do negro na sociedade de classes* (1965).

[26] Ibid, p. 132-134.

[27] Ibid.

[28] Octavio Ianni, *Crisis in Brazil*, 188-195.

[29] Emilia Viotti da Costa, 246.

[30] An electoral college established in 1982 chose provisional President Tancredo Neves who would lead Brazil back to democracy. Neves, who fell ill, was superseded by his Vice President José Sarney. The first popularly elected President, Fernando Collar de Mello came to power in 1990.

[31] The precursor to the MNU was the Movimento Unificado Contra a Discriminacão Racial (MUCDR) which later added the word 'negro' becoming the MNUCDR.

[32] Decreto no. 6627, March 21, 1983, instituted by the United Nation General Assembly in 1966.

[33] Abdias, Interview by author, 16 May 1991 Rio de Janeiro, tape recording, Abdias do Nascimento's residence, Rio de Janeiro. Many of these items are reprinted in *Povo Negro: A Sucessão e a Nova Republica*. p. 25.

[34] Ibid.

[35] See Darién J. Davis, 'Postscript', *No Longer Invisible: Afro-Latin Americans Today* (London: Minority Rights Group, 1995), p. 359-378.

[36] See 'Interview with Pelé', *Raça* Ano 2 No. 9 (May 1997). See also letters to the editor in response to Pelé's interview in *Raça* Ano 2 No. 11 (July 1997), 8.

[37] Gilberto Gil and Caetano Veloso, 'Haiti', *Tropicalia 2* (Polygram, 1993), CD, band 1.

[38] Abdias do Nascimento points out many of these expressions in his collection of essays. See *Brazil Mixture o Massacre?* (Dover, Massachusetts: The Majority Press, 1989). In Chapter 2, he quotes a Brazilian old saying, 'branca para casar, negra para trabalhar, mulata para fornicar' (white lady for marrying, black woman for working, mulatto woman for fornicating).

[39] Frantz Fanon, *Black Skin White Masks* (New York: Grove Weidenfeld, 1967), 113.

[40] The comment on the importance of race consciousness is taken from a discussion in V.P. Naipaul, *India: Wounded Civilization* (New York: Alfred A. Knopf, 1977).

[41] Black intellectuals pursued a similar process within their respective communities.

[42] Antonio Gramsci, *Selections from the Prison Notebooks* (London: Lawerence and Wishart 1971), 96-98.

[43] Juan Rial, 'El Imaginario Social Urugauyo y la Dictadura. Los Mitos Políticos (De-Re)-Construcción', *De Mitos y Memorías Políticos* (Montivideo: Ediciones de la Banda Oriental, 1986), 16-17.

[44] Frank Kermode, *The Classic* (New York: Viking Press, 1975), 40.

Bibliography

Archives and Special Collections

Arquivos das Poliçias Politicais do Estado de Rio de Janeiro. (APP)

Arquivo Nacional (AN). Rio de Janeiro.

Bibleoteca Nacional: Seção de Manuscritos. Rio de Janeiro.

Bibleoteca Nacional: Seção da Musica, Ministerio da Cultura. Rio de Janeiro. (BN)

Centro de Pesquisa e Documentação (CPDOC), Fundação Getúlio Vargas. Rio de Janeiro.

Library of Congress, Washington, D.C.

Museu da Imagen e do Som, Rio de Janeiro.

Museu Histórico do Estado de Rio de Janeiro, Rio de Janeiro.

Schomburg Center, New York Public Library.

Secretaria do Patrimônio Historico e Artístico Nacional, Ministerio da Cultura, Rio de Janeiro.

Journals/Newspapers

O Clarim D'Alvorada

Correio da Manha

Correio da Manha

Folha do Povo

O Estado de São Paulo

A Noite

Ordem

Quilombo

Voz da Raça

Interviews

Nascimento, Abdias do., interview by author, 16 May 1991 Rio de Janeiro, tape recording, Abdias do Nascimento's residence, Rio de Janeiro.

Souza, Ruth de, interview by author, June 1991 Rio de Janeiro, tape recording, Ruth de Souza's residence, Rio de Janeiro.

Miscellaneous Interviews, May-June 1991, Rio de Janeiro.

Miscellaneous Interviews, Summer 1993, Rio de Janeiro.

Books/ Manuscripts

Almeida, Martins. *Brasil errado*. Rio de Janeiro: Schmidt, 1932.

Amado, Jorge. O pais do Carnival. São Paulo: Martins, 1931.

Amaral Azevedo, Antonio José. *Ensaios brasileiros*. 2nd ed. Rio de Janeiro: Omena e Barreto, 1930.

Andrade, Mario de. *Macunaíma*. São Paulo: Livraria Martins, 1968.

--------. *Hallucinated City*. J. Tomlins. (trans.) Nashville, Tennessee: Vanderbilt University Press, 1968.

-------- *O movimento modernista*. Rio de Janeiro, 1942.

Andrade, Oswald de.   *Obras Completas* Vol 6   Rio de Janeiro: Civilização Brasileira, 1970

Alves Filho, Aluízo.   *Pensamiento político no Brasil: Manoel Bonfim, un ensayista esquecido*. Rio de Janeiro: Achiame, 1979.

Alves, Francisco. *Minha Vida*. Rio de Janeiro: Brasil Contemporaneo, 1937.

Amaral, Azevedo.   *O estado autoritário e a realidade nacional*. Rio de Janeiro: José Olympico, 1938.

Arinos de Mello Franco, Afonso.   *Introdção á Realidade Brasileira*. Rio de Janeiro: Schmidt-Editor, 1933.

Backauser, Everedo.   *Problemas do Brasil*. Rio de Janeiro: Ed. Omnia, 1932.

Barbosa, Francisco de Assis.   *Testamento de Mario de Andrade e outros reportagens*. Rio de Janeiro, 1954.

Barroso, Gustavo.   *A palavra e o pensamento integralista*.   Rio de Janeiro: Civilização Brasileira S.A., 1935.

--------. *O integralista e o mundo*.   Rio de Janeiro: Civilização Brasileira, 1936.

--------. *O integralismo de norte a sur*.   Rio de Janeiro: Civilização Brasileira, 1934.

Bastide, Roger.   *A poesia afro-brasileira*. São Paulo: Martins, 1943.

Bello, José María.   *Panorama do Brasil*. Rio de Janeiro: Imprensa Nacional, 1936.

--------. *A questão social e a solução brasileira*.   Rio de Janeiro: Imprensa Nacional, 1936.

Bevilaqua, Clovis. 'Gustave Le Bon e a psicologia dos povos'. *Revista Brasileira*, 5 (1896): n.p.

Boas, Franz.   *Race, Language and Culture*. New York: Free Press, 1940.

Boxer, Charles R. 'The Colour Question in the Portuguese Empire, 1415-1825'. *Proceedings of the British Academy* 47 (1961): 113-138.

--------. *Race Relations in the Portuguese Colonial Empire, 1415-1825.* London: Oxford University Press, 1963.

Cabral, Oswaldo R. 'Os grupos negros em Santa Catarina'. *Laguna e outros ensaios.* Florionopolis: Imprensa Oficial, 1939.

Cândido, Antônio. 'Literatura and the Rise of Brazilian National Self-Identity'. *Luso-Brazilian Review* 5 (1968): 27-43.

Caravalho, Elysio de. *A realidade brasileira.* Rio de Janeiro: Anuario do Brasil, 1922.

Cardoso Junior, Abel. *Carmen Miranda: a cantora do Brasil.* Rio de Janeiro, 1978.

Cardoso, Fernando Henrique and Otavio Ianni. *Cor and mobilidade social em Florionopolis: Aspectos as relações entre negros e brancos numa comunidade do Brasil meridonal.* São Paulo: Compañia Editora Nacional, 1960.

Carneiro, José Fernando. *Aprestação de Jorge de Lima.* Rio de Janeiro, 1954.

Carneiro, Edison and Abdias do Nascimento et al. *80 anos da abolição.* Rio de Janeiro: Editora Cadernos Brasileiros, 1968.

Caravalho de, Elysio de.   *A realidade brasileira.*   Rio de Janeiro: Anuario do Brasil, 1922.

Caravalho, Ronald de y Elysio de Caravalho. *Affirmações, um agapé de intellectuães.* Rio de Janeiro: Monitor Mercantil, 1921.

Celso, Affonso. *Porque me ufano do meu pais.* Rio de Janeiro: Liv Garnier, 1901.

Costa, Haroldo. *Fala Crioulo.* Rio de Janeiro: Editora Record, 1987.

Coleção das Leis do Brasil. Rio de Janeiro, 1939.

Da Cunha, Euclides. *Rebellion in the Backlands.* Samuel Putnam trans. Chicago: University of Chicago Press, 1944.

De La Torre, Victor Raul Haya. *A dónde va Indoamerica?* Santiago, Chile: Bibleoteca America, 1936.

Delafosse, Maurice. *The Negroes of Africa: History and Culture.* Washington D.C.: Associated Publishers, 1931.

Donald Pierson. *Negroes in Brazil: A Study of Race Contact at Bahia.* Chicago: University of Chicago Press, 1942.

Edmundo, Luiz. *O Rio de Janeiro de meu tiempo.* Rio de Janeiro: Imprensa Nacional, 1938.

Estellita Lins, Augusto E. ed. *A Nova Constituição dos Estados Unidos do Brazil.* Rio: José Konfino, 1938.

Ferreira, Orbelino Geraldes. *Brasil Pedagógico.* Lisboa: Edição da Académico da Escola do Magistério Primário, 1953.

Figueiredo, Jackson de. *Do nacionalismo na hora presente.* Rio de Janeiro: Livraria Católica, 1921.

--------. *Pascal e a Inquietação Moderna.* Rio de Janeiro: Anuario do Brasil, 1922.

--------. *In Memoriam.* Rio de Janeiro: Centro D. Vidal, n.a.

Filho, Mario. *O negro no futebol brasileiro.* São Paulo: Editôra Civilização Brasileira, 1964.

Forntoura, João Neves da. *A Alianza Liberal e a Revolução de 1930.* Memorias II. Porto Alegre: Editora Globo, 1963.

Freyre, Gilberto. *The Masters and the Slaves.* New York: Alfred A. Knopf, 1946.

--------. *Alem do apenas moderno.* Rio de Janeiro: José Olympico Editora, 1973.

--------. *The Mansions and the Shanties: Making of Modern Brazil.* New York: Alfred A. Knopf, 1963.

--------. *Interpretación del Brasil.* México: Fondo de Cultura Económica, 1945.

--------. *Novo Mundo nos Trópicos.* São Paulo: Cia Ed. Nacional/EDUSP, 1971.

--------. 'O homen brasileiro: formação étnica e cultural'. *Estudo de Problemas Brasileiros.* Recife: Universidade Federal de Pernambuco, 1971: 167-178.

--------. *Portuguese Integration in the Tropics.* Lisbon: Tipografia Silva, 1961.

--------. 'Social Life in Brazil in the Middle of the Nineteenth Century'. *Hispanic American Historical Review* 5 (1922): 597-630.

Geertz, Clifford (ed.) *Old Societies and New States: The Quest for Modernity in Asia and Africa.* Illinois: Free Press, 1963.

Gobineau, Artur de. *The Inequality of Human Races.* Vol I 1853-1855 London: Heineman, 1915.

Gordon, Eugene. *An Essay on Race Amalgamation.* Rio de Janeiro: Serviço de Puiblicações, 1951.

Goulart, Silvana. *Sob A Verdade Oficial. Ideologia, Propaganda e Censura no Estado Novo.* São Paulo: Editora Marco Zero, 1990.

Henriques, Alfonso. *Vargas o Maquiavelico.* São Paulo: Palacio do Livro, 1961.

Holanda, Sergio Buarque de. *Raizes do Brazil.* 2nd ed. Rio de Janeiro: José Olympio, Ed., 1948.

Lissovsky, Mauricio and Paulo Sergio Morães de Sá. (orgs.) *Colunas da Educação: A construcão do Ministério da Educação e Saude.* Rio de Janeiro: Fundação Getúlio Vargas/ CPDOC, 1996, 1996.

Marques dos Reis, Antonio. *A Constituição Federal Brasileira de 1934.* Rio de Janeiro: A. Ceolho Branco F. Editor, 1934.

Martí, José. *Obras Completas.* (Vol 6) La Habana: Editorial Lex, 1946.

--------. *Our America* Philip Foner ed. New York and London: Monthly Review Press, 1977.

Mello, Valdecir. *1978-1988: 10 anos de luta contra o racismo.* Salvador: Movimento Negro Unificado, 1988.

Mustelier, Enrique. *La Extinción del Negro.* Habana: Imprenta de Rambla, 1912.

Nabuco, Joaquim. *Abolutionism: The Brazilian Anti-Slavery Struggle.* Urbana, Chicago and London: University of Chicago Press, 1977.

Nachman, Robert G. 'Positivism, Modernization and the Middle Class in Brazil'. *Hispanic American Historical Review* 57 no. 7 (Feb 1977): 1-23.

Nascimento, Abdias do. *O genocidio do negro brasileiro: processo de un racismo mascarado.* Rio de Janeiro: Editora Paz e Terra, 1978.

--------. *Mixture or Massacre? Essays on the Genocide of a Black People.* Elisa Larkin Nascimento trans. New York: Afrodiaspora, 1979.

--------. *Drama para Negros, prólogo para brancos.* Rio de Janeiro: Teatro Experimental do Negro, 1951.

Nott, J.C. and G.R. Gliddon. *Types of Mankind or Ethnological Researches.* Philadelphia, Lippincoatt and London: Trubner, 1884.

Ortega y Gasset, José. *El tema de nuestro tiempo.* Buenos Aires: Espasa-Calpe, 1945.

--------. *The Revolt of the Masses.* New York: W.W. Norton andCompany, Inc, 1932.

Penna, J. Oliveira de Meira. *Em berço espléndido.* Rio de Janeiro: Liv. Gráfica, 1974.

Pereira, Astrojildo. *Crítica impura.* Rio de Janeiro: Civilização Brasileira, 1963.

Pererira, Loris Rocha. *Velhos carnavais.* São Paulo: Câmara Brasileira do Livro, 1994.

Pontes, Eloi. *Em defesa da raça.* Rio de Janeiro: D.I.P., 1940.

Prado, Paulo. *Retrato de Brasil*. São Paulo: Duprat, 1928.

Ramos, Artur. *A aculturação negra no Brasil*. São Paulo: Companhia Editora Nacional, 1942.

Ramos, Alberto Guerriero. *Patología social do 'branco' brasileiro*. Rio de Janeiro: Journal do Commercio, 1955

Ramos Tinhorão, José. *A historia social da música popular brasileira*. Lisboa: Editorial Caminho, S.A., 1990.

Ricardo, Cassiano. *Martim Cerreré*. São Paulo: Revista de Tribunais, 1928.

Rodrigues, José Honario. *Brasil e Africa*. Rio de Janeiro: Edições GRD, 1961.

Rodó, José Enrique. *Ariel* Margaret Sayers Peden trans. Austin, Texas: University of Texas Press, 1988.

--------. *Ariel*. 19th ed. London: Cambrdidge University Press, 1967.

Rosa, Virginio Santa. *Qué foi o tenetismo?* 1933 Reprint, Rio de Janiero: Civilização Brasileira, 1963.

Salgado, Plínio. *O Integralismo perante a nação*. 2a Edição. Rio de Janeiro: Livraria Clásica Brasileira, S.A., 1950.

--------. *Obras Completas*. São Paulo: Editora das Americas, 1955.

Saloutos, Theodore. *Populism Reaction or Reform?* New York: Holt, Rivehart and Winston, 1968.

Sarmiento, Domingo Faustino. *Facundo*. Mexico: Nuestros Clásicos, Universidad Nacional Autónoma de México, 1972.

Severiano, Jairio. *Getúlio Vargas e a música popular brasileira*. Rio de Janeiro: Fundação Getúlio Vargas/ CPDOC, 1982.

Silva Brito, Mario da. *Historia do modernismo brasileiro*. Antecedentes da Semana de Arte Moderna. São Paulo: Ed. Saraiva, 1958.

Torres, Alberto. *A organização nacional*. Rio de Janeiro: Imprenta Nacional, 1912.

--------. *O problema nacional*. (Reprint) São Paulo: Companhia Editora Nacional, 1938.

--------. *O problema nacional brasileiro*.   Rio de Janeiro, Impresa Nacional Brasileiro,   1914.

Vasconcelos, José.   *La raza cósmica: misión de la raza ibero-americana*. Mexico: Aguilar S.A. de Ediciones, 1961.

Vila-Lobos, Heitor.   *A Música Nacionalista no Governo Getúlio Vargas*.   Rio de Janeiro: Departamento de Imprensa e Propganda DIP), n/a.

Secondary Sources

Abreu,   Regina   Maria   do   Rego   Monteiro.   'Emblemas da nacionalidade: o culto a Euclides da Cunha'. *Revista Brasileira de Ciências Sociais*   Vol. 9, no.   24 (February 1994): 66-84.

Alba, Victor. *Nationalists Without Nations*. New York: Frederick A. Praeger Publishers, 1968.

Alencar, Edigar de. *O carnaval carioca através da música* 5 ed. São Paulo, Franciso Alves, 1985.

Amaral, Aracy A.   'Oswald de Andrade e as artes plásticas no modernismo dos anos vinte'. *Revista do Instituto de Estudos Brasileiros* 33 (1992):   68-75.

Amdao, Jorge. 'Gods and Men Have Mingled'. *Courier* (May-June 1986): 25.

Anderson, Benedict. *Imagined Communities*. London and New York: Verso, 1983.

Andrews, George Reid. *Blacks and Whites in São Paulo: 1888-1988*. Madison: University of Wisconsin Press, 1991.

Arnold, James A. *Modernism and Negritude*. Cambridge: Harvard University Press, 1981.

As culturas negras. Rio de Janeiro: Casa de Estudante do Brasil, 1972.

Azevedo, Thales de. *As elites de côr: Um estudo de ascensão social.* São Paulo, 1953.

--------. *Democracia racial: ideologia e realidade.* Petrópolis, Brazil: Editôra Vozes, 1975.

Barman, Roderick J. *Brazil: The Forging of a Nation, 1798-1852.* Stanford: Stanford University Press, 1988.

Bell, Era Thompson. 'Does Amalgamation Work in Brazil?' *Ebony* 20 (July 1956): 27-34.

Berger, Bennet M. 'How long is a generation?' *British Journal of Sociology*, Vol. II 1960: 1 -23.

Betancur, Arturo Ariel. *Getúlio Vargas: nacionalismo e industrialización en el Brasil, 1930-1945.* Montivideo: Fundación de Cultura Universitaria, 1991.

Brunetti, Almir de Campos. 'Abdias do Nascimento: Negro de Alma Branca'. *Revista Iberoamericana* Vol. 50, no. 126 January-March 1984): 203-209.

Burns, E. Bradford. 'Ideology in Nineteenth-Century Latin American Historiography'. *Hispanic American Historic Review* 58 (30): 409-431.

--------. 'The Destruction of a Folk Past: Euclides da Cunha and Cataclysmic Cultural Clash'. *Review of Latin American Studies* Vol. 3, no. 1 (1990): 16-35.

Butler, Kim D. *Freedoms Given Freedoms Won: Afro-Brazilians in Post-Abolition São Paulo and Salvador.* New Brunswick: Rutgers University Press, 1998.

Cabral, Sergio. *Ensaios de opinião.* Rio de Janeiro: Editora Inúbia, 1975.

Campbell, Joseph. *The Power of Myth.* New York: Doubleday, 1988.

Carbonell, Walterio. *Como surgió la cultura nacional.* Havana: Ediciones Yaka, 1961.

Carneiro, Edison de Sousa. 'La nacionalización del negro en el Brazil'. *Cuba professional* (Havana) 3, no. 10 (April-June 1954): 16-18.

Carneiro, Maria Luiza Tucci. 'Sob a máscara do nacionalismo: autoritarismo e anti-semitismo na era Vargas, 1930-1945'. *Estudios Interdisciplinarios de América Latina y el Caribe* Vol. 1, no. 1 (Jan-June 1990), 23-40.

Chiavenatto Julio José. *O negro no Brasil: Da senzala á Guerra do Paraguai* 4th ed. São Paulo: Editora Brasilaiense, 1987.

Compte, Auguste. *Auguste Compte and Positivism: The Essential Writings.* ed. Gertrud Lenzer. New York: Harper and Row, 1975.

Cooper, Barry. *The End of History: An Essay on Modern Hegelianism.* Toronto: University of Toronto Press, 1984.

Conliff, Michael Lee. 'Rio de Janeiro During the Great Depression 1928-1937. Social Reform and Emergence of Populism in Brazil' Ph.D. Diss. (Stanford, 1976).

Conrad, Robert. *The Destruction of Brazilian Slavery, 1850-1888.* Berkeley: University of California Press, 1972.

Costa, João Cruz. *A History of Ideas in Brazil.* Suzette Macedo (trans.) Berkeley and Los Angeles: University of California Press.

Coulthard, G.R. *Race and Color in Caribbean Literature.* New York: Oxford University Press, 1962

Crawford, William Rex. *A Century of Latin American Thought.* Cambridge, Mass: Harvard University Press, 1961.

Cunningham, Adrian. *The Theory of Myth.* London: Sheed and Ward, 1973.

Cunha, Lois Baena. *A Verdadeira História do Futebol Brasileiro.* Rio de Janeiro: Edicão Rua Araújo, 1994.

Da Costa, Emilia Viotti. *The Brazilian Empire: Myths and Histories.* Belmont, California: Wadsworth Publishing Company Inc, 1985.

Davis, Darién J. (ed.) *Slavery and Beyond: The African Impact on Latin America and the Caribbean.* Wilmington, Delaware: Scholarly Resources, 1995.

De Queirós Mattoso, Katia M. *To Be A Slave in Brazil, 1550-1880*. Arthur Goldhammer trans. New Brunswick: Rutgers University Press, 1986.

Degler, Carl. *Neither Black nor White: Slavery and Race Relations in Brazil and the U.S.* New York: Macmillian, 1972.

Della Cava, Ralph. 'Catholicism and Society in the Twentieth Century'. *Latin American Research Review* 11, 2 (1976): 7-50.

Dicionario Literario Brasileiro. Vol II São Paulo: Edição Saraiva, 1969.

Delafosse, Maurice. *The Negroes of Africa: History and Culture*. Washington D.C.: Associated Publishers, 1931.

Deutsch, Karl W. and William J. Freidrich. *Nation Building*. New York: Atherton Press, 1963.

Doob, Leonard W. *Patriotism and Nationalism: Their Psychological Foundations*. New Haven and London: Yale University Press.

Douglas, Mary. *Natural Symbols, Explorations in Cosmology*. London, 1970.

Drescher, Seymour. *The Abolition of Slavery and the Aftermath of Emancipation in Brazil*. Durham: Duke University Press, 1988.

Dulles, John Foster. *Anarchists and Communist in Brazil, 1900-1935*. Austin, Texas: University of Texas Press, 1974.

--------. *Vargas of Brazil*. Austin: University of Austin Press, 1969.

Dzidzienyo, Anani and Lourdes Cabral. *The Position of Blacks in Brazilian and Cuban Society*. London: Minority Rights Group, 1979.

Eisendstadt, Samuel. *Intellectuals and Tradition*. New York: Humanities Press, 1973.

Elkins, Stanley. *Slavery, a Problem in American Institutional and Intellectual Life*. Chicago, 1959.

Elliot, T.S. *Notes Towards The Definition of Culture*. New York: Harcourt, Brace and Company, 1949.

--------. *What is a Classic?* London: Faber and Faber Ltd, 1946.

Fanon, Franz. *Black Skin White Masks.* New York: Grove Weidenfeld, 1967.

Faustino Sarmiento, Domingo. *Facundo.* México: Nuestros Clásicos, Universidad Nacional Autónoma de México, 1972.

Feenberg, Andrew. *Luckás, Marx and the Sources of Critical Theory.* Oxford: Martin Robertson, 1981.

Fernandes, Florestan. 'El drama del negro e del mulato en una sociedad que cambia'. *Mundo Nuevo* 33 (March 1969): 11-21.

--------. 'Imigração e relações racias'. *Revista Civilização Brasileira* (Rio de Janeiro) 1, 8 (1966): 75-95.

--------. 'Immigration and Race Relations in São Paulo'. *Présence Africaine* (Paris) 61 (First Quarter, 1967): 103-120.

Fernández Robaina, Tomás. *El negro en Cuba.* La Habana: Editorial de Ciencias Sociales, 1990.

Filho, João Lyra. *Introducão à sociologia dos desportos.* São Paulo, 1974.

Fontaine, Pierre-Michele. (ed.) *Race Class and Power in Brazil.* Los Angeles: University of California, 1980.

Foucault, Michel. *Vigiliar y castigas.* México: Siglo XXI, 1976.

Fraginals, Manuel Moreno. *El ingenio.* La Habana: Editorial de las Ciencias Sociales, 1978.

Franco, Jean. *The Modern Culture of Latin America: Society and the Artist.* Middlesex, England: Pelican Books, 1967.

Frazer, Sir James George. *The Golden Bough.* T.H. Gaster. (ed.) New York: New American Library, 1964.

Freye, Northrop. *Anatomy of Criticism.* Princeton, N.J.: Princeton University Press, 1957.

Fundação CPDOC. *Dicionário Histórico Biográfico Brasileiro 1930-1983.* Vol. IV Rio de Janeiro: Editora Forense-Universitaria Ltd., 1984.

García-Zamor, Jean-Claude. 'Social Mobility of Negroes in Brazil'. *Journal of Inter-American Studies and World Affairs* Vol. 12, no. 2 (April 1970): 242-254.

Gellner, Ernest. *Thought and Change.* London: Weiderfeld and Nicolson, 1964.

G.R. Gliddon and J.C. Nott. *Types of Mankind or Ethnological Researches.* Philadelphia, Lippincoatt and London: Trubner, 1884.

Graham, Lawerence S. *Civil Service Reform in Brazil Principles and Practice.* Austin: University of Texas Press, 1968.

Graham, Richard. ed. *The Idea of Race in Latin America, 1870-1940.* Austin: University of Texas Press, 1990.

Gramsci, Antonio. *Gli Intellecttuali e l'organizzazione della cultura.* Giulio Einaundi Editore, 1964 .

--------. *Los intellectuales y la organization de la cultura.* México: Juan Pablos Ed, 1975.

--------. *Selections From The Prison Notebooks.* New York: International Publishers, 1987.

Guillén, Nicolás. 'Nación y mestizaje'. *Casa de Las Americas* Vol. 6, nos. 36-37 (May-August, 1966): 74.

Guilherme, Olympio. *O nacionalismo e a política internacional do Brazil.* São Paulo: Editôra Fulgos, 1957.

Haberly, David T. *Three Sad Races: Racial Identity and National Consciousness in Brazilian Literature.* Cambridge, England: Cambridge University Press,   1983.

Halloway, Thomas H. *Policing Rio de Janeiro: Repression and Resistance in a 19th Century City.* Stanford: Stanford University Press, 1993.

Hanchard, Michael George. *Orpheus and Power: The Movimento Negro of Rio de Janeiro and São Paulo, Brazil, 1945-1988.* Princeton University Press, 1994.

Hanke, Lewis. *Gilberto Freyre Vida y Obras.* New York: Instituto de las Españas nos Estados Unidos, 1939.

Havighurts, Robert J. and J. Roberto Moreira. *Society and Education in Brazil.* University of Pitsburgh Press, 1965.

Hellwig, David J. 'Racial Paradise or Run-around?:   Afro-North American Views on Race Relations in Brazil'. *American Studies* 31 (Fall 1990): 43-6

Hegel, Georg Wilhem Freidrich. *The Phenomenology of the Mind.* London: G. Allen and Unwing, 1971.

--------. *The Philosophical History.* (J. Sibree trans.) New York: Dover Publications Inc, 1956.

Hernández, Eugenio. *Cuba-Soviet Relations: Divergence and Convergence.* Washington: Georgetown University Press, 1980.

Horwitz, Irving Louis. (ed.) *Revolution in Brazil.* New York: Dutton, 1964.

Humbert, Elie. *C.G. Jung.* Wilmette, Illinois: Chiron Publications, 1984.

Ianni, Octavio. *Crisis in Brazil.* (Phyllis B. Eveleth trans). New York and London: Columbia University Press, 1971.

--------. *Escravidão e racismo.* São Paulo: Editora Hucitec, 1978.

Jackson, Richard L. *The Black Image in Latin American Literature.* Alburquerque: University of New México, 1976.

Jesus, Maria Carolina de. *Child of the Dark.* New York: New American Library, 1962.

Jorrín, Miguel and John D. Martz. *Latin American Political Thought.* Chapel Hill: University of North Carolina Press, 1970.

Karasch, Mary. *Slave Life in Rio de Janeiro, 1808-1850.* Princeton: Princeton University Press, 1987.

Kermode, Frank. *The Classic: Literary Images of Permanence and Change*. New York: Viking Press, 1975.

Kojeve, Alexandre. *Introduction to Hegel*. New York: Basic Books, 1969.

Lardies, Miguel. *Coletânea de leis e regulamentos dos desportes*. (6th edition) Porto Alegre: Edicão Sulina, 1971.

Lamounier, Bolivar. 'Raça e Classe na Politica Brasileira'. *Cuardernos Brasileiros* 47 (May-June 1968): 39-50.

Lerner, Gerda. 'Reconceptualizing Differences Among Women'. *Journal of Women's History* (Winter 1990): 106-123.

Levine, Robert M. *Historiographical Dictionary of Brazil*. Metuchen. N.J.: The Scarecrow Press, 1979.

--------. *Father of the Poor? Vargas and His Era*. Cambridge: Cambridge University Press, 1998.

--------. *The Brazilian Photographs of Genevieve Naylor, 1940-1942*. Durham: Duke University Press, 1998.

--------. *The Vargas Regime: The Critical Years 1934-1938*. New York and London: Columbia University Press, 1970.

Levine, Robert M. and José Carlos Sebe Bom Meihy. *The Life and Death of Carolina Maria de Jesus*. Alburquerque: University of New Mexico Press, 1995.

Levi-Strausse, Claude. 'The Structural Study of Myth'. *Structural Analysis*. Claire Jacobson and Brooke Grundfest Schoepf trans. New York: Basic Books, 1963.

Lira, José Perreira. *Temas de nossos dias: Nacionalismo, corrupção, presença das massas*. Rio de Janeiro: J. Olympio, 1955.

Lowenstein, Karl. *Brazil Under Vargas*. New York: Macmillan, 1942.

Luhr, William. (ed.) *World Cinema Since 1945*. New York: Ungar, 1987.

MacLachlan, Colin M. 'Slavery, Ideology and Institutional Change: The Impact of the Enlightenment on the Slavery in Late

Eighteenth Century Maranhão'. *Journal of Latin American Studies* (May 1979): 1-17.

Macedo, Jorge de. 'Portugal é a economia pombaline. Tesis e hipótesis'. *RHSP* no. 19 (July-Spetember 1954): 83-84.

Mancuso, Flora Edwards. 'The Theater of Black Diaspora: A Comparative Study of Drama in Brazil, Cuba and the United States' Ph.D. Diss., New York University, 1975.

Mannheim, Karl. *Essays on the Sociology of Knowledge.* London: Routledge and Kegan Paul Ltd, 1952.

Marías, Julian. *El método histórico de las generaciones.* Madrid: Revista de Occidente, S.A., 1961.

Martins, Wilson. *The Modernist Idea.* (trans. Jach E. Tomlin) West Port, Conn: Greenwood Press Publishers, 1971.

Neiva de Matos, Cláudia. *Acertei no milhar: malandragem e samba no tempo de Getúlio.* Rio de Janeiro: Paz e Terra, 1982.

Mazzoni, Tomás. *Historia do Futebol no Brasil.* São Paulo, 1950.

Melo Franco, Virgilio A. *Octubre 1930.* Rio de Janeiro: Nova Fronteira, 1980.

Mendonça, Renato. *A influencia africana do portugues do Brasil.* 3rd ed. São Paulo: Companhia Editora Nacional, 1935.

Miceli, Sergio. *Intelletuais e classe dirigente no Brasil, 1920-1945.* São Paulo and Rio de Janeiro: Difusão Editorial S.A., 1979.

Minority Rights Group. *The Position of Blacks in Brazilian and Cuban Society.* London: Minority Rights Group, 1979.

Mulvey, Patricia Ann. 'The Black Lay Brotherhoods of Colonial Brazil' Ph.D. Diss. New York City University, 1976.

Myerson, Michael. *Memories of Underdevelopment.* New York: Grossman Publishers, 1973.

Nascimento, Abdias do. *Quilombismo.* Retrópolis, Brazil: Vozes, 1980.

--------. *Combate ao Racismo* Vol. 6. Brasilia: Coordenação de Publicações, 1983-1986.

Needell, Jeffrey D. 'History, Race, and the State in the Thought of Oliviera Viana'. *Hispanic American Historical Review* Vol. 75 no. 1 (1995): 1-30.

--------. 'Identity, Race, Gender and Modernity in the Origins of Gilberto Freyre's Oeuvre'. *American Historical Review* Vol. 100 no. 1 (February 1995): 51-77.

Nist, John. *The Modernist Movement in Brazil*. Austin and London: University of Austin Press, 1967.

Novo Diccionario de Historia do Brasil. São Paulo: Indústrias de Papel, 1971.

Oliveira, Lúcia Lippi. *A questão nacional na Primera República*. São Paulo: Editora Brasiliense, 1990.

Otero, Lisandro. *Cultural Policy in Cuba*. Paris: Unesco, 1972.

Peel, J.B.Y. (ed.) *Herbert Spencer on Social Evolution*. Chicago and London: University of Chicago Press, 1972.

Perelli, Carina and Juan Rial, Jand (ed.) *De mitos y memorias politicas*. Montevideo: Ediciones de la Banda Oriental, 1986.

Pierson, Donald. *Negroes in Brazil*. Southern Illinois, 1967.

--------. 'Diluição da linha de côr na Bahia'. *Revista do Arquivo Municipal* (São Paulo) Vol. 8, no. 89 (March-April 1943): 105-127.

--------. 'Os africanos da Bahia'. Revista do Arquivo Municipal (São Paulo) Vol. 7, no. 78: (August-September 1941): 39-64.

Pike, Frederick B. and Thomas Stritch (eds.) *The New Corporatism*. Notre Dame: University of Notre Dame Press, 1974.

'Publisher's Weekly Interviews: Jorge Amado'. *Publisher's Weekly* 23, June 1975, 2.

Quierós Mattoso, Katia. *To Be a Slave in Brazil, 1550-1880*. New Brunswich: Rutgers University Press, 1986.

Ilan Rachun, Ian. Feminism, Women's Suffrage and National Politics in Brazil: 1922-1937'. *Luso Brazilian Review* 14 (1977): 118-134.

Rama, Angel. *La ciudad letrada*. New Hampshire: Ediciones del Norte, 1984.

Ramos, Alberto Guerriero. *Patología social do 'branco' brasileiro*. Rio de Janeiro: Journal do Commercio, 1955.

Ramos, Julio. *Desencuentros de la modernidad en America Latina*. Mexico: Fondo de Cultura Económica, 1989.

Raphael, Alsion. 'From Popular Culture to Microenterprise: The History of the Brazilian Samba Schools'. *Latin American Music Review* Vol. 11, no. 1 (June 1990): 73-83.

Rodriquez-Castro, Maria Elena. 'La escritura de lo nacional y los intelectuales puertorriqueños'. Ph.D. Diss. Princeton University, 1988.

Rout, Leslie. The African Expereince in Spanish-America, 1502-Present. Cambridge: Cambridge University Press, 1976.

Said, Edward W. *Literatura and Society*. Baltimore: John Hopkins University Press, 1980.

Sánchez Vásquez, Adolfo. *Las ideas estéticas de Marx: ensayos de estética marxista*. México: Ediciones Eva,1965).

Santos, Joel Rufino dos. *Historia política do futebol brasileiro*. São Paulo: Brasiliense, 1981.

Saunders, J.V.D. 'A Revolution of Agreement Among Friends: The End of the Vargas Era'. *Hispanic American Historical Review* (May 1964): 197-213.

Schwartz, Stuart. *Slaves, Peasants and Rebels: Reconsidering Brazilian Slavery*. Urbana and Chicago: University of Illinois Press, 1992.

--------. 'Resistance and Accommodation in 18th Century Brazil: The Slave's View of Slavery'. *Hispanic American Historical Review* Vol. 57, no. 1 (February 1977): 69-81.

Scott, Rebecca. *The Abolition of Slavery and the Aftermath of Emancipation in Brazil*. Durham: Duke University, 1988.

--------. *Slave Emancipation in Cuba*. Princeton: Princeton University Press, 1985.

Senken, Leonardo. 'La lógica populista de la identidad y alteridad en Vargas y Perón: algunas implicaciones para los inmigrantes'. *Cuadernos Americanos*, 66, (Nov-Dec 1997), 130-152.

Severiano, Jairo. *Getúlio Vargas e a Música Popular Brasileira*. Rio de Janeiro: Fundação Getúlio Vargas/ CPDOC, 1982.

Slenes, Robert W. 'O que Rui Barbosa não queimou: Novas fontes para o estudo da escravidão no século XIX'. *Revista de Estudios Econômicos* Vol. 13, no. 1: 117-50.

Skidmore, Thomas. *Black Into White: Race and Nationality in Brazilian Thought*. (New York: Oxford University Press, 1974.

--------. *Politics in Brazil 1930-1964: an Experiment in Democracy*. New York: Oxford University Press, 1967.

Sodré, Nelson Werneck. *Raízes históicas do nacialismo brasileiro*. 2nd edition Rio de Janeiro: Ministério da Educação e Cultura, 1960.

Spencer, Hebert. *Classics in Anthropology*. Robert L. Carneiro (ed.) University of Chicago Press, 1967.

Spengler, Osvald. *The Decline of the West*. New York: Alfred A. Knopf, 1926.

Stabb, Martin S. *In Quest of Identity: Patterns in the Spanish American Essay of Ideas, 1890-1960*. Chapel Hill: University of South Carolina Press, 1967.

Stam. Robert. *Tropical Multiculturism: A Comparative History of Race in Brazilian Cinema and Culture*. Durham and London: Duke University Press, 1997.

Stephans, Nancy Ley. *The Hour of Eugenics: Race Gender and Nation in Latin America*. Ithaca and London: Cornell University Press, 1991.

Swan, Harry. 'The Nineteen Twenties: A Decade of Intellectual Change in Cuba'. *Revista Interamericana* Vol. 8, no. 2 (Summer 1978): 275-288.

Tannenbaum, Frank. *Slave and Citizen: The Negro in the Americas.* New York: Vintage Books, 1946.

Taylor, Brian K. 'Culture: Whence, Wither and Why?' *The Future of Cultural Minorities.* New York: The Macmillan Press Ltd, 1979: 9-29

Taylor, William. 'The Social History of Colonial Latin America: Evolution and Potential'. *Latin American Research Review* (Spring 1972): 6-7.

Tivey, Leonard. *The Nation-State.* New York: St. Martin's, 1981.

Toplin, Robert B.(ed.) *Slavery and Race Relations in Latin America.* Westport Press: Greenwood Press, 1974.

--------. *Freedom and Prejudice.* Westpoint, Conn: Greenwood Press, 1940.

--------. 'Brazil: Racial Polarization in the Developing Giant'. *Black World* 22 (November 1972): 15-22.

Torre, Guillermo. *Historia de la literatura de la vanguardia.* Madrid, 1965.

Tudor, Henry. *Political Myth.* New York: Praeger, 1972.

Udom, E.E. Essien. *Black Nationalism.* Chicago: University of Chicago Press, 1962.

Velez, Claudio. 'Centralism, Nationalism and Integration'. Published report. Budapest: Center for Afro-Asian Research, 1969.

Velloso, Monica Pimenta. 'A Ordem: uma revista de doutrina, política e cultura católica'. *Revista de Ciencia Política* 21, 3 (1978): 127-128.

--------. 'A brasilidade verde-amarela: nacionalismo e regionalismo paulista'. *Estudos Históricos*, Vol. 6, no. 11 (Jan-June 1993), 89-112.

Viotti da Costa, Emilia. *The Brazilian Empire Myths and Histories.* Belmont, California: Wadsworth Publishing Company, 1985.

Vivas, Eliseo. 'Myth: Some Philosophical Problems'. *Southern Review* 6, no.1 (1970): 92 and 1.

Wagley, Charles. *Introduction to Brazil.* New York: Columbia University Press, 1971.

---------. 'Attitudes in the 'Backlands'. *Courier* (Paris) 5 (August-September, 1952): 12-14.

Francisco Weffort. *O populismo na política brasileira.* Rio de Janeiro: Paz e Terra, 1978.

White, Hayden. *Tropics of Discourse.* Baltimore: John Hopkins University Press, 1978.

Williams, Margaret Todaro. 'Integralism and the Brazilian Church'. *Hispanic American Historical Review* 53, no. 3 (1974): 431-452.

Winthrop R. Wright, Winthrop R. *Cafe con Leche Race Class and National Image in Venezuela.* Austin: University of Texas Press, 1990.

Woodward, Ralph Lee Jr. (ed.) *Positivism in Latin America, 1850-1900.* Toronto and Lexington: D.C. Heath and Company, 1971.

Zunz, Oliver. ed. *Reliving the Past: The Worlds of Social History.* Chapel Hill: University of North Carolina Press, 1985.

Index